WRITERS' REVISIONS

AN ANNOTATED BIBLIOGRAPHY OF ARTICLES AND BOOKS ABOUT WRITERS' REVISIONS AND THEIR COMMENTS ON THE CREATIVE PROCESS

DAVID MADDEN
AND RICHARD POWERS

THE SCARECROW PRESS, INC.
METUCHEN, N.J., & LONDON 1981

Library of Congress Cataloging in Publication Data

Madden, David, 1933-
Writers' revisions.

Includes index.
1. Literature, Modern--History and criticism--Bibliography. 2. Creative writing--Bibliography. I. Powers, Richard, 1928- joint author. II. Title.
Z6519.M28 016.808 80-22942
ISBN 0-8108-1375-0

Manufactured in the United States of America

The art of writing is rewriting. Sean O'Faolain

People deeply interested in an art are interested in the "how." Robert Penn Warren

The innocent eye sees nothing. W. H. Auden

[The writer] must ... suppress much and omit more. Robert Louis Stevenson

I've never had a sentence turn up in the final form as it was in the beginning. Evan S. Connell

A work that aspires, however humbly, to the condition of art should carry its justification in every line. Joseph Conrad

After writing a poem, one should correct it all over. Alexander Pope

to the memory of Vernon Sternberg
one of the great editors
and
for Susan Powers

CONTENTS

PREFACE

We imagine the practical users of this annotated bibliography to be teachers, students, creative writers, editors, and scholars.

We imagine teachers consulting this book if they want to find quickly articles or books dealing with a specific work in order to discuss that work with a class by comparing versions in the revision process. Or one may study the creative process itself from conception, through revisions, to the finished work.

A major premise of this book is that a study of the writer's techniques in the various versions of works in which he employs those techniques develops the student's receptivity to the effects of those techniques; such a study also enables the student to understand the nature and concepts of the various literary genres. This approach helps teachers and students focus on the creative process itself. It may be used in the teaching of literature in both high school and colleges. Emphasis on discussion of meaning and symbol alone often hold the living work at too great a distance. Examinations of revisions stimulate concrete comparisons that inevitably raise important and useful questions even as one uses the more familiar strategies of discussion of theme, and of biographical, historical, sociological, and psychological elements.

A study of revision offers a close-up encounter with literature as it is being shaped. Starting in high school, students find it difficult to accept the fact that one human being wrote a well-known work. That difficulty is demonstrated every time a student prefaces a statement about a work with "they say," as if something as impressive as a book could be written only by a committee. A careful comparison of a work in several stages of composition should convince the student that writers, like themselves, are fallible and limited. Such an examination offers proof finally that one person really does possess the powers to compose a work of complex beauty and intelligence alone, and that in concentrating on the actual practice of his craft he or she does use symbols and other techniques in shaping that work. This approach not only helps students to read more creatively and critically, it contributes directly to the improvement of their own writing skills.

We imagine creative writers, working alone or in classes, making practical use of this book. A study of the creative process in all genres provides writing students with opportunities to study various versions of a specimen work, from notebook entries to final editions.

For students who want to consider a writer's creations in the light of his methods, goals, and values, Part II, in which writers talk about the creative process and about their own work, will be helpful.

In some of the pieces cited in this book, the role of the reader himself is discussed. Robert Frost states the direct relationship of writer and reader: "No tears in the writer, no tears in the reader." Frank O'Connor comments on the writer as reader: "... the rest is rereading and rewriting. The writer should never forget that he is also a reader, though a prejudiced one, and if he cannot read his own work a dozen times he can scarcely expect a reader to look at it twice." Or more than twice. Wright Morris sees an even more complex relationship: "The writer learns to write, the reader learns to read.... It seems the writer's intent to involve the reader not merely in the reading, but in the writing ...." These three related comments become more richly suggestive as one analyzes revisions.

Enough material is cited here to provide a student, scholar, or imaginative writer with the means for making a rather full study of Faulkner, James, Hardy, Joyce, Richardson, Whitman, and Yeats at various stages. Joyce's notebooks, manuscripts and marked galley proofs have been thoroughly examined. Henry James more than any other writer revised serial installments for the book publication and again for later editions. Variants among Hardy's serial versions and the British and American editions have been examined. Conrad, Lawrence, and Woolf revised between British and American editions.

The revisions of some writers have been studied more often than others. The novelists most often examined are Faulkner, James, Hardy, Joyce, Samuel Richardson; the poets are Whitman, Yeats, and Dickinson. Others are Conrad, Stephen Crane, Thackeray, Dickens, Fitzgerald, Lawrence, Wolfe, and Woolf among novelists; T. S. Eliot, Keats and Byron among poets. One way to study the creative process at length and in depth is to choose one of the writers most often cited and read all the studies devoted to his work. Faulkner's various versions of his short stories provide a major opportunity for studying the creative process through an examination of revisions.

Some of the entries are simply citations of works that remain to be studied, so that they offer students of literature and creative writers exercises in comparison of versions without scholarly commentary. A number of the entries suggest work to be done. "A reader with the published text before him," says one scholar, referring to Faulkner's _Sanctuary_, "can reconstruct the original version for himself." The reader may make his own comparison between Joyce's _Stephen Hero_ and the final version, _A Por-_

trait of the Artist as a Young Man. Compare Wright Morris's short story, "The Ram in the Thicket," with the later novel version, Man and Boy. One may compare Flannery O'Connor's first story, "The Geraniums," with her last, "Judgment Day," which is the first rewritten. Compare stories in the first edition of Ray Bradbury's The October Country with the revised edition. Compare John Fowles' two published versions of The Magus. Gore Vidal has published two versions of The City and the Pillar. John Seelye's The True Adventures of Huckleberry Finn offers a unique opportunity for comparative study: how does his Huck compare with Twain's? One may develop one's ability to analyze by comparing versions of The Way of All Flesh, Tess of the D'Urbervilles, Middlemarch, Daisy Miller, given, without comment, in Hildick's Word for Word. Many writers have not yet been thoroughly explored, and many others not at all.

Among other practical users of this book are the editors of books and magazines who may wish to extract from these annotations a kind of rhetoric of revision of their own for use in dealing with problem manuscripts. The index of revision problems will help in that task.

Obviously, this book is of practical use to scholars who are writing about a specific work, especially those engaged in the analysis of revisions and textual criticism. As one sets out upon a new project in these fields, it is good to be able to survey conveniently what has been done. Also, this book implicitly suggests the numerous areas in which little or no work has been done, especially in relatively neglected genres, such as playwriting and imaginative nonfiction.

This book is divided into two parts: Part One: "Articles and Books about Writers' Revisions," the main concern of the book; and Part Two: "Writers Talk About the Creative Process," which augments Part One.

We assume that the reader is looking generally for items pertaining to a specific work, not, normally, for a specific essay by a scholar about that work. Part One, therefore, is organized by creative author, alphabetically, with individual works arranged alphabetically under the author's name; the essays and books about each work are, then, arranged chronologically by the date on which the piece appeared, not alphabetically by the critic's name. When the item cited deals with more than one work by a writer, that item appears at the end of the section.

The information in each of the more than 350 items cited includes:

1. Name of author
2. The work or works discussed
3. The extent to which the work under study is reprinted in the book or article
4. The method the scholar uses to compare or display versions

5. The conclusions the scholar draws, or his or her purpose for making the revisions available
6. The order in which the scholar's information is presented
7. Kinds of revisions the scholar discusses
8. Whether for maximum benefit from the item the reader need have in hand the author's published work.

All the pieces cited are in English, but the authors discussed are not all American and British. Included are French (Flaubert), Russian (Dostoyevski), and German (Mann). Classes in foreign literature may find this book useful, but sufficient work in this area has yet to be done (Spanish and Italian writers go unrepresented).

In the introduction, we offer a checklist of revision problems discussed in the items cited in both Parts I and II. The Revision Problems Index is more detailed. An even more detailed handbook on "the rhetoric of revision," with examples, is in preparation.

In Part Two, "Writers Talk About the Creative Process," there are over 120 entries for articles and books in which writers talk about writing in general, their own in particular; revision is not a subject in all cases. We offer only a sampling of authors' notebooks, journals, diaries, letters, and autobiographies and biographies.

Most of the information conveyed in the entries in Parts One and Two is given in direct quotations from the authors of the pieces. We feel that the variety of voices makes the book more readable. And we do feel that beyond its usefulness as a reference volume, this annotated bibliography offers a reading experience.

Most of the genres are represented, poetry and novels commanding the greater attention. Also represented are short stories (Hemingway, Faulkner); plays (Galsworthy, Ibsen, O'Neill, O'Casey, Shakespeare, Shaw, Tennessee Williams), including the plays of poets Shelley, Byron, Yeats; writing for movies; adaptations of novels into film (Ben Maddow's adaptation of Intruder in the Dust); nonfiction (Emerson, Ruskin, Gibbons); autobiography (George Moore, Franklin, Yeats). Areas that demand further exploration are the various nonfiction categories and drama and film.

Using the same characters, theme, and story in two or three different media (novel, play, movie), whether working on them simultaneously or at different times, a writer may learn about one genre while working in another. And so students, comparing versions of a work in two or three different media, may gain deeper insights into the nature of each medium. Bushrui concludes that Yeats's full-time devotion to dramatic writing for more than five years enabled him to find new expression in his lyricism.

Some of the entries enable the reader to compare short story with novel versions of the same elements, and fiction versions with play or film versions. Thomas Mann's The Magic

Mountain, like Joyce's Ulysses, was conceived as a short story but grew into a monumental novel. Virginia Woolf's Mrs. Dalloway grew out of a short story; having finished the novel, she revised the short story version. One may compare Tennessee Williams' story, "Portrait of a Girl in Glass," with a long one-act play version, then with the full-length play, The Glass Menagerie. After fiction and poetry, the genres most represented, in order of emphasis, are playwriting, nonfiction, and filmwriting. We believe that a study of revisions helps one to understand not only the individual work and the creative process in general but also the nature of the work's genre.

A study of the changes a writer (or his or her adaptor) makes in adapting a work from one medium to another (and sometimes to two different other media) is the subject of another work in preparation.

At the risk of a little initial confusion but in the service of greater ease in reader use of this book, we have prepared five indexes:

For us, this is a new field of study. This book is as complete as we know how to make it. The study of revisions is a somewhat new field; textual criticism has a longer history but is comparatively new also. Most entries are dated in the 1960s and 70s. Books and articles in these fields and in the area of writers' commentary on the creative process are spread out; there is no central reference volume that brings them all together. This book is a first attempt to do that. In future editions, we will attempt to be more inclusive.

Acknowledgments

We are grateful to Peggy Bach for invaluable editorial assistance. The librarians of the Louisiana State University, Humanities Division and Library School Library, were very helpful.

David Madden,
Writer in Residence,
Louisiana State University

Richard Powers,
Assistant Principal for Instruction,
McKinley High School

Baton Rouge, Louisiana
1980

INTRODUCTION

1. What Is the Value of Studying Revisions?

The study of writers' revisions has been so long one of the more esoteric suburbs of the scholarly province that perhaps one needs to claim its practical value. Walker Gibson asks a basic question: "How does a study of the creative process facilitate an understanding of literature generally?" Cleanth Brooks answers that question succinctly:

> What we learn about the origin of a poem may, if we do not confuse origin and poem, enlarge our understanding and deepen our appreciation.... This gain in understanding and appreciation is not merely, in fact not primarily, of the poem whose development we can trace.... It is, rather, a gain in our understanding and appreciation of poetry in general; when we learn about the materials of poetry and about the poetic process, we also learn something about the nature of poetry.

There are, of course, specific values. Carter A. Daniel assures us that an examination of Nathanael West's revisions of *Miss Lonelyhearts* will throw "light on the basic conception and meaning of the book" and "clarify the author's aims, some features of his thought, and the technical means by which he solved certain problems of style and structure." Michael C. O'Neel makes an even more general claim for the value of his study of Sir Thomas Wyatt's revisions: one may arrive at "several statements about Wyatt's life as artist and man." Revisions may, then, tell us about the author's original intentions, the process by which the author makes choices, the growth and changes in the author himself during the interim.

Students often complain that analysis distracts from when it does not destroy enjoyment and appreciation. But having studied Flannery O'Connor's revisions, Margaret Harrison concludes: "Analysis ... should only deepen respect for those mysteries known as artistic development and the creative process." Beyond understanding a writer's body of work or a specific work more deeply, "our interest," says John Livingston Lowes, in his giant study of two of Coleridge's greatest poems, "is in a study of the imaginative processes themselves." Coleridge himself said: "nothing can permanently please which does not contain in itself the reason why it is so, and not otherwise." Revisions help us to see that reason more clearly.

Some writers share the scholar's, the teacher's, the student's interest in their own revisions. R. P. Blackmur describes Henry James's task in the prefaces: James tried to "remount" "the stream of composition," "to make an ex post facto dissection, not that we may embalm the itemized mortal remains, but that we may intellectually understand the movement of parts and the relation between them in the living body we appreciate." And some writers share our interest in the revisions of other writers. Even a popular writer, W. Somerset Maugham, offered his Notebook on the assumption that it would interest other writers: "I publish it because I am interested in the technique of literary production and in the process of creation, and if such a volume as this by some other author came into my hands I would turn to it with avidity. By some happy chance what interests me seems to interest a great many other people." The purpose of this volume is to expand that interest beyond the realm of scholarly specialization, with gratitude for the work scholars have done.

We argue that the study of revision will interest and specifically benefit teachers and students of literature in all genres, from early high school through doctoral programs in universities; writers, from those just beginning through the most accomplished; and, of course, literary scholars, whatever their specialty. Ironically, a book whose purpose is to appeal to and benefit so broad an audience must consist, at this stage in the development of revision studies, mostly of articles and books written by and for specialists. The aims of these specialists are varied: to show the genesis of a work, to examine closely the technical revisions, to discover textual discrepancies, with the purpose of deepening one's understanding of a specific work, of the body of a writer's work, of the writer's life and the world in which he lived, of understanding the creative process in general, and of making a more authentic text of a specific work possible.

Discussing the art of James Joyce, Walton Litz sees a parallel between the writer rewriting and the reader re-reading: "In a sense the process of composition parallels the process we follow as readers: a gradual accretion of details which finally form themselves into related patterns. To trace the evolution of an episode is to re-enact our own gradual apprehension of the work."

By bringing together into a single volume bibliographical information about much of the work that has been done in this field, we hope, among other goals, to contribute to an effort to derive from these studies a pedagogy for teaching an understanding of the nature of literature and an appreciation of its effects. That value is seldom directly expressed but frequently implicit in these annotated entries.

Vincent Tartella is one of several scholars who point to another value; he claims for his study of Henry James's revisions "some value to the novice in creative writing." We are convinced that one of the most effective supplements to the usual practice in creative writing workshops, of discussing student works in progress, is an examination of the revisions of published writers. There is general agreement among writers who conduct these workshops that one of the few really effective textbooks is Kuehl's Creative Vision and Revision.

Our own experiences in the classroom convince us that one way to study the nature of literature and writing is to analyze the creative process itself. If in one story, for instance, students can see instances in which the author made a series of choices in various drafts and see relationships between the way it was done and the effects of the finished work, they may understand better how those elements function in other works. We urge then the development of a pedagogy for teaching literature and creative writing through an examination of the revision (or re-vision, re-seeing) process in which the reshaping imagination functions.

It is by no means reaching to assert that another value of this book will be to editorial practice; editors of magazines and books of all kinds may gather both a clearer general view and specific skills from a study of revisions. Several entries cite works in which the editorial process is directly depicted; for instance, J. M. Howells concludes that his study of variants among four revisions of "The Short Happy Life of Francis Macomber" supplies a view of magazine editing practice.

In the area of scholarly benefits, one of the major consequences of studies of manuscript versions, along with galleys, page-proofs, and various editions, is that more authoritative texts are established.

Because most of these entries describe work done by scholars, we also claim a value for those who wish to survey the work already done and derive some view of work yet to be done. Some scholars study revision, as Vinton A. Dearing studies Dryden's, to make "a case for authorial revision" itself. Dante Gabriel Rossetti's case may seem extreme. R. N. Keane tells us that "one can see him involved in every facet of the book: adding and removing poems, rearranging the order of the poems, revising and re-revising the text--literally composing in the margins--and giving attention to type size, margins, punctuation, arrangement of headlines, pagination, and finally, binding and endpapers." Some activities described in these entries do not fall under the rubric "revision," but they help shape an enhancing context for analyses of revision. There are those few, I. A. Richards, for one, who argue against the value of such studies. The problematic aspects of this field of study leads one to Robert L. Beare's question, posed in his study of variants in the texts of Eliot's poetry, "At what point does a modern poem or a play--or novel--cease to be in a state of 'becoming' and reach a state of 'being'?"

2. How Does the Study of Revision Enhance Our Understanding of Individual Writers and Their Individual Works?

A major value lies in studying the creative process itself but, of course, most of these items do that by focusing on a single writer, and usually a single work. What may we learn about individual writers and their individual works?

Very basically, we may begin with the knowledge that a particular writer does indeed revise. Yeats "was never content, he revised constantly, and he almost always improved." Hardy was "an inveterate reviser." Even minor revisions suggest "the minute care and critical intelligence" that Shelley, for instance, "brought to his art." Adams offers evidence for his contention that Shakespeare's Titus Andronicus is an extensively revised version of an earlier play. We learn that Edward Taylor was a "conscientious reviser ... a craftsman concerned with increased dramatic expression, simpler syntax, clearer images, and smoother rhythms." It is valuable in certain contexts to know that Edwin Arlington Robinson did not, as Dauner concludes, revise his works extensively but that when he did revise, the effects were many-faceted. Monod concludes that "one of our rewards was, and is, an increased respect for Dickens' conscientious craftmanship"; his revisions of Hard Times were "eager, lucid and passionate." For some writers revision may be perfunctory drudgery, but "for James," says Isadore Traschen, "revision was not a matter of choice, but of immediate and absolute necessity. That is, it was a moral act of the highest kind."

Manuscript evidence often contradicts a writer's claim to have written solely out of inspiration; we learn nothing from a stance that has no basis in reality. George Eliot's revisions of Middlemarch refute her "claim to have written it in a frenzy of inspiration, and never to have revised it." His public claims to the contrary, Stephen Crane revised The Red Badge of Courage extensively.

Some scholars charge writers with failure to revise. A study of Dante Gabriel Rossetti's "The Blessed Damozel" defends his integrity as an artist. Swinburne's worksheets for "Hymn to Proserpine" tend to prove that he was "not the automatic writer, the gushing verse geyser, of legend." Whitman's manuscripts show that he was "a conscious artist." The revisions of Dorian Gray "suggest that the stereotyped view of Wilde as a careless and hasty writer may need reassessment." Branda refutes the often repeated charge that D. H. Lawrence did not revise, and Ross contends that Lawrence's "resourceful and exploratory artistry is beyond doubt." Garrett refutes a mistaken view that Faulkner did not revise. Shannon's comparison of revisions and texts shows that Tennyson's Wellington poem is "far from a perfunctory funeral panegyric." Sutherland sets out "to determine whether Thackeray, in writing Vanity Fair, was a careful planner or a brilliant improviser"; Thackeray's notes show him "inventing, outlining, measuring, altering, experimenting...."

Another value of studying revisions is to help resolve critical disputes about a specific work. Fadiman says, "In light of the disputes over the novel," (Faulkner's Light in August), "a thorough analysis of the revisions is greatly needed." Langford concludes that "examination of the manuscript" of Faulkner's Absalom, Absalom! "clears up many inconsistencies and ambiguities that have caused critical controversies." Rene Kerf shows the peril of interpreting Conrad's works in ignorance of the fact that Rescue was written before Nigger of the "Narcissus" though published afterwards--a fact her scrutiny of both manuscripts establishes. On the other hand, Alspach's caution about Yeats applies to many other cases: "Scholars and critics should be careful in drawing conclusions from Yeats's revisions."

3. What May We Learn About the Revision Methods of Individual Writers?

Joyce's method was meticulous and exacting; he could never be completely satisfied with anything he wrote. He had "an almost psychotic compulsion." Ulysses was "literally an organically evolving book." Philip Herring discovered that "each of the eighteen episodes was continually revised and expanded (almost never condensed) from early sketches right up to a few days before the date of publication." Joyce is a "mosaic craftsman," says Herring. Discussing Finnegans Wake, Thomas Connolly says, "Now his method resembled that of an expert Japanese lacquerer who begins with a basic coat and then, layer upon layer, builds up his medium so that the final product is a highly polished surface that reveals a warm and rich depth down to the basic wood." Joyce's revisions offer an opportunity to study six methods of composition: 1) straight composition; 2) revise-and-complete; 3) episodic; 4) episodic fusion; 5) piecemeal or mosaic; 6) framing.

In her study of Light in August, Regina Fadiman describes Faulkner's work habits. She concludes that Faulkner was not a systematic writer, that he worked on small independent units, that the final order of those units was of primary importance to the meaning of the book, and that the final order successfully expressed his intentions for this novel. Joanne Creighton concludes that Faulkner's craft of revision was generally flexible. Samuel Richardson made four kinds of revision of Clarissa: 1) simple revision: addition, rejection, substitution; 2) reverse revision: return to original; 3) continued revision: new material substituted for rejected revision; 4) combination of 2 and 3. We learn from R. H. Wilson that Aldous Huxley "rarely cancelled material without replacing it." The most significant kinds of revision Huxley made in Brave New World were additions. James Stephens' most frequent type of revision is substitution. Conrad has special problems with English idioms, as we see especially in versions of his first novel, Almayer's Folly. Harden shows that Thackeray deleted passages from The Newcomes for no reason that can be seen in context. Sutherland's study of the revisions prove that Thackeray wrote his later novels with fewer changes than in his earlier work. David Mann reveals that John Crowe Ransom's lesser-known poems were revised significantly, while his best-known poems were little revised.

Tennyson's method of composition was to rough out the pattern for a poem in his head before writing; in later years he wrote prose versions first; he revised extensively in the proof stage and before each new edition. Helene Harvitt's study of James's revised _Roderick Hudson_ (1924) was a seminal study of revision; one may see James employ basic approaches. Gettman does not discern a set theory of revision guiding even the analytical James. Sometimes the author looks at what he has done and sees a value for himself. Dickens made numbered plans for _Dombey and Son_ and "found the practice profitable and continued it for the remainder of his monthly number novels."

One way to enhance our understanding of the creative process is to see how one work grew out of a similar but different work, as Beaty did in the case of George Eliot's _Middlemarch_. C. G. Hoffman and Jacqueline Latham, in separate essays, argue that Woolf's _Mrs. Dalloway_ grew out of a short story and that the story became an integral part of the novel. Litz was interested to see how the techniques of Joyce's _Finnegans Wake_ developed out of _Ulysses_.

Lyndon Shanley tells us that "only the manuscript could reveal to how great an extent _Walden_ is the result of a gradual re-creation of his [Thoreau's] experience rather than simply a recounting of that experience as he had entered it in his journal when it happened."

4. How Do Revisions Show the General Aesthetic Development of the Writer?

Many scholars point out the development of general aesthetic aspects of individual writers. In an examination of revisions, "we come as close as possible to the writer at the moment of composition," says Martin Battestin, and in the case of Fielding's _Joseph Andrews_, "an examination of the novel in process can tell us much about Fielding's craftsmanship and his purpose." Frank McShane tells us that Ford Madox Ford "is ... remembered ... as one of the few novelists of modern times who tried to explain why technical consciousness was necessary in writing." Margaret Harrison sees in Flannery O'Connor's revisions of _Wise Blood_ a "growing awareness of her own peculiar thematic and technical aims." James T. Boulton concludes that the revisions of "Odour of Chrysanthemums" testify to Lawrence's "growth in self-criticism." Sucksmith concludes that Dickens's "vision and rhetoric compelled him to make major modifications to his original plans for the construction of _Bleak House_." Robert Scholes finds that "Joyce had either an actual or a literary source in mind for almost every passage in" _Portrait of the Artist_. Students of James, says Vincent Tartella, will find a comparison of two published versions of "Four Meetings" interesting and valuable. Isadore Traschen sees in the revisions of The American a demonstration of James's conviction "that reality was to be understood through form." Most of James's revisions "furnish evidence," as Albert Gengenheimer says in his study of "A Passionate Pilgrim," "that James grew as an artist and improved his work with every opportunity for revision." James Early says that Go Down, Moses offers students of Faulkner "an almost unique opportunity to study Faulkner's creative activity." We see examples of the "supreme achievements of Faulkner's synthesizing imagination."

Revisions of Drayton's Four Legends "show how his development reflects a transition from Elizabethan to Jacobean poetic attitudes." The intermediate version of Poe's "Lenore" shows him "moving from a somewhat strained lyrical subjectivity to the firmness of dramatic dialogue." Even revisions in his reviews "reveal a shift in Poe's style as a writer," says Walter Evans, and "his valuing of the literary concepts involved." G. T. Tanselle discusses ways in which revisions of James Russell Lowell's The Cathedral "reveal certain aspects of his poetic personality." In Yeats at Work, Curtis B. Bradford's claim for a study of Yeats's revisions applies to all writers as well: we gain "new critical insights into the work."

5. What Specific Changes in Technique Does a Study of Revisions Reveal?

In a study of revisions, we increase our understanding of the way that various techniques function in a work. Fitzgerald discovered in revision of "The Debutante" "a major new theme--the role of money in our lives." The several versions of "Author's House" show Fitzgerald struggling "to gain distance and detachment from his material." We may watch the writer at work on general technical areas. The revisions of "Crazy Sunday," says Bronson, show F. Scott Fitzgerald "working skillfully with problems of style, structure, and characterization...." The revision of Sanctuary shows Faulkner at "a turning point in his experimentation," as he altered his narrative method. We understand the Christian symbolism of The Sound and the Fury better when we see Faulkner add the birthday passages. Changes in Go Down, Moses reveal Faulkner's "entirely new conception of Lucas' role...." We see Faulkner's "structural skills" at work. Langford found that "to trace the process" of the revision of Faulkner's Absalom, Absalom! "is to experience a sharp focusing of the dominant theme of the novel, and to witness a demonstration of how the meaning of a fictional work can shape its structure and thus stand revealed by what has become the outward and visible signs, or form, of that meaning."

In two preliminary outlines for Ellen Glasgow's Virginia we see the stages by which "the hypothetical and abstract become concrete and actual" for the writer. Scrutiny of his manuscripts show Nathanael West's "personal preferences in diction and phrasing." Sir Thomas Wyatt's manuscripts aid us "in defining his poetical style." The important revisions James made in "Four Meetings" "reveal his anxiety to realize all the possibilities latent in character and situation." By "smoothing or sharpening his style," says Battestin, referring to revisions of Joseph Andrews, Fielding breathed "the breath of life into scene and character, whetting the edge of his satire." We may come to a negative but useful conclusion, as Measures does in his study of revisions for Diana of the Crossways: "the source of Meredith's stylistic complexity is not his practice of revision."

Questions about the evolution of a writer's purpose or intentions in a particular work are often answered partly in an examination of revisions, such as Virginia Woolf's of Orlando, Joyce's of Ulysses, Dickens' of Hard Times. Or we may discern the work's basic conception and meaning, as Carter Daniel shows in his analysis of Nathanael West's revisions of Miss Lonelyhearts. We may also discern, Krauss points out, the intentions of the revisions themselves, as in the case of James's The Portrait of a Lady.

6. What Effect Do Editors and Publishers Have on the Revision Process?

One may study extra-literary reasons for revision, external influences that affect a writer before, during, and after publication. Some revision studies reveal the effect of the editor upon a writer. Saxe Commins seems unsympathetic to Faulkner's artistic aims in Requiem for a Nun. One scholar declares that Thomas Wolfe's outline for The Web and the Rock is the work of his editor, Edward Aswell; another scholar refutes that claim. Hardy's editor helped him clarify meaning in later editions of The Woodlanders. Editor to Author: The Letters of Maxwell Perkins and Stephen Berg's biography Max Perkins, Editor of Genius reveal interactions between Perkins and F. Scott Fitzgerald, Hemingway, Sherwood Anderson, and Thomas Wolfe in all phases of publishing, including the revision process.

The role of the editor in putting together a work-in-progress for posthumous publication is special but suggestive. "It is evident," says Matthew Bruccoli, "that in the case of work-in-progress authorial intention is the crucial consideration for interpretation and evaluation." He charges that Edmund Wilson's doctored text of F. Scott Fitzgerald's The Last Tycoon is "misleading because it presents Fitzgerald's working drafts in a finished form.... The only way to regard it is as material toward a novel." Victor Kramer argues that certain passages in James Agee's unfinished manuscript, A Death in the Family, should have been included by the editors, and concludes that the editors did not come as close to Agee's intentions as the manuscript would warrant. Editors or publishers sometimes persuade writers to change their entire approach. The uncut version of Willard Motley's first novel, Knock on Any Door, is more experimental, bolder in technique. Some publishers act as censors. Random House persuaded Robinson Jeffers to tone down his anti-American poems, published during World War II. Some of Joyce's corrections were never incorporated into Dubliners because the publishers acted as censors. Frank sexual material was omitted from Hardy's The Woodlanders in the serial version. Huxley exercised self-censorship regarding sex and religion in revising Brave New World.

Changes made for serial publication often impair but sometimes improve the artistic unity of a work. Deletions in the serial version of Sinclair Lewis' Arrowsmith actually "removed irritating blemishes."

Some scholars argue that portions of a work were omitted, deliberately or inadvertently, by the publishers and should therefore be restored in future editions. Publishers rejected, against his wishes, lines 314-322 of Keats's "The Eve of St. Agnes"; Stillinger argues that they should be restored. Or a scholar may argue for leaving the text incomplete. The American publisher of Lawrence's Kangaroo lost the last page, but Jarvis concludes the novel is the better for that loss.

7. What Non-literary Aspects of a Writer's Life Influence the Revision Process?

Some revisions reveal non-literary aspects of a writer's life that influence the revision process before and after first publication.

Kallich charges that Dos Passos' revisions of Rosinante to the Road Again for inclusion in Journeys Between Wars show changes aimed at covering up his earlier enthusiasm for the Communist movement and at playing down a youthful romantic mysticism. Bernardin defends Dos Passos' changes as reflecting natural and normal growth for a writer as he reacts to a time of great change (particularly in Spain). Steffan points out that in his revisions of Don Juan Byron made changes in social or political areas. Some changes in Joseph Andrews reflect, says Battesin, "Fielding's shifting political loyalties." George Orwell came to see that "it is invariably where I lacked political purpose that I wrote lifeless books." The opposite is true of many writers, especially those who wrote proletarian novels during the thirties.

Revisions of "Pandora," says Vandersee, reveal James's more intense disparagement of America. Some of Fielding's revisions of David Simple were prompted by his knowledge of law. To avoid the charge of blasphemy, Twain altered some of his remarks in Innocents Abroad. "Keats's revisions on his manuscript 'Ode on Melancholy' distinctly confirm a movement in his mind towards a philosophy of stoic acceptance...." Lawrence's revisions of "Odour of Chrysanthemums" were affected by his growing understanding that his mother was also responsible for the failure of her marriage.

Friends sometimes get caught up in the creative process. Richardson kept up a lively correspondence with a large number of acquaintances while writing Charles Grandison and Clarissa, asking for and getting suggestions for improvement; their advice was also reflected in revisions for later editions. Dante Rossetti had help from Swinburne and other friends in reading proof and making improvements for Poems. Mary Shelley's suggestions were incorporated into Byron's Don Juan. Hume advised Gibbon to soften positives and reduce superlatives in composing Decline and Fall. John Burroughs' remarks affected Whitman's revisions of "Lilacs." The relationship between Eliot and Pound produced the unusual example of one poet (Pound) cutting and revising the work of another (Eliot's The Waste Land).

Hawthorne's wife had a "purefying" influence on his work, sometimes between serial and book publication. The criticism of actors in rehearsal apparently affected Shakespeare in bringing Titus Andronicus to the form we now know. Revisions in Drayton's Idea sonnets reflect changes "in manner towards the method of Donne." Some of Joyce's revisions of the language of Finnegans Wake are intended to force the reader "into a realization of the Vichian continuity of history, myth, and language."

Response to the public is not unusual. Frank Norris revised both McTeague and A Man's Woman in response to public criticism that they contained objectionable material. Richardson made changes in Clarissa in response to the public's misreadings and objections after the first and second editions. Pressure from reviewers moved Tennyson to make several changes in Ode on the Death of the Duke of Wellington; the revisions themselves were then reviewed. In revising later editions of several of his novels, Hardy took some suggestions from editors, reviewers and readers pertaining to sex and religion, but rejected others.

8. What Does the Study of Revisions Contribute to Textual Criticism?

One of the purposes of studying revisions and variants among texts is to establish the proper text, which Stillinger and others take to be the one that is true to the latest reading intended by the writer. In Yeats at Work, Curtis B. Bradford demonstrates a practical reason for studying the manuscripts: to correct or improve the texts. In his study of the versions of Joyce's Portrait of the Artist as a Young Man, Hans Walter Gabler strives for "textual validity."

"The main burden" of Donald L. Lawler's article on Wilde's The Picture of Dorian Gray "is to prove by detection the existence of an earlier manuscript, now lost." Kenneth Allott argues that six quatrains of Matthew Arnold's "The River" found in an early manuscript version and never included with the published versions should be added in future editions. Stallman argues that a passage deleted from Crane's Maggie should be reinstated. D. J. Leary gives reasons why a passage cut from George Bernard Shaw's John Bull's Other Island should be reinstated. Patricia B. Craddock shows that Gibbon's revisions of Chapter One, Volume I, were never "incorporated" into subsequent editions of *Decline and Fall.* Adams suggests that eight pages of one late version of Joyce's only play, *Exiles,* be considered to "have special authority as a gloss on" the published version.

Many writers make significant revisions in galley or page proof stages: Conrad's *Almayer's Folly* (we see also the editor's changes); O'Casey's *Red Rose for Me* (galley and page proof stages); Tennyson's *Idylls of the King* (heavily revised); most of Balzac's work, more extensively than most; George Moore's *Esther Waters,* extensively as in most of his works; Joyce, most of his works, a great deal; Hardy's *The Woodlanders;* Dante Gabriel Rossetti's *Poems* through eight proof stages. Scholars sometimes discover errors caused by careless proof-reading, as in Fitzgerald's *This Side of Paradise.* Langford argues that the galley version of Faulkner's *Sanctuary* is in some ways superior to the "rearranged" published version. (The galley version was finally published in 1980.)

One result of working on a particular manuscript is that a scholar may begin to develop a methodology that is generally useful in determining whether variants are the result of authorial revision or of other causes: Dearing's work on Dryden's *Mac Flecknoe.* Sloppy printing produces errors that affect our interpretation of a poem, as with Coleridge's "The Friend," and of novels, as with Fielding's *Joseph Andrews.* Printers deleted many commas from a faulty late impression of James's *Portrait of a Lady.*

E. F. Shields, studying Woolf's *Mrs. Dalloway,* sets his task: "to evaluate the relative authenticity of the two editions (both are of equal value, but different)...." J. A. Lavin argues that the revised American edition of Woolf's *To the Lighthouse* is superior to the English edition. American editions of Anthony Burgess's *A Clockwork Orange* omit the last chapter included in the English edition. Burgess himself argues that his intentions are frustrated by such an omission. Even James, who revised his work in almost every edition, never discovered the major error of the misplaced chapter of his masterpiece, *The Ambassadors.* The first American edition of Conrad's first novel, *Almayer's Folly,* was based on the unrevised proof sheets from the first English edition. This sort of discovery warrants some change in future editions.

Sometimes the author expands his manuscript in the serial stage. The author may make revisions between serial and book publication: Moore added about fifteen pages to and deleted about four from the serial text of *Esther Waters.* To fill out a magazine installment, Thackeray added material to *The History of Pendennis* that altered the characterization of John Finucane. Wilde added five chapters, introducing many new characters to *The Picture of Dorian Gray.* Lewis's *Arrowsmith* is over 336 paragraphs longer in book than serial form. James withheld three and a half chapters from the serial version of *The Ambassadors.* When a comparison of serial versions with book publication reveals passages cut for serial publication simply because of space limitations, scholars may urge that they be included in future editions of books, as in the case of Dickens' Bleak House.

Sometimes the discovery of a misplaced passage raises a quandary, as in the case of James's The Ambassadors; put in its proper place it resolves inconsistencies but diminishes the ironical effect. Scholes cautions that when materials are insufficient, passages omitted from earlier editions, as in the case of Joyce's The Dubliners, "can be restored, in some instances, however, at the risk of error in judgment." In other cases, the solution is clear. Forty-five of Emily Dickinson's poems were originally published with one or more stanzas missing.

9. At What Stages in Composing and Publishing a Work Are Revisions Normally Done?

A work--a novel, for instance--may go through six distinct stages, at each of which an author may make revisions.

1. Notebook entries
2. Drafts
3. Serial publication
4. Book publication
5. Reprints and complete works
6. Foreign publications, editions

One may study three well-defined stages in Melville's composition of Moby Dick; three major stages in Shelley's play The Cenci; three distinct conceptual and compositional stages in Wordsworth's "Prelude." Conrad's revisions of Almayer's Folly, Lord Jim, and The Nigger of the "Narcissus" went through six stages: manuscript, typescript, serial, English publication, American publication, and definitive edition. Crane's The Red Badge of Courage may be studied in seven stages: 1) original composition of first draft; 2) revision of first draft; 3) original composition of second draft; 4) first revision of second draft; 5) last revision of second draft; 6) pagination changes and major textual deletions; 7) marginalia and typographical changes not in Crane's hand. One may examine eight versions of Yeats's "Under Ben Bulben," in four stages of composition. Madtes sees in the revisions of the seventeenth chapter alone of Joyce's Ulysses nine stages of composition: 1) notes; 2) rough draft; 3) fair copy; 4) revision of fair copy; 5) revision of first typescript; 6) revision of second typescript; 7) revision of first galley proof; 8) revision of second galley proof; 9) revision of final page proof. One may trace thirteen stages in the development of a single sentence in Joyce's Finnegans Wake over fourteen years.

Study of a writer's notebooks may offer insight into a writer's method. Notebooks show plans for and give accounts of individual works in progress. Using the term in its broadest sense, notebook entries and notes on loose sheets of paper are a kind of "revision." One may examine early notes on the conception, the narrative outline, the characters, thematic intentions and techniques of a work. Beaty is convinced that "a study of the notebook" for an unwritten novel "is essential for scholars reconstructing George Eliot's creative process or tracing the development of her mind and art." We have access to the memoranda and number plans for installments of Dickens' novels; material pertaining to *Bleak House* is especially interesting. The notes James made as he originally conceived several tales are available for study. Meredith's notes and notebooks reveal "the long gestation of much of his fiction" and his various preoccupations. The manuscript notebooks of *The Years* reveal Virginia Woolf's practice in writing the first section by alternating chapters of factual exposition with chapters of fiction in an attempt to develop an essay-novel form. In later revisions, she integrated the essay chapters into the fictional ones. In Joyce's notebooks for *Finnegans Wake* we may follow his deletions, substitutions, and additions. Joyce's notesheets for *Ulysses* were used to "assure that patterns and relationships" were realized. Gertrude Stein's notebooks show the steps that led to the first draft of *The Making of Americans.* Ronald Firbank's notebooks reveal "several important features of his style and technique." Steele examines two preliminary outlines for Ellen Glasgow's novel *Virginia.* Carson McCullers' outline for "The Mute" (*The Heart Is a Lonely Hunter*), included in *The Mortgaged Heart,* is an excellent example of a conceptualized outline. Camus' notebooks contained material for his fiction, often transcribed verbatim. John Braine comments on extracts from his notes and the second drafts of his first novel, *Room at the Top.* Not all notebooks relate significantly to an author's works. One may conclude, as in the case of Arnold Bennett's *Riceyman Steps,* that "the notebook was not a necessary prologue to the novel."

Poets' notebooks often include early versions of entire poems, as in the case of Milton, Tennyson, and Housman. Peters comments line by line on Swinburne's worksheets for "Hymn to Proserpine." White reproduces the notes for Whitman's "Lilacs" with corresponding passages in the poem.

We have access to only a few playwrights' notebooks: Ibsen's, Shaw's, and Tennessee Williams'. We have access to even fewer notebooks for works in the non-fiction genres. Howarth compares Thoreau's journal entries with the transcribed versions of "Moonlight," a kind of successor to *Walden.*

We see some poets go from prose versions to verse versions. Yeats made three prose drafts of "Under Ben Bulben." Prose and poetry versions of William Carlos Williams' "The Last Words of My English Grandmother" are given in *I Wanted to Write a Poem.* In revising his novel *The Dynasts,* Hardy converted prose materials to verse. The works of McCullers, Hemingway, and Camus provide several instances of the prefiguration of a later piece fiction in an earlier one. Bruccoli's *The Last of the Novelists* is an excellent study of the genre "work-in-progress." Fitzgerald's death left *The Last Tycoon* uncompleted.

Writers may make revisions after varying lengths of time between versions. This time lapse may have varying effects upon the kinds and quality of revisions. Many errors, as in Fielding's Joseph Andrews, come in "the rapidity of the original composition." Huxley made "constant piecemeal" revisions of Brave New World in every stage of revision. Benjamin Franklin reviewed and revised each segment of four pages of his Autobiography before going on with the next four pages. Usually, Dickens corrected as he wrote, sentence by sentence. Some writers make changes on impulse, as e. e. cummings did in "Buffalo Bill's Defunct" ; or as an afterthought, as Crane did when he made his characters anonymous in The Red Badge of Courage. The formal correspondences between the Homeric epic and the episodes of Joyce's Ulysses were produced in late revisions. The revisions of Chapter XII of Hardy's Mayor of Casterbridge were not made until over half of the novel was written. Faulkner added episodes and passages to Light in August after the early version was nearly complete. Shakespeare appears to have made changes in Julius Caesar after the prompt or fair copy was prepared. Joseph Heller revised Catch-22 over a decade. One may study documents showing the twenty-year evolution of Petrarch's Canzone XXIII.

A survey of the entries reveals that when new editions are planned, most writers seize the opportunity to make revisions, and at that stage improvements usually result. George Moore revised his earlier work within a year or two of original publication. Tennyson revised before every new edition of his work. Simms revised his first novel, Guy Rivers, twenty years later for a uniform edition of his works. Smollett made more revisions in the third and fourth than in the second edition of Roderick Random. Fielding revised five editions of Joseph Andrews. Several recent writers have revised their early novels extensively after first publication. John Fowles has rewritten several scenes of The Magus, added one or two new ones, and revised the style throughout. Gore Vidal has rewritten The City and the Pillar. Scholars have made studies of complete editions of Blake, Byron, Whitman, Yeats, Housman, among others, noting variations. Several of the entries deal with variorum editions of Yeats and others. Sometimes a revision is published posthumously--Thoreau's fourth version of "A Walk to Wachusett," for instance.

10. What Are Writers' Typical Reasons for and Intentions in Revision?

Writers revise, in most instances, for a variety of reasons: aesthetic, political, socio-economic, to adjust to the medium or to an audience. An examination of revisions of Ulysses "yields much new light on Joyce's intentions and methods." By examining the 1801 edition of Richardson's Pamela we see the author's "last intentions regarding the work." Yeats revised the Hanrahan stories simply because he had come to hate them, but in most of his revisions he had a higher purpose: "It's myself that I remake." Faulkner revises stories to make them into novels because novels sell better than story collections. In his revisions of Hard Times Dickens tried "to appeal to as wide and popular audience as possible." In revising A Passage to India, E. M. Forster's "goal is to entertain the reader by means of contrast." Henry James revised "Lady Barbarino" and "Glasses" to achieve "a more gradual, more rounded presentation." One may trace, through major revisions over twenty years, Michael Drayton's "gradual but persistent rejection of sonnets of hyperbolic sadness, of excessive conceit, and of undue religious fervor."

Out of general motivations to revise come more specific objectives: to improve the line-by-line texture of the writing; to change a character; to alter a philosophical position; to communicate more clearly; to tighten up the piece; to change the pace; to emphasize or de-emphasize an early element because of a later development. In revising "For the Time Being" Auden aimed mainly at clarity. Twain's revisions of The Innocents Abroad aimed for coherence and continuity. All Conrad's revisions of The Secret Agent, says Davis, were "toward precision, toward more direct rendering through the implication of sensory detail."

11. What Types of Revisions Do Writers Make?

With fair consistency among the entries, the term "revision" is used the same way by most scholars, but we ought to secure a workable definition of "revision." The most specific use applies to changes made line by line after the first draft, while "rewrite" is sometimes applied to major structural changes. In his essay on Lawrence's Women in Love, Branda describes a charge made against Lawrence: he "did not revise, only rewrote his work." What is the difference? "Emendation" is used, loosely, as a synonym for revision, usually pertaining to line-by-line changes. Sacco, discussing Meredith's The Ordeal of Richard Feverel, says, "my analysis suggests that 'excision' is a more precise term than 'revision.'" What, then, *is* revision? Madtes, discussing the seventeenth chapter of Joyce's Ulysses, says that "'revision' is a misleading word; 'expansion' would be more accurate." Again, what then *is* 'revision'? Here are some of the many terms used as synonyms for revision: rewrite, authorial revisions, reverse revision, continued revision; correct, emend, redact, change, alter, repair, modify, adjust, adapt, revisualize, re-evaluate, perfect, prune, burnish, play down, file. "Authorial revisions" is redundant; any changes made by anybody but the author are not revisions, but conscious or unconscious errors. We feel that the most workable overall term for anything written after the first note is "revision." The writer has a vision--fragmentary or conceptual--and makes a note, from a word to a phrase to a line to several paragraphs or pages. When he rewords or adds to that initial note, he begins the revision process, which ends when he has made the last change, as late as the fifth edition, in some cases, thirty years perhaps after the first note was made. The scholar or student of the creative process then asks, "What kind of revision has the author made?"

(We should point out here that not all the entries, especially those in Part II, deal with "revision" in the purest sense. For instance, in Part II, writers most often comment on aspects of their finished work or on the creative process itself in general terms. In Part I, many of the entries direct the reader to analyses of various texts of a work; long after the author has made the last change, editors and publishers make "corrections" or commit errors. The scholar's task is to undo what others than the author have wrought, to return the reader to the work the author finished. We have included entries in a few special categories; for instance, there is John Seelye's The True Adventures of Huckleberry Finn, an imitation that illuminates our understanding of the original--a sort of, as if, revision, by another hand.)

To arrive at a working vocabulary let us look at terms that recur throughout the entries in discussions of types of revisions. The first term listed in each of the seven categories is the one we prefer; similar terms that the reader will encounter follow. The most generally used terms for types of revisions are:

1. Additions: insert, increase, maintain, enrich
2. Expansions: enlarge, amplify, elaborate, develop, evolve
3. Deletions: cut, excise, drop, remove, cancel, reject, omit, exclude, eliminate, decrease, shorten, reduce, cut down, lessen, tighten, de-emphasize, suppress
4. Substitutions: replace, reverse
5. Re-Orderings: rearrange, shift, recast, refocus, reassign, redispose, transpose
6. Combinations: fuse, episodic fusion.

To describe the general aim or purpose of revisions, the following terms are often used in the entries: to simplify (or complicate); clarify; be more overt; emphasize; stress; heighten; underscore; strengthen; enhance; subtilize; tone down; to avoid or ameliorate problems; to improve what is written or to realize what was conceived.

Joyce's method was mainly expansion, and especially elaboration; in the "Ithaca" episode of Ulysses, forty-two per cent of his revisions are additions; he made additions to additions; he made 348 word changes, including substitutions and deletions. Wilde added five new chapters to The Picture of Dorian Gray. Richardson added over 200 pages to Clarissa to "develop more clearly and fully psychology of character and the high moral purpose of the novel." By inserting "O Soul" into "Passage to India" Whitman had to revise extensively the lines that followed. James's revisions added 2,000 words to "Four Meetings." Wolfe added 5,000 while cutting 95,000 words. Some writers do more of one type of revision than another. Additions more than any other type characterize Huxley's.

Revising six major poems for the 1842 Poems, Tennyson added no new material but excised or "ameliorated" faulty passages. Simms deleted many "authorial intrusions" in Guy Rivers. Meredith's revisions of *Richard Feveral* consist mainly of "the wholesale omission of sequential passages." Sidney deleted the first person and "apostrophes to the audience" from *Arcadia*.

12. What Basic Elements of Revision Can One Extract from These Entries?

We have said that the study of revisions has value for readers pursuing varied interests and that this bibliography is of practical value in several areas. Not only may this handbook be used as a starting point for the development of pedagogy for teaching literature and creative writing; it may also serve as a primary source for deriving a rhetoric of revision of immediate value to those who study literature, to scholars who continue work in this field, and to writers engaged in original work in all genres, and to editors.

We may imagine the writer, in the revision process, asking: What effect did I want to achieve here? Have I achieved it? If not, how may I revise to achieve my purpose? We may imagine the writer saying, *do* this, do that.

The following list of elements most often considered in the revision process suggests what to look for, what to consider as one reads these entries or conducts one's own original studies. (The entries yield few specific terms for poetry and playwriting):

1. Style
2. Figures of Speech
3. Grammar: usage; concrete nouns, pronoun reference; modifiers (adjective, adverb); verb tense, punctuation, commas; syntax; mechanics
4. Wording
5. Avoid affected words
6. Avoid wordiness
7. Phrasing
8. Sentence structure (simplify *or* make complex)
9. Paragraphing
10. Names of people and places, titles
11. Concreteness: clarity, clarify the obscure
12. Avoid vagueness, ambiguity
13. Create effective ambiguity
14. Simplify, be specific
15. Complicate
16. Overstatement
17. Understatement
18. From general to specific
19. From abstract to concrete (don't tell, show)
20. Implication (suggestivity)
21. Allusions (references)
22. Compress
23. Avoid inconsistencies
24. Avoid redundancies
25. Avoid repetition
26. Repeat for effect
27. Irrelevant material
28. Accuracy
29. Conception
30. Theme, meaning
31. Point of view
32. Authorial intrusion (commentary), editorializing
33. Characterization
34. Motivation
35. Psychological complexity
36. Emotional qualities
37. Clarify character relationships
38. Dialog
39. Colloquialism
40. Time

41. Setting
42. Situation
43. Scenes
44. Episodes
45. Plot
46. Action
47. Narration
48. Dramatic elements
49. Exposition
50. Description
51. Details
52. Imagery
53. Beginnings
54. Chronology
55. Resolution
56. Endings
57. Chapters
58. Re-order chapters, sections, episodes
59. Length
60. Form, order
61. Structural control
62. Structural symmetry
63. Pattern
64. Relation of parts to whole
65. Balance
66. Variety
67. Shifts from comic to serious
68. Shifts from serious to comic
69. Irony
70. Tension
71. Tone
72. Suspense
73. Sentimentality
74. Key elements
75. Pace
76. Tempo
77. Energy
78. Effects
79. Techniques
80. Devices
81. Juxtaposition
82. Transitions
83. Focus
84. Emphasis

Poetry: Prosody (Many of the above terms also apply)

1. Meter
2. Rhyme
3. Sound
4. Rhythms
5. Stanzas
6. Assonance
7. Alliteration
8. From prose drafts to poetry

Plays: Various Dramaturgical Considerations (Many of the above terms also apply)

The Index to Revision Problems is in itself a checklist, more detailed, more descriptive and analytical.

13. What Are Some Possible Beneficial or Harmful Effects of Revision?

Many of the scholars conclude with value judgments as to the effect of revisions. In most cases, the general effect of revisions is improvement. Some of the entries direct the reader to studies of cases in which the author, the scholar concludes, does harm to his work in revision. In only a few cases is the effect one of little difference.

Generally, there is some controversy as to whether James improved or impaired his work in the revisions he made for successive editions. The effects of revision among the works of James, as in every other aspect of his work, are complex. In his study of the revisions of Portrait of a Lady, Krause generalizes: "revision for James meant nothing less than the complete reactivation of the work in his imagination...." James revised Portrait of a Lady so intensively that the 1881 American and the 1908 New York editions strike Mazzella as two different works. Baym concludes that revisions of Portrait of a Lady "cloud the original dynamics of the story," and cause "dislocations of emphasis." Fish concludes that James "polished and refined a mediocre story," Watch and Ward. Vincec charges that James's failure to re-read The Wings of the Dove before publication resulted in "a too-lengthy novel with structural imbalances." Harvett charges that some changes in Roderick Hudson obscure "spontaneous, natural passages, making them labored, heavy, ambiguous, and sometimes almost impenetrable." To Harvett some revisions of Roderick Hudson seem "completely unimportant." Vandersee can see no observable reason for James's revision of some words in "Pandora." He concludes that "the net result is neither striking improvements nor fatal tampering."

Schweik describes the general effect of Hardy's revision of Far from the Madding Crowd: "By adding the dramatizations of Fanny Robin's story and developing Boldwood as another major character, Hardy laid the groundwork for a broader treatment of human feeling...." In A Passage to India, says Levine, E. M. Forster's characters "were gradually reshaped as Forster's theme of fissure and connection grew more prominent." Simms improved passages of conversation in his revolutionary war novels. Much of the material Conrad added to The Secret Agent, says Davis, "enhanced the impressionistic effect." Marchesani points out that Drayton's revisions in Four Legends, "in syntax and rhetoric provide a sensitive gauge for changes in structure and attitudes throughout the legends." Most of the revisions of Johnson's The Vanity of Human Wishes "show Johnson strengthening his writing by enforcing finer discriminations of sense and feeling in both word and rhythm." The revised Every Man in His Humor by Jonson is "by almost every criterion," says Dutton, "an improvement on the original." Alspach concludes that Yeats's revisions almost always improved his plays. Samuel Richardson's slight changes in Sir Charles Grandison improved the novel. Gettman shows that "the prose style of the original is often wretched," but that Moore's revisions improved Esther Waters. Stallman claims that some of Crane's revisions of Maggie improve the novel, some don't.

Some scholars attempt to determine whether and how revisions result in harm to a work. Hunt feels that usually, and especially in the Wellington sonnet, "Wordsworth's first thoughts ... may have been better than his second, third, or fourth thoughts." Hergenhan contends that Meredith's Harry Richmond is better in the original edition than in his revised edition. Jonah Raskin shows the consequences of both ineffective revisions and a lack of revision in Conrad's The Heart of Darkness. Langford observes that the published version of Faulkner's Sanctuary "simplifies Benbow's story to accommodate a new ending." Klotz contends that Faulkner's revisions harmed the short stories that made up Go Down, Moses: "great chunks of unassimilated, mostly expository, prose almost everywhere blurring thematic focus, destroying established characterization." James Early shows "abortive efforts to achieve aesthetic unity" in Go Down, Moses.

Bruccoli concludes that both Fitzgerald and his publisher made a mess of the first printing of This Side of Paradise with avoidable errors. Higgins attempts to show that Fitzgerald's reordering of the parts of Tender Is the Night in 1936 rendered it inferior to the 1934 version. Sinclair Lewis's revisions of The Man Who Knew Coolidge only "increase the incidence of banalities and ungrammatical expressions," says Richardson. Higdon says Greene's 158 changes in the published text of The Heart of the Matter "result in demonstrably inferior readings or obvious grammatical and logical errors." Sometimes it is the author who decides revisions have wrecked the work, as Woolf says about The Voyage Out in her letters. The minor changes in Woolf's To the Lighthouse "are all significant because individually and collectively they have a cumulative effect."

One may quarrel with those scholars who imply a hierarchy of value when they call revisions in style "minor." A presumption that style is a minor element emerges in several of the items cited. We contend that nothing could be more major than words, the medium in which the writer works.

14. What Formats Do Scholars Use to Show Revisions?

Among the approximately 200 journal articles and 75 books listed in Part One, scholars use several common formats for showing revisions.

1. COLUMNS: two, three, or four columns showing different versions are presented side by side on the same page. This method is most often used.
2. VERSO/RECTO: one version on the left (verso) usually an early version, another version on the right (recto), usually a revised version.
3. DIPLOMATIC PRINTING: an attempt to reproduce in print the appearance of an original manuscript; deletions in a version are indicated by striking through the cancelled material and adding new material between the lines.
4. FACSIMILES (PHOTO COPIES)
5. Revised versions of some length follow each other over several pages, forcing the reader to go back to make comparisons.
6. A few lines are quoted, then shown as revised, with commentary before and after.
7. COMBINATIONS of the above.

The formats described above show:

1. HOLOGRAPHS (autographs): material wholly in the author's handwriting.
2. TYPED DRAFTS of various versions, rough or "good."
3. FAIR COPIES of the work after all corrections and revisions have been completed.
4. GALLEY PROOF: printer's proof made to allow printer, copy editor, and author a chance to detect errors.
5. PAGE PROOF: printer's proof incorporating corrections made in the galley stage, set up as the page will appear in the book.
6. VARIOUS PRINTINGS, EDITIONS, REPRINTS.
7. AUTHOR'S NOTES, NOTEBOOK ENTRIES, OUTLINES, MARGINALIA, ETC.

Scholars may also include material never reprinted before: explanatory notes, cross references, appendices.

Some scholars simply discuss revisions without showing versions. James Early compares versions of Faulkner's _Go Down, Moses_ through his own exposition rather than by showing versions. D. S. R. Welland doesn't systematically study revisions of any single poem of Wilfred Owen's but describes the poet's revisions in a general manner. Steegmuller discusses the genesis and development of Flaubert's _Madame Bovary_ in general terms; his study is best read along with _Flaubert's letters_.

Biographical as well as artistic considerations become part of the work of some scholars. H. P. Sucksmith relates Dickens' "blueprint" for _Bleak House_ to his narrative technique and his complex vision as an artist. We see Dickens "translating his vision, by means of a rhetoric itself complex, into the substance of a work of art." P. D. Herring presents Dickens' entire Number Plans, including memoranda for material to be used, chapter divisions, summaries of contents, and titles, for _Dombey and Son_. His commentary relates each number plan to external biographical information. Howard G. Baetzhold gives a detailed biographical account of Twain's writing of _A Connecticut Yankee_. John Dozier Gordan shows how Conrad's "perseverance against unfavorable environments, his worry over health and money, his periods of nervousness and sudden spurts of creation are reflected in the copious corrections of the manuscripts" of his fiction.

The methods used by some scholars to show revisions may put the reader to work that may be either frustrating or beneficial. In our annotations to some of the entries, we advise the reader that to make the best use of the piece cited, the reader needs a copy of the complete text in hand; or the scholar may advise the reader that while analyzing a particular work one needs also to examine the pertinent manuscripts of other works. One may be left to draw one's own conclusions. For instance, Fredson Bowers in his study of the manuscript of Whitman's "Passage to India" does not make critical generalizations, but he makes the revisions easily accessible to those who would.

15. What Do Writers Say About Their Own Work and About the Creative Process in General?

The entries on revision are augmented by general and specific comments on the creative process, including revision, that writers themselves make in Part Two, "Writers Talk About the Creative Process." We have access to writer's comments through notebooks (Camus, Maugham), diaries (Woolf), journals (Gide, Mansfield, Steinbeck), letters (Woolf), interviews (the Paris Review series), collections of pieces by or about writers (works edited by Kuehl, McCormack, Allott, Allen), books by writers themselves (Wright Morris, R. V. Cassill, Henry James, Joyce Cary, John Braine), autobiographies and memoirs (Erskine Caldwell, Ford Madox Ford, Hemingway), and books by or about editors (Maxwell Perkins). In Novels in the Making, for instance, Buckler offers access to Defoe, Fielding, Smollett, Cooper, Dickens, Flaubert, Turgenev, Tolstoy, Eliot, Zola, de Maupassant, Conrad, James, Bennett, Lawrence, Gide, and Bowen at work through excerpts from author's notebook entries, sketches, outlines, letters, prefaces.

What do the writers discuss? In The Creative Vision: Modern European Writers on Their Art, the artist, the nature of art, the artist's relation to the audience, language, structure are among topics discussed.

In these entries, writers express and demonstrate love of the craft itself. We may observe the reshaping imagination at work. Often, they are inspired by some technical or stylistic solution to the problems raised in the revision process. How many revisions are necessary really to finish a story? Our investigations provide no answer. Writers themselves never seem to feel that a story is ever really finished. As one writer has said, one must finally abandon a work.

In "The Philosophy of Composition," Poe explains his own impulse to describe the process that produced "The Raven": "I have often thought how interesting a magazine paper might be written by any author who would--that is to say who could--detail, step by step, the processes by which any one of his compositions attained its ultimate point of completion...." Some writers find value themselves in their own old versions of a work; O'Casey retained early revisions throughout his lifetime as reference materials for new composition. Many writers testify to the value of writers talking about writing. Sinclair Lewis called Ford Madox Ford's Joseph Conrad: A Personal Remembrance "the one great book on the technique of writing a novel that I have ever read." Richard Wright advised Ralph Ellison to "learn how Conrad, James, Dickens got their effects."

In some of these collections, the editor asks writers to describe the creative process, as Thomas McCormack does in Afterwords: Novelists on Their Novels: describe "how it began, what it looked like to you at various stages, what problems came up and what solutions you devised, how explicit were the considerations of craft we think we see--in other words, what was going on when you worked?" Paul Engle, a poet and teacher who created one of the earliest and most effective writing workshops, observes in Poet's Choice: "Nor were we startled at the intensity of devotion to the craft of poetry expressed by many poets ... many of them speak with an almost painful affection of the number of times they revised a favorite poem." For Conrad, writing his prefaces was "a nearly ecstatic reminiscence of the adventures of composition." Some of those who analyze the revisions of other writers are themselves novelists whose conclusions have added authority: Wallace Hildick believes that "the alteration of a single word can transform completely one's view of a character."

In Making a Poem, Melville Cane conducts the reader through the entire creative process that produced several of his poems; he reports "the step-by-step, trial-and-error operations" from start to finish. John Braine uses versions of his own first novel, Room at the Top, to illustrate his "discussion of basic techniques of fiction" in his book on Writing a Novel. The writing methods of some writers are unusual: Katherine Anne Porter says, "I must know a story 'by heart' and I must write from memory." Christopher Isherwood says, "What I tend to do is not so much pick at a thing but sit down and rewrite it completely." The writers who are most articulate and voluminous in their comments on their own work and on creativity generally are Henry James, Joseph Conrad, Ford Madox Ford, Wright Morris, and John Braine.

Aside from their intrinsic value to the reader in search of them, comments on commercial writing in all genres illuminate by contrast the discussions of "serious" writing techniques. Glenn Gundell in Writing--From Idea to Printed Page shows with facsimile pages and commentary the detailed and practical author-editor collaboration process at the old Saturday Evening Post that produced their short stories and articles. In The Writer's Craft, Frederick A. Birmingham offers comments on writing commercial non-fiction, fiction, and poetry. Robert C. Meredith in Structuring Your Novel deals with problems in writing commercial fiction that prompt revision. In Writer to Writer, Floyd C. Watkins offers "down-to-earth advice about writing," quoting many writers in all literary genres. W. R. Burnett, in The Modern Short Story in the Making, quotes writers by fictional categories and techniques. In another book, This Is My Best, Burnett asks writers in all genres to choose their best work and comment on it.

Not all genres are equally represented. Screenwriting and playwriting have not received the attention they deserve. Richard Corliss gives his assessment of 38 screenwriters in Talking Pictures. William Froug allows twelve screenwriters to talk about their craft in The Screen Writer Looks at the Screenwriter. In Playwrights on Playwriting, Toby Cole reprints pieces by playwrights of several nationalities from Ibsen to Ionesco. And William Frenz's American Playwrights on Drama reprints pieces by playwrights as early as O'Neill, no later than Albee. Non-fiction is perhaps the most neglected genre.

Some writers talk of the influence upon their work of other art forms; Mann learned from music, Hemingway from painting, Madden feels a compulsion to explore all media, all genres, including criticism. Creators in other fields beyond art speak of inspiration and conceptualization and other concepts normally associated with art in Brewster Ghiselin's unusual book, The Creative Process.

Some writers talk about the effect upon their work of teaching literature and writing, as in Jonathan Baumbach's Writers as Teachers: Teachers as Writers and in John Graham's condensed version of The Writer's Voice called Craft So Hard to Learn. In Writing Fiction, generally acknowledged to be one of the best books of its kind, R. V. Cassill, himself a novelist, "emphasizes analytical reading as an integral part of learning to write fiction." The reading process is often paralleled with the writing process; as they read, general readers, critics, and even other writers revise, in a sense, what they read, prompting Henry James to caution that "we must grant the artist his subject, his idea, his donnee; our criticism is applied only to what he makes of it." In the revision process, we see quite clearly what the writer is attempting to "make of it."

In On Creative Writing, poet Paul Engle stresses the importance of self-criticism to the writer. Criticism is "a constant part of the writer's job, beginning with his rejection of one concept in favor of another, one image, one phase, rather than others." Block and Salinger observe that the essays in their book The Creative Vision: Modern European Writers on Their Work "are decisive evidence of the dominance of critical intelligence in recent European literature. Any sharp distinction between critical and creative activity has all but fallen away." In the United States the situation is not yet quite that extreme, but Philip Roth, in Reading Myself and Others, comes close; in a note, he tells us what he sees in the pieces he has written about his own works.

It is appropriate that writers have the last word. Here are some comments on aspects of the creative process arranged in a kind of progression, one comment deliberately juxtaposed to another.

ROBERT PENN WARREN: "The idea of writing a first draft with the idea of revising the first draft is repugnant to me.... I have to play for keeps on every page."

TOLSTOY: "In a writer there must always be two people--the writer and the critic." He seldom re-read his published work, "but if by chance I come across a page, it always strikes me: All this must be rewritten; this is how I should have written it."

DOSTOEVSKY: "Yes, that was and ever is my greatest torment--I can never control my material."

FORD MADOX FORD: "Consciously strive for an art that will seem artless."

ROBERT FROST: "The whole thing is performance and prowess and feats of association. Why don't critics talk about those things--?"

JAMES WHITEHEAD: "A writer is a performer ... at some point or another he becomes aware of his audience, and begins to calculate effects...."

HENRY JAMES: "Questions of art are questions of execution."

ALBERT CAMUS: "It is in order to shine sooner that authors refuse to rewrite. Despicable. Begin again." "Rewrite--the effort always brings some profit, whatever this may be. Those who do not succeed fail because they are lazy."

EVELYN WAUGH: "I regard writing not as investigation of character, but as an exercise in the use of language, and with this I am obsessed."

WILLIAM GASS: "There are no events but words in fiction."

ANAÏS NIN: "Spontaneity belongs in the first jet of writing, but some disciplined selectivity and cutting should follow in editing."

HENRY MILLER: "Work according to program and not according to mood. Stop at the appointed time."

ERNEST HEMINGWAY: "... I learned not to think about anything that I was writing from the time I stopped writing until I started again the next day. That way my subconsciousness would be working on it...."

FLAUBERT: "Feeling does not make poetry."

A. E. HOUSMAN: "Poetry is not the thing said but a way of saying it."

PAUL HORGAN: "Revision word by word and sentence does follow, for me, not once, but many times, each for a different value."

WILLIAM STYRON: "I seem to have some neurotic need to perfect each paragraph--each sentence, even--as I go along"--an average of three pages a day.

KATHERINE MANSFIELD: "In 'Miss Brill' I chose not only the

length of every sentence, but even the sound of every sentence. I chose the rise and fall of every paragraph to fit her, and to fit her on that day, at that very moment."

GERTRUDE STEIN: "So now to come to the real question--of punctuation, periods, commas, colons, semi-colons, and capitals and small letters. I have had a long and complicated life with all these."

JOSEPH CONRAD: "Give me the right word and the right accent and I will move the world."

JOY ANDERSON: "Some things in every story are necessary for the author to write, but not for the reader to read--the first few pages, usually."

GEORGE ELIOT: "Beginnings are always troublesome."

CHEKHOV: "And at the end of a novel, I must artfully concentrate for the reader an impression of the entire work."

DAPHNE du MAURIER: "No sentimentality about this job. I was ruthless, and crossed out passages that had given me exquisite pleasure to write."

SEAN O'CASEY: "Work? Ay, manalive, it is, and I don't like it, and never shall!"

VIRGINIA WOOLF: "Next morning I proceeded to slash and rewrite, in the hope of animating it; and ... destroyed the one virtue it had--a kind of continuity; for I wrote it originally in a dreamlike state, which was at any rate unbroken.... I have kept all the pages I cut out; so the thing can be reconstructed precisely as it was."

W. B. YEATS: "We must labour to be beautiful."

WALLACE STEVENS: "It is not every day that the world arranges itself into a poem."

JOHN FOWLES: "I make myself revise whether I like it or not." "All the best cutting is done when one is sick of the writing."

GORE VIDAL: (twenty years after publication) "I have rewritten the entire book."

These scholarly journals and books have proved to be good sources in the past; they are especially useful as sources of information about related books and articles in other periodicals.

1. Periodicals

American Literature
Annual Bibliography of the History of the Printed Book and Libraries
Bulletin of the New York Public Library
Dissertation Abstracts
Modern Fiction Studies
Papers of the Bibliographical Society of America
Princeton University Library Chronicle
Proof
Studies in Bibliography
Texas Studies in Literature and Language

2. Books and Articles

"The Aims, Methods, and Materials of Research in the Modern Languages and Literature." PMLA, LXVII (1952), No. 6, pp. 3-37.

Altick, Richard Daniel, and Andrew Wright. Selective Bibliography for the Study of English and American Literature. New York: Macmillan, 3rd edition, 1967.

American Literary Manuscripts: A Checklist of Holdings in Academic, Historical and Public Libraries in the United States. Austin, Texas, 1960.

"Annual Bibliography." PMLA, 1922- .

Bowers, Fredson. "Textual Criticism and the Literary Critic," Textual and Literary Criticism (Cambridge, 1959).

Downs, Robert B. American Library Resources: A Bibliographical Guide. Chicago, 1951.

Gohdes, Clarence. Bibliographical Guide to the Study of Literature of the U. S. A. Durham: Duke Univ. Press, 1959.

Hamer, Philip M. A Guide to Archives and Manuscripts in the United States. New Haven, 1961.

Harkness, Bruce. "Bibliography and the Novelistic Fallacy," Studies in Bibliography, vol. 12, 1958, pp. 59-73.

Ivy, G. S. "The Bibliography of the Manuscript-Book," in Frances Wormald and C. E. Wright, eds., The English Library before 1700 (London, 1958), pp. 32-65.

Modern Language Association of America, American Literature Group, Committee on Manuscript Holding. Austin: Univ. of Texas Press, 1961.

Richardson, Ernest Cushing. A List of Printed Catalogs of Manuscript Books. (Part III of a Union World Catalog of Manuscript Books.) New York, 1935.

Tanselle, G. Thomas. "Some Principles for Editorial Apparatus," Studies in Bibliography, vol. 25, 1952, pp. 41-88.

Taylor, Robert H. Authors at Work...: An Address Delivered at the Opening of an Exhibition of Literary Manuscripts at the Grolier Club together with a Catalogue of the Exhibition by Herman W. Liebert and Facsimiles of Many of the Exhibits. New York: Grolier Club, 1957.

These are of special interest:

Hildick, Wallace. The Rewriting of Fiction. New York: Norton, 1965.

In his introduction, Hildick, himself a novelist, discusses the various types of revision. "... an author makes only three kinds of alterations: he substitutes, he deletes, and he inserts." He then points out many sub-divisions, using examples. The book consists of excerpts from revisions of George Eliot's Middlemarch, D. H. Lawrence's The White Peacock, Odour of Chrysanthemums, The Rainbow, Samuel Butler's The Way of All Flesh, Thomas Hardy's Tess of the D'Urbervilles, Henry James's The Portrait of a Lady, Virginia Woolf's Mrs. Dalloway. Hildick presents most of the above examples without comment, allowing the reader to analyze the revision process.

Hildick, Wallace. Writing With Care. New York: Davie White, 1967.

An examination of manuscript revisions made by: 1. Samuel Butler, The Way of All Flesh; 2. Thomas Hardy, Tess of the D'Urbervilles; 3. George Eliot, Middlemarch; 4. Henry James, Daisy Miller. An excellent study, in which Hildick's method provides clear demonstrations of kinds of alterations made by the author: deletions, insertions, substitutions, running substitutions, insertions into insertions, to show attempts to improve the work that range from grammatical and stylistic points, logic and vocabulary choice, and complex adjustments of tone. The book ends with further problems from the four novels, representing "a wide range of problems in the use of language." "A change of tense can produce a heightening of tension; and the alteration of a single word can transform completely one's view of a character."

PART ONE:

ARTICLES AND BOOKS ABOUT WRITERS' REVISIONS

JAMES AGEE

Kramer, Victor A. "A Death in the Family and Agee's Projected Novel," Proof, 3 (1973): 139-154.

"From the working notes for the novel it appears that Agee must have been planning a much longer autobiographical work, and the sequential narrative as published would probably finally have formed only the concluding portion of a projected longer novel." Kramer stresses the importance of "Dream Sequence" as prologue over "Knoxville 1915" and discusses the effect it would have on the novel. He offers variants, side by side, of various passages in the novel. He argues that portions of the manuscript not used in the published version are more "detached" and complete than certain passages that were used. He explains why he thinks certain passages should have been included by the editors, and concludes that the editors did not come as close to Agee's intentions as the manuscript would warrant.

Kramer, Victor A. "James Agee Papers at the University of Texas," Library Chronicle of the University of Texas, 8 (Spring 1966): 33-36.

This article contains a facsimile of an autograph, with revisions, of an unpublished sonnet by Agee that can be read with a magnifying glass.

MARK AKENSIDE

Hart, Jeffrey. "Akenside's Revision of The Pleasures of Imagination," Publications of the Modern Language Association, 74 (1959): 67-74.

Two versions of a poem by Mark Akenside are compared: The Pleasures of Imagination (1744) and The Pleasures of the Imagination (1757 and 1765). Some of the changes apparent in the second version of Book I are (1) an increase in archaisms, reflective of an interest in Spenser; (2) simplified diction; (3) more syntactical inversion; (4) less rebelliousness and more sympathy for traditional religion and social institutions; (5) a sense of the limits of the power of human reason; and (6) an increase in the poet's powers of observation. Hart points out that "Akenside took pains with his revision, and the changes he made reflect both an increase in his poetic powers and his intense involvement with the political and cultural history of his time."

MATTHEW ARNOLD

Allott, Kenneth. "Matthew Arnold's Original Version of 'The River'," Times Literary Supplement, March 28, 1958, p. 172.

Allott reproduces here an early manuscript version of "The River" that includes six quatrains that have not appeared before and argues for the validity of that inclusion. "The poetic work of Arnold's best period is not so extensive that we can afford to do without a charming poem which its author has not clearly condemned." Allott contends that these verses were left out of the published version by Arnold only because they were too intimately revealing.

W. H. AUDEN

Morse, Donald E. "Two Major Revisions in W. H. Auden's 'For the Time Being'," English Language Notes, 7 (June 1970): 294-97.

W. H. Auden made two major changes "in the Christmas Oratorio, 'For the Time Being,' between its first publication with 'The Sea and the Mirror' as For the Time Being (New York, 1944, and London, 1945), pp. 61-124, and its appearance as the concluding piece in The Collected Poetry of W. H. Auden (New York, 1945), pp. 405-466." Auden changed the phrase HE IS, in reference to God to THOU ART; and he added three lines near the end of the oratorio to clarify an "unnecessarily dense passage."

HONORE DE BALZAC

Dargan, E. Preston, and Bernard Weinberg, editors. The Evolution of Balzac's Comédie Humaine. Chicago: University of Chicago Press, 1942.

See especially Chapter I, "Introduction: Balzac's Method of Revision." "The object of this Introduction is to show, within a limited area of inquiry, how Balzac's abundant revisions follow the lines of his general method and of his realistic processes. The material for such an investigation in any given case is almost overwhelming. Balzac's corrections and additions are likely to appear first on the manuscript of the story, then on the numerous proofs thereof, then in successive editions, up to and including the first collected edition of the Comédie humaine." "We have here attempted to show the principles which activated Balzac in making certain corrections, the results which he hoped to attain, and the methods which he used for this purpose." Various scholars examine the twenty-six works in the Comédie humaine.

ARNOLD BENNETT

Hepburn, James G. "The Notebook for Riceyman Steps," Publications of the Modern Language Association, 78 (1963): 257-261.

The thirty-six pages of Arnold Bennett's notebook for Riceyman Steps alter the conventional image of Bennett as the keeper of organized notes with all details of his plans for books written down ahead of time. The notebook jottings seem to have been more necessary for psychological reasons than they were for the craftsman in planning a piece of work. "The notations rarely deal with the external setting; they reveal a clear interest in psychology; they focus upon the novel as an isolated work, with its own internal demands. At the same time, the fragmentary and unsystematic quality of the material, the disproportionate development of minor scenes, the perfunctory notation of major points, and the omissions of significant and complex material suggest that the notebook was not a necessary prologue to the novel."

WILLIAM BLAKE

Moore, Donald K. "Blake's Notebook Versions of Infant Sorrow," Bulletin of the New York Public Library, 76 (1972): 209-219.

Blake's Notebook contains six stanzas in addition to the two engraved by Blake under the title "Infant Sorrow." These six stanzas are presented here and the stages of their composition discussed. Three photo-reproduced pages from the Notebook are included. "The Notebook poem goes on for six additional stanzas shown below, continuing the infant narrator's growth and search for delight (c) and introducing wandering vines and a mirtle tree (d). In (e), (f), and (g) the narrator describes how a hypothetical priest first prohibited him from enjoying the fruit (i. e., of the vines) or blossoms (of the tree), but then embraced the mirtle himself. The idea of hypocrisy is reinforced in the seventh stanza by the implied equation of priest with serpent. Finally, in the eighth stanza, the narrator destroys the priest, but not without staining the roots of the mirtle."

Nurmi, Martin K. "Blake's Revisions of The Tyger," Publications of the Modern Language Association, 71 (September 1956): 669-685.

William Blake's two notebook drafts of The Tyger and their revisions are presented in typographic transcription along with the final printed version. Nurmi describes the progress of composition in the context of contemporaneous world affairs and Blake's other writings and divides the development of the poem into three stages: (1) the first draft and revisions of the second stanza of this draft; (2) the second draft and an entire new stanza that becomes stanza five in the final draft; and (3) the final poem with stanzas two and four restored. "In the final stage he emphasizes the tiger's dreadfulness, portraying the beast as a cruel and bloody horror and asking pointed questions concerning its origin; in the second stage he swings to the opposite pole, shifting his emphasis to the divine origin by adding a stanza which rhetorically suggests that the tiger and the lamb do have a common creator and by omitting most of the tiger's dreadful attributes; in the third stage he retains the positive elements of the second stage, using the suggestion of the tiger's divine origin for the climax, but he also restores some of the dreadfulness of the first stage, though none of its horror, to effect a positively weighted synthesis of the two earlier stages in the complex affirmation of the final poem."

Blake, William. "The Tyger," The Norton Anthology of English Literature, Vol. II, M. H. Abrams, et al., eds. New York: Norton, 1979, pp. 2514-16.

"Our transcriptions from the poets' drafts attempt to reproduce, as accurately as the change from script to print will allow, the appearance of the original manuscript page."

Blake, William. The Pickering Manuscript. Introduction by Charles Ryskamp. Charlottesville: University of Virginia Press, 1972.

Included are "The Smile," "The Golden Net," "The Mental Traveler," "The Land of Dreams," "Mary," "The Crystal Cabinet," "The Grey Monk," "Auguries of Innocence," "Long John Brown and Little Mary Bell," "William Bond," with 22 pages of facsimiles.

Keynes, Geoffrey. The Complete Writings of William Blake, With Variant Readings. London: Oxford University Press, 1966.

"Reading a poem by Blake with the lines broken up by his hesitations and alterations will often be found to give fresh beauty and new light to its meaning by engaging the reader's closer attention and illustrating the poet's method of composition. The outstanding example of the second advantage is, of course, in 'The Tyger' where the MS Note-book provides two early versions and the printed Songs of Experience gives the final form." Keynes uses brackets and the notation del. to indicate deleted words, phrases, and lines. Footnotes offer interpretations of doubtful words and also changes made by Blake with pen on printed versions. The Index of First Lines can be used to locate the several versions of some of the poems, e.g., "Tyger, Tyger, burning bright: pp. 172, 173, 214." The Notes describe the manuscripts used and include, in some cases, fair copies of poems that do not appear in their entirety in any other form.

JAMES BOSWELL

SEE Smith, Chapman, and Powell, Johnson and Boswell under Samuel Johnson.

RAY BRADBURY

Bradbury, Ray. The October Country. New York: Ballantine Books, Inc., 1955.

Ray Bradbury notes that 15 of the stories in this collection were published in August Derleth's Arkham House edition of his first book Dark Carnival, a limited edition, now out of print. He says he has rewritten several of his favorite stories from the early work, but does not name them. If one is to compare early versions with later ones, one must scan the early collection, comparing it with The October Country.

ROBERT BROWNING

Maynard, John. "Browning's 'Sicilian Pastoral'," Harvard Library Bulletin, 20 (1972): 436-43.

Maynard presents the variants among three versions of a poem by Robert Browning: "Sicilian Pastoral" (a manuscript in the Harvard College Library); "Love Among the Ruins" (1855 first edition); and "Love Among the Ruins" (1919 standard text). Browning made minor phrase changes and changes in punctuation and single words for purposes of clarity and smoothness. These changes tended to increase the contrast between the pastoral world of the speaker and the bustling, dissonant city of the past. "As we have seen, Browning worked in a consistent way in his revision to heighten the traditional and essential dichotomy of the pastoral vision: celebration of country innocence and condemnation of urban corruption."

ANTHONY BURGESS

Cullinan, John. "Anthony Burgess' A Clockwork Orange: Two Versions," English Language Notes, 9 (June 1972): 287-92.

Both the Norton and Ballantine editions of A Clockwork Orange, published in the United States, leave out the last chapter which is included in the English edition by Heinemann. Norton apparently negotiated with Burgess to omit the twenty-first chapter in which the protagonist, Alex, begins to grow out of his compulsion to gang violence. The fact that the Stanley Kubrick film version is based on the American edition further frustrates Burgess' complete intentions regarding this work. "The last chapter in the English edition presents Alex in a somewhat different light. Now eighteen and attired as a 'Skinhead' with a new gang, he seems as ready for a night of violence as before; yet he is curiously bored by the prospect, and a baby's photograph he carries in his wallet indicates the onset of paternal feeling."

ROBERT BURTON

Hallwachs, Robert G. "Additions and Revisions in the Second Edition of Burton's Anatomy of Melancholy: A Study of Burton's Chief Interests and of His Style as Shown in His Revisions," Dissertation Abstracts, 12 (1952): 300-301.

"The changes appearing in the second edition, which are representative of those in later editions also incorporating Burton's revisions and editions, show much about Burton and his book. They reveal, first, the deliberate care Burton took in revising and adding to the Anatomy of Melancholy. They also make clear the conscious artistry of his prose style and show in what ways he worked deliberately to improve that style in the new edition of his work. Finally, and perhaps most important of all, they emphasize and throw into sharp relief his predominant interests and opinions, and thereby point to what were his real purposes in writing this book."

LORD BYRON

Steffan, Truman Guy, editor. Lord Byron's "Cain": Twelve Essays and a Text with Variants and Annotations. Austin: University of Texas Press, 1968.

Steffan gives a detailed account of the gestation of the play. Variants and annotations accompany the text. Steffan reproduces a sample page of manuscript.

McGann, Jerome. "The Composition, Revision, and Meaning of Childe Harold's Pilgrimage III," Bulletin of the New York Public Library, 71 (1967): 415-30.

Three manuscripts of Childe Harold's Pilgrimage once existed; "the fair copy" was lost. "The history of the poem's composition has always remained largely a matter of conjecture.... Even without the lost fair copy, however, one can arrive at a fairly precise account of when Byron began and finished his poem, and how it developed in the interim." A tabular collation of the two manuscripts is provided at the end. This article deals more with historical matters than with actual revisions.

Steffan, Truman Guy. "Byron's Focus on Revision in His Composition of Don Juan," University of Texas Studies in English, 31 (1952): 57-67.

A study of the manuscripts reveals the kinds of writing that seemed more difficult for Byron, as indicated by the kinds of lines that were heavily revised. "His most concentrated revision appears when he deals with five kinds of materials: (1) psychological analysis; (2) physical description of place and person; (3) vehement abuse and satiric or serious reflection on social or political topics, especially when he was personally involved; (4) images and allusions; and (5) trifling frivolity, where he often tries by clever revision to bolster and enliven manner, as a kind of reparation for tenuous matter."

Steffan, Truman Guy, and Willis W. Pratt. Byron's "Don Juan." A Variorum Edition. 4 vols. Austin: University of Texas Press, 1957.

Volume I, The Making of a Masterpiece, by T. G. Steffan, offers a three-way view of Don Juan. Part One, the "Chronicle," presents Byron's various descriptions of the writing of the poem; Part Two, "The Anvil of Composition," offers insight into the changes Juan underwent as it grew; Part Three, "An Epic Carnival," examines the finished product. "The Anvil of Composition" is divided into four chapters: 6. "Accretion"; 7. "Extent of Revision"; 8. "Focus of Revision"; and 9. "Furbishing." Accretive stanzas are categorized as (1) "exhuberant expansion, allusive accumulation, imagemaking"; (2) "serious or satiric excursion with social, psychological, and philosophical ideas"; (3) "structural supports of pattern, narrative, and characterization"; and (4) "autobiographical pressures (personal echoes)." "Most surprising is the evidence that much of his writing did not come easily. One could expect Keats, intensely self-conscious about his artistry, to make many changes in certain stanzas of a poem so elaborate in texture as the 'Eve of St. Agnes.' But one does not expect a Donny Johnny in a bedroom farce to cause a Byron to worry with a word or phrase. Yet a very large number of stanzas are almost as much juggled with, staggered through, pushed all over the page, and blotted as those about old Angela, the beadsman, Madeline, and Porphyro." In Chapter 9, "Furbishing," Steffan categorizes the kinds of revisions in Juan and gives specific examples of each: packing, new substance, images and allusions, energy, precision, implication, colloquialism, propriety, rhetoric, rhyming, Mary Shelley's changes, and perspective. Appendix C enumerates and describes the accretive stanzas, and Appendix D, "Stanzas Showing the Full Process of Manuscript Composition," presents twenty-four stanzas with all of the line-by-line revisions of each so that the order in which the revisions occurred is clear.

Byron, Lord George Gordon. "Don Juan," The Norton Anthology of English Literature, Vol. II, M. H. Abrams, et al., eds. New York: Norton, 1979, pp. 2517-18.

"Our transcriptions from the poets' drafts attempt to reproduce, as accurately as the change from script to print will allow, the appearance of the original manuscript page."

Butler, Maria Hogan. "An Examination of Byron's Revision of Manfred, Act III," Studies in Philology, 60 (1963): 627-636.

Byron wrote the first version of Act III (1816) under the influence of the Shelleys in the Swiss Alps, making the Abbot an iniquitous and worldly figure and setting up Manfred for certain damnation. He wrote the second version (1817) after an association with an American bishop in Venice and made the Abbot a kindly Christian friar who may or may not have made Manfred's salvation possible. "That Byron chose to transform a veritable 'Witch Drama' in such a way that his 'magician' must 'leave off magic,' must be a man, not a magician, to face Death, not 'untended,' not devoured by his own magic, but in the presence of Holy Church, seems to indicate that the drama is intended to represent the full cycle of man's eternal struggle for a 'way out' which is not devoid of hope, even for the 'lost man'."

JAMES M. CAIN

Cain, James M. The Postman Always Rings Twice. New York: Alfred A. Knopf, 1934. SEE Camus, The Stranger, Madden.

ALBERT CAMUS

A Happy Death. New York: Alfred A. Knopf, 1972. Translated by Richard Howard.

The purpose of the Afterword by Jean Sarocchi is "to sketch a literary genesis." He claims that "despite the obvious differences in plot, structure, and intention we may see in A Happy Death a prefiguration of The Stranger and even, setting aside the biological sense of the term, its matrix. To be convinced of this, we need merely compare the structure of the two works...." And since Camus admitted the influence upon The Stranger of James M. Cain's The Postman Always Rings Twice, it is instructive to compare that novel with both A Happy Death and The Stranger; one sees a great difference in style between the two novels by Camus and similarities between Cain's novel and The Stranger. Sarocchi provides twenty pages of notes and variants that trace the revision process and relate A Happy Death to The Stranger. SEE ALSO Camus' own notebook entries pertaining to both novels. SEE The Stranger and Madden, "James M. Cain's The Postman Always Rings Twice and Albert Camus' L'Etranger."

Madden, David. "James M. Cain's The Postman Always Rings Twice and Albert Camus' L'Etranger." Papers on Language and Literature, VI (Number 4, Fall, 1970), 407-419.

Madden shows specific similarities and contrasts between the two novels. "While one cannot say with certainty that Camus deliberately used The Postman as a model, it can be said that every element in Camus' novel that parallels an element in Cain's novel has been transformed into something finer." While there is nothing here about revisions, a close study of influence enhances our study of Camus' early novel A Happy Death as it relates to The Stranger. SEE A Happy Death and The Stranger.

Camus, Albert. The Stranger. 1946; reprint. New York: Vintage Books, 1958. SEE A Happy Death and Madden, "James M. Cain's The Postman Always Rings Twice and Albert Camus' L'Etranger."

LEWIS CARROLL

Carroll, Lewis. The Annotated Alice. Alice's Adventures in Wonderland and Through the Looking Glass, illustrated by John Tenniel, with introduction and notes by Martin Gardner. New York: Clarkson N. Potter, 1960.

The process of composition and revision are discussed in some of the notes.

Godman, Stanley. "Lewis Carroll's Final Corrections to 'Alice'," Times Literary Supplement, May 2, 1958, p. 248.

Lewis Carroll's revisions for the Christmas, 1896, edition of Alice and Through the Looking Glass were made upon copies of the 1882 edition of Alice and 1880 edition of Through the Looking Glass borrowed from the seventeen-year-old daughter of a girls' boarding school mistress. The changes were mostly in punctuation, capitalization, spelling, and italicization; but Lewis Carroll made a number of textual alterations. For example, "These were the verses the White Rabbit read:" changed to "There was dead silence in the court, whilst the White Rabbit read out these verses...." Copies of the books in hand would facilitate an understanding of the revisions, presented in this article in their entirety.

SAMUEL L. CLEMENS

Baetzhold, Howard G. "The Course of Composition of A Connecticut Yankee: A Reinterpretation," American Literature, 33 (May 1961): 195-214.

This detailed biographical account of the writing of the novel includes some information about revision. "This article will rechart the course of that composition to show that the first three chapters were planned and written (earlier than Hoben thought) between December, 1885 and March, 1886; that during the summer of 1887 when A Yankee supposedly lay untouched, Twain wrote some sixteen chapters; and that the manuscript was finished by May, 1889."

Dickinson, L. T. "Mark Twain's Revisions in Writing The Innocents Abroad," American Literature, 19 (May 1947): 139-157.

Mark Twain sent fifty letters to the Alta California during his voyage on the Quaker City and spent the six months after his return revising and reordering them for book publication with an Eastern audience in mind. Dickinson describes the rewriting process under the headings of clarity, variety, propriety, and humor. In order to achieve clarity, Mark Twain excised redundancies, cleared up pronoun references, made additions for coherence and continuity, and reordered details and longer sections. "In recognition of the more genteel taste of his new readers, Clemens tried in several ways to adapt his writing to them--by purifying his expression, by deleting or modifying coarse passages, and by altering his remarks in order to avoid the charge of blasphemy."

Hill, Hamlin L. "The Composition and Structure of Tom Sawyer," American Literature, 32 (January 1961): 379-392.

An examination of the manuscript of Mark Twain's Tom Sawyer reveals that the first part of the writing was mostly fictionalized anecdotes from the author's childhood and that the original plan was to continue the story into Tom's manhood. The later writing, however, involved a decision to end the book with Tom still a boy, but a boy who has been made to mature through the moving around of events and chapters so that a logical growth pattern can be discerned. "The original outline indicated that [the book] was begun with a definite structure in the author's mind. And the rearrangement of the later material shows that, instead of growing 'as grows the grass,' the book was considerably altered to conform to a bisected version of the outline...."

SAMUEL TAYLOR COLERIDGE

Coleridge, Samuel Taylor. The Annotated Ancient Mariner. With an introduction and notes by Martin Gardner. Illustrated by Gustave Doré. New York: Clarkson N. Potter, Inc./Publisher, 1965.

Some of the notes deal with revisions. A final chapter summarizes critical interpretations of the poem.

Bailey, June D. "Coleridge's Revisions of The Friend: A Study of

His Thought and Method," Dissertation Abstracts, 15 (January-June 1955): 120-121.

"Minor revisions are confined to grammatical and rhetorical problems which the long, involved sentences and the sloppy printing of the first edition, along with Coleridge's desire for clarity of phrase and precision of diction, made for. And his reworking of materials shows, as do all the revisions he made, that Coleridge was motivated by a desire to clarify and simplify his prose, to sharpen the focus of his point of view, and with these to make more incisive his criticism of the popular political and moral opinions of his day."

Lowes, John Livingston. The Road to Xanadu. New York: Vintage Books, Random House, Inc., 1955 (1927).

One of the most exhaustive studies ever made of the imaginative processes of a poet. "I propose to tell the story, so far as I have charted its course, of the genesis of two of the most remarkable poems in English, 'The Rime of the Ancient Mariner,' and 'Kubla Khan.'" Lowes states that "our interest is in a study of the imaginative processes themselves," to "discover how, in two great poems, out of chaos the imagination frames a thing of beauty." The notes are voluminous.

Martin, C. G. "Coleridge's 'Lines to Thelwall': A Corrected Text and A First Version," Studies in Bibliography, 20 (1967): 254-257.

First and second drafts of a poem Samuel Taylor Coleridge did not publish in his lifetime are presented and compared. "Though the final couplet of the second draft is not represented in the first, its drift is clearly enough implied, so that first draft's broken conclusion can be read as an attempt to condense the second part of the poem within the compass of a sonnet."

Zall, P. M. "Coleridge's Unpublished Revisions to 'Osorio'," Bulletin of the New York Public Library, 71 (1967): 516-23.

Zall examines three manuscripts of "Osorio" and concludes that Poetical Works, edited by E. H. Coleridge, presents two of them accurately but omits from the third important passages that demonstrate Coleridge's method of revision. "Aside from this extrinsic interest, MS III retains considerable intrinsic value for showing how Coleridge worked by trial and error to create a successful play without benefit of Sheridan's expert assistance after all." The revisions noted have more to do with clarifying ambiguous plot development than they do with improving the artistic value of the play.

Coleridge, Ernest Hartley, editor. The Complete Poetical Works of Samuel Taylor Coleridge, Including Poems and Versions of Poems Now Published for the First Time. 2 volumes. Oxford: Clarendon Press, 1912.

All detailed variants are given in footnotes. In Appendix I of Vol. 2, eighteen poems are printed in two or more different drafts; or an earlier version is printed (as in the case of "The Rime of the Ancient Mariner"). "His erasures and emendations are not only a lesson in the art of poetry, not only a record of poetical growth and development, but they discover and reveal the hidden springs, the thoughts and passions of the artificer."

JOSEPH CONRAD

Eddleman, Floyd E., David L. Higdon, and Robert W. Hobson. "The First Editions of Joseph Conrad's Almayer's Folly." Proof, 4 (1975): 83-108.

The first American edition of Conrad's first novel (Macmillan, 1895) was based on the unrevised proof sheets from the first English edition (Unwin, 1895). These proof sheets, however, were revised by Conrad for the Unwin edition, which represents a later state of the novel. Eddleman et al. examine the changes made by the Macmillan editor and the revisions Conrad effected in the proof stage for the Unwin edition. "Conrad's revisions, astonishingly diverse and numerous, demonstrate his preoccupation with the problems of repetition and redundancy, idiomatic rephrasing..., more precise images, and grammatical consistency." Of particular interest is Conrad's problem with English idioms.

Eddleman, Floyd E., and David L. Higdon. "The Typescript of Conrad's Almayer's Folly," Texas Studies in Literature and Language, 18 (Spring 1976): 98-123.

"The sheer number of substantive revisions may be misleading. No major revisions of action, motivation, description, or characterization are effected. Rather, the 440 changes in wording, 162 additions, 93 deletions, and 14 oddities concentrate primarily on increased grammatical correctness, precision of imagery, idiomatic phrasing, and refocused details." Eddleman and Higdon present these revisions with relevant commentary.

Gross, Seymour L. "Conrad's Revision of 'Amy Foster'," Notes and Queries, 208 (1963): 144-146.

Joseph Conrad revised "Amy Foster" between its serial publication in The Illustrated London News in December of 1901 and its appearance in Typhoon, and Other Stories (1903). "In addition to several changes in word-order and paragraphing, and numerous alterations in punctuation (which may of course be editorial rather than authorial), Conrad made over fifty changes in diction (either substitution, addition, or deletion of words) and altered the names of two characters." Some of the categories of the changes in diction are (1) preferences of the moment; (2) corrections for accuracy; (3) corrections of usage; (4) additions that increase the visual character of the prose; and (5) changes to affectedly elevated rhetoric.

Raskin, Jonah. "Heart of Darkness: The Manuscript Revisions," Review of English Studies, n. s., 18 (1967): 30-39.

"The MS. contains both single-word variants and long, fairly comprehensive changes. I have dealt with the larger, more important alterations which reflect on Conrad's themes, for most of the single-word changes are unimportant in evaluating Conrad's technique and theme. Five major revisions are under consideration; those concerning the historical analogy between Roman and modern times, the metaphor 'the heart of darkness,' the imperial establishment in the Congo, the description of Kurtz, and Conrad's treatment of the primitive." Raskin relates what he considers some of Conrad's failures in the novella to his revisions and to a certain lack of revision.

Davis, Harold E. "Conrad's Revisions of The Secret Agent: A Study in Literary Impressionism," Modern Language Quarterly, 19 (1958): 244-254.

Joseph Conrad added descriptive details, intermediate length passages, and one whole chapter to the American serial version of The Secret Agent (Ridgeway's Militant Weekly: October 6, 1906 to December 15, 1906) in order to produce the novel in book form (1907). Much of the added material enhanced the impressionistic effect of the novel, and Davis documents this change by furnishing many specific examples. "The Secret Agent is almost a mid-point in Conrad's development of impressionism, and this development is perhaps the most important single technical change evident in the revisions from serial to novel. The central tendency of all the changes is toward precision, toward more direct rendering through the implication of sensory detail, rather than telling through a point-by-point chronological narrative."

Gordan, John Dozier. Joseph Conrad: The Making of a Novelist. New York: Russell & Russell, 1963.

Chapter IV, "The Growth of the Text," deals with Conrad's revisions in completing six states of work--manuscript, typescript, serial, English publication, American publication, and definitive edition--for three novels: Almayer's Folly, The Nigger of the "Narcissus," and Lord Jim. "The study of Conrad's habits of composition substantiates his claim that he wrote first and theorized later. His perseverance against unfavorable environments, his worry over health and money, his periods of nervousness and sudden spurts of creation are reflected in the copious corrections of the manuscripts. The cancellations, new attempts, economies, incoherence, and sudden changes of those blackened pages are evidence of his perplexities. He felt his way towards the plot of his stories and towards the best presentation of his material. The labor with which he evolved some of his most moving passages explains his dissatisfaction with the rewards of his work. One is able to see through Conrad's eyes that writing is 'un art trop difficile'."

Kerf, Rene. "The Nigger of the 'Narcissus' and the Ms. Version of The Rescue," English Studies, 44 (1963): 437-443.

"Together with the nautical setting and the imagery used to deal with it, the common sailor type and the way in which he is described are elements of The Rescue, Part I, which foreshadow The Nigger of the 'Narcissus'." Kerf establishes that Rescue was written before Nigger, though published afterwards, and shows the peril of interpreting Conrad's works in ignorance of that fact. Kerf quotes a long passage Conrad omitted from Nigger and explains Conrad's reasons.

Ordonez, Elmer A. "The Early Development of Joseph Conrad: Revisions and Style," Dissertation Abstracts, 23 (April-June 1963): 4362.

Ordonez studies Almayer's Folly (1895); An Outcast of the Islands (1896); The Nigger of the "Narcissus" (1898); Tales of Unrest (1898); Lord Jim (1900); Youth and Two Other Stories (1902); and Typhoon and Other Stories (1903). "The initial step in this analysis has been to examine the revisions made by Conrad in two phases--from manuscript to print (serial or book) and from serial to first edition--of the early works given above. The revisions indicate that during this period he was concerned largely with stylistic matters. Apparently only a few structural changes--in plot and character--were made in these stories; for on the whole he was interested in improving the verbal means and elements of his prose fiction."

JAMES GOULD COZZENS

Ludwig, Richard M. "A Reading of the James Gould Cozzens Manuscripts," Princeton University Library Chronicle, 19 (Autumn 1957): 1-14.

This general discussion of Cozzens' career also describes the fifteen file boxes of papers and manuscripts he gave to the Princeton University Library. Three versions of the opening page of By Love Possessed (early manuscript version, first text, and second text) are presented in sequence with Ludwig's comments. Photographic reproductions of typescript with Cozzens' revisions penned upon them make available four versions of the first page of Part Three of By Love Possessed: "B" Version, "G" Version, "H" Version, and Final Version. "All seven of these manuscripts deserve close study..., but none is as rewarding as By Love Possessed. Cozzens has preserved a first and second text (so labeled by his own hand), the final printer's copy, the corrected galleys, and hundreds of assorted sheets of versions abandoned or altered during the novel's eight years of incubation."

Meriwether, James B. "The English Editions of James Gould Cozzens," Studies in Bibliography, 15 (1962): 207-217.

Cozzens is quoted: "All the English editions have a certain number of changes. They were always published later and in English proof I had a chance to change things I'd come to wish I'd changed in the American proof...." Meriwether spotchecks two novels in their American and English editions and fully collates another. Michael Scarlett contains at least one example of improvement in the English edition, but Castaway shows revision for the better in the American version. In a complete collation of S. S. San Pedro, seventeen of nineteen revisions demonstrate the American version to be the later, revised one. Meriwether does not necessarily draw the conclusion that Cozzens' statement is incorrect but calls for a careful examination of all major American writers in their British editions as well as in their American ones. Meriwether establishes five categories of changes in S. S. San Pedro: (1) spelling;

(2) punctuation; (3) hyphenation; (4) paragraphing; (5) authorial revision.

STEPHEN CRANE

Stallman, R. W. "Stephen Crane's Revision of Maggie: A Girl of the Streets," American Literature, 26 (January 1955): 528-536.

Following the first edition (1893) of Maggie, Stephen Crane revised the novel for publication by Appleton in 1896. The main thrust of his changes was to tone down the curse words spread so thickly through the first edition, but he also excised some words that had unfortunate sentimental and melodramatic effects. One deleted passage that Stallman feels should be reinstated describes an additional character in the procession of men Maggie meets in her walk to the river. Some of the revisions, then, are improvements, and some are not. "The striking thing about the 1893 edition is that it is far more picturesque in phrasing than the 1896 edition."

Crane, Stephen. The Red Badge of Courage and Selected Stories. Edited by R. W. Stallman. New York: New American Library, 1952.

This edition includes the same notes, the same text of The Red Badge of Courage, and the same bracketed indications of textual variants as Stallman's Stephen Crane: An Omnibus; but it does not include the complete essay on the manuscripts. The paperback format, however, facilitates its use in class-sized quantities.

Crane, Stephen. Stephen Crane: An Omnibus. Edited by R. W. Stallman. New York: Knopf, 1952.

Stallman makes comparisons among three versions of The Red Bad of Courage: (1) the second draft manuscript; (2) the final manuscript; and (3) the first American edition. In a section of one of his introductory essays, "The Original Manuscripts of The Red Badge of Courage," pp. 201-224, Stallman describes the writing and early publishing history of this novel, which is presented here in its entirety. Footnotes and brackets in the text of the novel, pp. 225-370, indicate additions and excisions, including a whole chapter that was removed after the second-draft manuscript. Three versions of the ending demonstrate Crane's concern with the paradoxical nature of the human condition. Two conclusions drawn by Stallman are (1) that Crane, despite his public claims to the contrary, revised extensively, and (2) that the anonymity of the characters was an afterthought developed and applied during revision.

Stallman, R. W. "The Red Badge of Courage: A Collation of Two Pages of Manuscript Expunged from Chapter XII," Papers of the Bibliographical Society of America, 49 (1955): 273-277.

Stallman arrays the original and two revised versions of several paragraphs from a chapter that Stephen Crane later expunged entirely from The Red Badge of Courage. The second revised version contains an example of Crane's moving away from the use of specific names of characters. Fleming is canceled, and the youth is written in. An example of the kind of change made by Crane to make his imagery more concrete is also available here.

> Manuscript SV 84:
> "... All possible forces and fates which were swelling down upon him like storms."
>
> Berg 98:
> "... All possible forces and fates which were swelling down upon him in black tempests."

Howarth, William L. "The Red Badge of Courage Manuscript: New Evidence for a Critical Edition," Studies in Bibliography, 18 (1965): 230-247.

Through an examination of the two manuscript drafts of The Red Badge of Courage by Stephen Crane, Howarth identifies seven different states of writing: (1) the original composition of the first draft; (2) the revision of the first draft; (3) the original composition of the second draft; (4) first revision of the second draft; (5) last revision of the second draft; (6) pagination changes and major textual deletions; and (7) marginalia and typographical changes not in Crane's hand. Howarth describes several kinds of changes: (1) improving chapter endings by dropping exposition and adding specific action; (2) changing from the regular use of characters' names to the use of descriptive phrases such as "a blatant young soldier" for allegorical effect; (3) dropping the terms young and youthful in most of their applications to other characters so as to emphasize youth as a dimension of Henry Fleming; (4) normalizing the dialect of some of the main characters; and (5) deleting some of Fleming's interior monologues in favor of dramatic action.

E. E. CUMMINGS

Kidder, Rushworth M. "'Buffalo Bill's'--An Early E. E. Cummings Manuscript," Harvard Library Bulletin, 24 (1976): 373-380.

Kidder presents a manuscript, in photo-reproduction and in diplomatic transcription, that may be the first draft of "Buffalo Bill's defunct." The final version of the poem also appears in this creative analysis of the changes Cummings wrought. "Essentially, it gives us an insight into his creative process: it helps us understand the particular blend of the mundane and the poetic that informs his work. Cummings drew his ideas, as other men do theirs, not out of thin and magic air but out of the context of his daily experience. Unlike many, however, he discovered in the context symbols of potentially penetrating significance. Seeing that potential, he proceeded to craft a poem--not in a sudden blast of vatic inspiration, nor in an offhand and cavalier flourish, but, like other men, in a deliberate and step-by-step manner full of trial and error, impulses and deletions."

DONALD DAVIDSON

Young, Thomas Daniel, and M. Thomas Inge. "Lee in the Mountains: The Making of a Poem," Donald Davidson, An Essay and a Bibliography. Nashville: Vanderbilt University Press, 1965.

Young and Inge examine closely the five versions of Davidson's best-known poem. Allen Tate comments on how the fourth version affected the final version. "An examination of the extant drafts of 'Lee in the Mountains' and the Tate comments demonstrates concretely the manner in which the criticism of the Fugitive Group assisted its member poets in their creative efforts; this examination may also give some insight into the mysterious process of creativity itself."

CHARLES DICKENS

Sucksmith, H. P. "Dickens at Work on Bleak House: A Critical Examination of His Memoranda and Number Plans," Renaissance and Modern Studies, 9 (1965): 47-85.

"The interesting memoranda and number plans Dickens used in writing Bleak House have never been published or considered in their entirety.... I shall try to relate the author's blueprint for Bleak House to both his narrative technique and his complex vision as an artist to give, that is, a glimpse of Dickens at the very moments when he is translating his vision, by means of a rhetoric itself complex, into the substance of a work of art." "A general survey of the notes for Bleak House affords fascinating glimpses into Dickens' mind, disclosing the manner in which he saw, imagined and manipulated the main threads and pieces of his narrative design." "Everywhere in the notes for Bleak House we find Dickens exploiting irony." "We can ... find evidence in Dickens' notes of two striking instances where the requirements of both his vision and his rhetoric compelled him to make major modifications to his original plans for the construction of Bleak House." The twenty pages of Dickens' Memoranda and Number Plans are published with the article.

DeVries, Duane. "The Bleak House Page-Proofs: More Shavings from Dickens' Workshop," Dickensian, 66 (1970): 3-7.

DeVries publishes here three pages of passages Dickens cut from the serial version of Bleak House, in response to space limitations, a situation that argues "sufficient justification for printing the deletions here and even for including them, within brackets, perhaps, as part of the text of the novel."

Herring, P. D. "The Number Plans for Dombey and Son: Some Further Observations," Modern Philology, 68 (November 1970): 151-187.

Charles Dickens' number plans for Dombey and Son, presented here in their entirety, include memoranda for material to be used, chapter divisions, summaries of contents, and titles. Herring's commentary relates each number plan to external biographical information and to the inside of the novel itself, resulting in an extensive account of the making of the novel. "Whether the number plans were necessitated by the difficulties Dickens experienced in writing at this time ... or whether they were a result of the conscious intention expressed in the preface to the preceding novel, Martin Chuzzlewit ..., he obviously found the practice profitable and continued it for the remainder of his monthly number novels."

Monod, Sylvere. "Dickens at Work on the Text of Hard Times," Dickensian, 64 (1968): 86-99.

Monod co-edited Hard Times for the Norton Critical Edition and in this article makes direct comparisons of versions. A photo reproduction of a manuscript page (magnifying glass needed) is included. Monod's intention is "to present and discuss a sampling of the more interesting kinds of textual observations suggested by Dickens' work on Hard Times ... for a better knowledge of Dickens the craftsman and the artist." "The changes he made may have resulted from some aesthetic or moral intention and therefore deserve close examination." "Dickens' work on his style proper, and the evolution of his purposes, are most interesting to observe." In his revisions, he tried to preserve "the consistency of each of his characters," to preserve "within his narrative a certain unity of tone," to "appeal to as wide and popular audience as possible." "One of our rewards was, and is, an increased respect for Dickens' conscientious craftsmanship. His work on the text of Hard Times, though not impeccable, was certainly eager, lucid and passionate."

Butt, John, and Kathleen Tillotson. Dickens at Work. London: Methuen, 1957.

Dickens' methods of working are described through examinations of his number plans for the installments of his novels. Publication of the first volume of a work normally proceeded before the writing of the second volume was completed, and notes for numbers were revised after changes in actual writing were made in order to have a corrected reference for the author as he moved on to compose additional installments. "The different shades of ink which he used from time to time show that his habit was to correct as he wrote, sentence by sentence, and that though he subsequently read through the whole of his chapter, he rarely needed to make any later alteration." Butt and Tillotson have included studies of (1) Sketches by Boz; (2) Pickwick Papers; (3) Barnaby Rudge; (4) Dombey and Son; (5) David Copperfield; (6) Bleak House; (7) Hard Times; and (8) Little Dorrit.

EMILY DICKINSON

Bingham, Millicent Todd. "Poems of Emily Dickinson: Hitherto Published Only in Part," New England Quarterly, 20 (1947): 3-50.

"Forty-five poems by Emily Dickinson originally published with one or more stanzas missing are here made available in their entirety. With them are eleven others: three which have appeared piecemeal, here brought together for the first time; four heretofore printed as prose in Emily's letters; and four which are best described as variant versions." Bingham makes these additional stanzas and variant versions available without critical comment except to notice that in Emily Dickinson's very productive last period she was writing more new poems and spending less time on revising old ones. Bingham also notes that the stanzas and variants presented here are not necessarily ones that were preferred by Emily Dickinson.

Johnson, Thomas H. The Poems of Emily Dickinson. Including variant readings critically compared with all known manuscripts. 3 vols. Cambridge, Massachusetts: The Belknap Press of Harvard University Press, 1955.

"For one thing, the several stages demonstrate the extent to which she adopted her own suggested changes. They show a worksheet draft redacted into a semifinal one, and that into a fair copy which clearly is the text that satisfied her.... Above all, they show her filing her lines to gain that economy of expression which, when achieved, is the mark of her special genius." Volume I includes twenty pages of photographic reproductions of manuscripts.

JOHN DOS PASSOS

Kallich, Martin. "A Textual Note on John Dos Passos' Journey Between Wars," Papers of the Bibliographical Society of America, 43 (1949): 346-348.

A comparison of John Dos Passos' Rosinante to the Road Again (1922) with his Journeys Between Wars (1938) reveals that he included most of the earlier publication in the later one but revised it significantly, making four kinds of changes: (1) altering the order of chapters; (2) combining chapters; (3) deleting material; and (4) emending the text. Kallich maintains that Dos Passos suppressed certain passages in order to cover up his earlier enthusiasm for the Communist movement and to play down a youthful romantic mysticism. "Naturally, it is the privilege of the author to edit the text of his own publications. But such changes, made about twenty years after the original publication, should not obscure significant facts of personal history, psychological and social, and prevent, in this special instance, understanding of an intellectual position held in the years 1916-1920."

Bernardin, Charles W. "John Dos Passos' Textual Revisions," Papers of the Bibliographical Society of America, 48 (1954): 95-97.

Bernardin contends that the changes Dos Passos made in Rosinante to the Road Again (1922) to prepare it for publication in Journeys Between Wars (1938) reflect natural and normal growth for a writer as he reacts to a time of great change (particularly in Spain). Bernardin appears in the role of defender of Dos Passos against criticism leveled by Martin Kallich five years earlier. A reply from Kallich immediately follows this article.

SIR ARTHUR CONAN DOYLE

Doyle, Sir Arthur Conan. The Annotated Sherlock Holmes. Two volumes. Edited, with an Introduction, Notes and Bibliography by William S. Baring-Gould. New York: Clarkson Potter, 1979.

The two volumes include the four novels and the fifty-six short stories complete. While the book contains very little on revision, the material Doyle uses as a writer and sources and background for his works suggest a good deal about the creation of the works.

MICHAEL DRAYTON

Marchesani, Joseph J. "The Revisions of Michael Drayton's Four Legends," Dissertation Abstracts International, 37 (August 1975): 905A.

"This study closely examines the major revisions which Michael Drayton made in his four legends, Gaveston, Matilda, Robert, and Cromwell, poems derived from the didactic tradition of the Mirror for Magistrates and the modification of that tradition which flourished after Samuel Daniel's Complaint of Rosamond. These revisions help to define Drayton's development as a poet and to show how his development reflects a transition from Elizabethan to Jacobean poetic attitudes. The examination of these revisions develops three themes: first, that the progress of the revisions is marked by an increasing integration of technique; second, that the progress develops in two stages; third, that the revisions in syntax and rhetoric provide a sensitive gauge for changes in structure and attitudes throughout the legends."

Schroder, William T. "Michael Drayton: A Study of the Idea Sonnet Revisions," Dissertation Abstracts, 20 (October-December 1959): 2277-2278.

"Drayton's gradual but persistent rejection of sonnets of hyperbolic sadness, of excessive conceit, and of undue religious fervor is traced through the major revisions of 1599, 1600, 1603, 1605, and 1619. Here is noted the depersonalizing of the sequence through the removal of those sonnets most closely identifiable with its original inspiration (Anne Goodere), a change paralleled, somewhat paradoxically, by revisions in manner towards the method of Donne."

JOHN DRYDEN

Dearing, Vinton A. "Dryden's Mac Flecknoe: The Case for Authorial Revision," Studies in Bibliography, 7 (1955): 85-102.

"There are those general types of revision that may occur: simple revision, which may be addition, rejection, or substitution; reverse revision, returning to the original reading; and continued revision, where a new revision is substituted for the rejected one. Combinations of two or all three types are also possible. Simple revision results from a single decision on the author's part (pattern ab), reverse revision from two (pattern aba), continued revision from two or more (pattern abc, abcd...), and combinations of types from three or more (simple and reverse abab, ababa ... ; continued and reverse: abac, abca, abcb ... ; all three: ababc...)." Dearing attempts to develop an approach to deal with large bodies of data in collation problems and to determine whether variants are the result of authorial revision or of other causes.

ECA DE QUEIROZ

Nuzzi, Carmela Magnatta. "Analysis and Comparison of Two Versions of *a Ilustre Casa de Ramires* by Eca de Queiroz," *Dissertation Abstracts International*, 37 (September 1976): 1597A.

"After an analysis of the *Revista Moderna* version, the book version is compared for both story content and linguistic expression with bilateral quotes from both versions. Two styles, two structures in the earlier version are thus examined against Eca's final book rendition. His process of perfecting his work is studied 'in the making,' so as to arrive at his ultimate philosophy of art and life as related to his fiction."

GEORGE ELIOT

Wiesenfarth, Joseph. "George Eliot's Notes for *Adam Bede*," *Nineteenth Century Fiction*, 32 (September 1977): 127-165.

Wiesenfarth presents all the notes pertaining to *Adam Bede* (18 pages in this article) from a book of notes also containing other material. Wiesenfarth's editorial notes and commentary (17 pages) follow.

Beaty, Jerome. *"Middlemarch" from Notebook to Novel: A Study of George Eliot's Creative Method.* Urbana: University of Illinois Press, 1960 (*Illinois Studies in Language and Literature*: Vol. 47).

In Chapter One, "'Middlemarch' and 'Miss Brooke'," Beaty's study reveals how *Middlemarch* grew out of a similar but different effort. In Chapter Two, he discusses the "publication in parts" of Chapters 19-32. In Chapter Three, he traces the evolution of "Books 4-8: From Notebook to Novel." The most detailed study of revision is Chapter Four, "The writing of Chapter 81." Eliot claims to have written it in a frenzy of inspiration and never to have revised it. Beaty offers columned comparisons. An appendix offers "Facsimiles of Four Significant Pages from the *Middlemarch* manuscript."

Beaty, Jerome. "George Eliot's Notebook for an Unwritten Novel," *Princeton University Library Chronicle*, 18 (Summer 1957): 175-182.

"A study of the notebook is essential for scholars reconstructing George Eliot's creative process or tracing the development of her mind and art." The plans are published for the first time. Eliot projected a "melodramatic story set in England during the Napoleonic wars. The aristocratic characters, the international intrigue, and the particular historical period are uncharacteristic of George Eliot's fiction." Several leaves "seem to be a rough draft of actual introductory or opening pages of a novel." The text "may contain George Eliot's last words of fiction."

T. S. ELIOT

Gardner, Helen. The Composition of "Four Quartets." New York: Oxford University Press, 1978.

"... Four years spent with abandoned fragments, discarded readings, and what Eliot called the 'Litter' of composition has not diminished my love for these poems or my conviction of their greatness. It has, indeed, contributed to an increase of that 'understanding and enjoyment' which Eliot in later life thought it was the prime function of criticism to promote." Ms. Gardner describes "the documents in the case," gives a full account of the sources for and the growth of the poems, and provides notes on revisions. In Appendix A, she reproduces the first draft of "Little Gidding."

Marshall, William. "The Text of T. S. Eliot's 'Gerontion'," Studies in Bibliography, 4 (1951-1952): 213-217.

The sponsors of a seminar on T. S. Eliot's poetry at the University of Virginia constructed an eclectic text of "Gerontion" from seven collected editions (sixteen impressions), and the poet himself later marked this text, changing two of the readings and agreeing with others by making check marks. The author of this study displays the variants among the editions and Eliot's checks and alterations. The reader should have a complete text of the poem from another source in hand to benefit fully from this study.

Eliot, T. S. The Waste Land: A Facsimile and Transcript of the Original Drafts Including the Annotations of Ezra Pound. Edited by Valerie Eliot. New York: Harcourt Brace Jovanovich, 1971.

"In this book each page of the original manuscript has been produced in facsimile, with a clear transcript on the facing page. Mrs. Valerie Eliot, the poet's widow, has meticulously supervised the design and production, provided explanatory notes, cross-references, and written a revealing introduction.... The text of the first published version is also included." A very interesting and unusual case of one major poet, Pound, cutting and revising another. Eliot's first wife's comments are also reproduced. Did Pound help or harm the poem? Mrs. Eliot uses many quotes from Eliot's letters "to describe some of the events and emotions of the year leading up to The Waste Land."

Browne, E. Martin. The Making of T. S. Eliot's Plays. London: Cambridge University Press, 1969.

"This book is a record of the way in which T. S. Eliot's plays came to be written and of their first appearances on the stage. Much of its contents are from Eliot's pen. I have been generously given leave to peruse drafts, notes and letters in a number of collections apart from my own, and to publish those passages which seemed to further the understanding of the growth of each play. The unique advantage which I enjoy in doing this is that I worked with Eliot from 1933 to 1958, directing the first productions of all the plays written during that time, and acting as consultant in their making." Browne reproduces many passages, showing revisions.

Beare, Robert L. "Notes on the Text of T. S. Eliot: Variants from Russell Square," Studies in Bibliography, 9 (1957): 21-49.

Variants in every major play and poem by T. S. Eliot are recounted in some detail. Two principles of revision are stated: (1) Concentration is achieved by eliminating punctuation and deleting words and phrases, and (2) the final copies of poems and plays that are offered for sale are nearest in form to the author's intention. "And finally, in the light of all these problems, I should like to raise the ultimate question appropriate to a symposium on modern authors: 'At what point does a modern poem or a play--or novel--cease to be in a state of 'becoming' and reach a state of 'being'?"

RALPH WALDO EMERSON

Lauter, Paul. "Emerson's Revisions of Essays (First Series)," American Literature, 33 (1961): 143-158.

Lauter compares the 1840-1841 first version of the first series of Emerson's Essays with the 1847 Munroe edition. In his stylistic revisions Emerson eliminated modifiers, "rhetorical baggage," and phrases that unnecessarily repeated his point. He also worked to simplify his prose and to achieve more concreteness and clarity. "Emerson's revisions of sense concentrate primarily on man's relationship to the world around him, the quality of virtue, and the nature of spirit." In part three of this study, Lauter arrays in parallel columns three versions (the manuscript journal, the first edition, and the revised edition) of four selections to illustrate Emerson's progress through revision to vividness and clarity.

WILLIAM FAULKNER

Langford, Gerald. Faulkner's Revision of "Absalom, Absalom!" A Collation of the Manuscript and the Published Book. Austin: University of Texas Press, 1971.

Langford makes excellent use of columned comparisons without comment. Langford confines his observations to a long introduction, discussing major changes chapter by chapter. "Some of the revisions are structural, and it is particularly interesting to learn that, while writing and reworking the novel, Faulkner altered in several ways his original design.... To trace the process of such revision is to experience a sharp focusing of the dominant theme of the novel, and to witness a demonstration of how the meaning of a fictional work can shape its structure and thus stand revealed by what has become the outward and visible signs, or form, of that meaning." "Faulkner reworked his first version so as to regulate the tempo of his narrative, to build suspense where the flow has slackened, to highlight his characters so that we glimpse the flicker or twitch of live flesh, and finally to get a firm hold on the theme toward which he had felt his way in the manuscript." Examination of the manuscript clears up many inconsistencies and ambiguities that have caused critical controversies. Langford emphasizes that Faulkner's revisions were not the polishing of a finished creation but rather results of rethinking and reworking situations and problems so that the structure of the novel becomes one with its meaning.

Bleikasten, Andre. Faulkner's "As I Lay Dying." Bloomington: Indiana University Press, 1973.

"My purpose in writing this study was to offer a comprehensive approach to As I Lay Dying, based on a close reading of the novel's text (from the initial stages of its composition to the final version of the published book) and on a detailed examination of its formal and technical aspects (language, style, structure, creation of character) as well as of its thematic design." The material on revision is short but useful.

Faulkner, William. A Fable. New York: Random House, 1954.

This novel includes, in pages 151-189, the rewritten version of the stolen racehorse story originally published as Notes on a Horsethief. Two examples of changes Faulkner made are (1) breaking extremely long sentences into shorter ones, and (2) making additional paragraph divisions.

Faulkner, William. Flags in the Dust. New York: Random House, 1973.

Compare with Sartoris (Harcourt, Brace, 1929). Faulkner reluctantly allowed his agent to cut a fourth of the original manuscript. Flags in the Dust "aims at being a faithful reproduction," says Douglas Day, the editor, in his introduction, of the composite typescript Faulkner continued to work on, hoping someday to see the original published. "Flags in the Dust is far more complicated: primary focus is still on the Sartorises, but Faulkner clearly wished to make of his novel an anatomy of the entire Yoknapatawpha social structure, excluding only the Indians."

Millgate, Jane. "Short Story into Novel: Faulkner's Reworking of 'Gold Is Not Always'," English Studies, 45 (1964): 310-317.

"Gold Is Not Always" (Atlantic Monthly, November 1940) is included as Chapter Two of the section, "The Fire and the Hearth," in Go Down, Moses (1942). "The modifications which Faulkner made in the story when reworking it into the fabric of the novel are in the main concerned with the placing of Lucas in relation to the other characters, so that the story plays its part in the structure of the section and of the work as a whole. The attitude of Lucas to the salesman and to the other Negro, as well as to Roth Edmonds, is clarified in various ways--by modifying the dialect, by broadening the comic aspect of George, by giving concrete examples of Lucas' refusal to submit to the salesman or even to Edmonds himself, and, at the end, by introducing external comparisons which elevate him. Though the changes at first appear small, their total effect is considerable, and examination of them reveals the care for essential details with which Faulkner revised the story for the later work.... The changes, in fact, involve an entirely new conception of Lucas' role, and this conception seems comprehensible only in terms of an overall intention on Faulkner's part to write Go Down, Moses as a novel rather than simply a collection of stories." Excellent direct comparisons are worked into the body of the essay.

Klotz, Marvin. "Procrustean Revision in Faulkner's Go Down, Moses," American Literature, 37 (March 1965): 1-16.

Klotz contends that the short stories that were joined together to make the novel Go Down, Moses ("The Bear," "Was," "The Fire and the Hearth," "Delta Autumn," "Pantaloon in Black," "The Old People," and "Go Down, Moses") were harmed by the revisions necessary to make them, however loosely and incongruously, comprise one novel, and that the motivation for creating this amalgamation was the fact that novels sell better than books of short stories. "If we trace the biography of the matter in the book from its pristine state, we discover over a hundred pages of additions tucked and sometimes jammed into the tightly structured and lucid magazine stories, great chunks of unassimilated, mostly expository, prose almost everywhere blurring thematic focus, destroying established characterization."

Early, James. The Making of "Go Down, Moses." Dallas: Southern Methodist University Press, 1972.

Early bases his study on the magazine versions of some of the stories that make up the book and the unpublished typescripts in the Faulkner collection in the Alderman Library of the University of Virginia. The stories are "Go Down, Moses"; "Was"; "A Point of Law"; "The Old People"; "Pantaloon in Black"; "Gold Is Not Always"; "Delta Autumn"; and "The Bear." "Despite its fragmentary nature, Go Down, Moses is more impressive in its totality than any of its parts. And it provides--to some degree because it is fragmentary--an almost unique opportunity to study Faulkner's creative activity." "This book contains both examples of abortive efforts to achieve aesthetic unity and, in 'The Bear' and to a lesser extent in 'Delta Autumn,' supreme achievements of Faulkner's synthesizing imagination." Early compares later versions with their predecessors by means of his own exposition rather than by direct comparisons of quotations.

Creighton, Joanne V. William Faulkner's Craft of Revision, The Snopes Trilogy, "The Unvanquished," and "Go Down, Moses." Detroit: Wayne State University Press, 1977.

"My method is strictly inductive, based on a word-by-word comparison of multiple versions of the texts. In other words, I first recorded the textual changes between an earlier and later version of a story and then attempted to explain the apparent rationale behind them. What did Faulkner have to do to satisfy himself that he had incorporated an independent story into a larger context? What do his changes reveal about the ideas and the structure he was trying to implement in the evolving larger work?" "The works to be examined in this study all commonly incorporate pre-existent short stories, but they offer interesting and illuminating contrasts, growing out of remarkably different geneses and taking markedly different shapes." The longest section deals with Go Down, Moses, especially "The Fire and the Hearth." Creighton concludes with four general observations about Faulkner's craft of revisions: it was flexible; it proceeded from the part to the whole, from simplicity to complexity, from the comic to the serious or vice versa; it retains the narrative frame of the original story; it strives for a profusion of details and a precision of style.

Fadiman, Regina K. Faulkner's "Intruder in the Dust," Novel Into Film. Knoxville: University of Tennessee Press, 1978.

In a context consisting of chapters on the process of adapting a novel into a film, an examination of the novel itself and of the film, Fadiman examines Ben Maddow's revisions of his screenplay adaptation of Faulkner's novel. Also included are the final script with Fadiman's notations to show specific revisions, titles of episodes in the treatment, pages from the continuity script, and a page of the director's shooting script. "In general, Maddow's original concept employed a wider range of cinematic techniques than was used in the final screen version." The "process" script "illustrates clearly the script 'in process' as well as the process of collaboration between screenwriter, director, and producer." Faulkner himself made a few contributions. Compare the script with the novel.

Fadiman, Regina K. "Faulkner's Light in August: Sources and Revisions," Dissertation Abstracts International, 32 (July 1971): 427-A.

"This study examines the genesis and revisions of Light in August. In a detailed description of the documents which precede the published novel, it not only illustrates the author's work habits but also traces the kinds of revisions he made and the stages through which the novel evolved. The conclusions are drawn from the external and internal evidence in the Virginia manuscript and typescript, the four-page manuscript at the University of Texas, and the published text."

Ficken, Carl. "The Opening Scene of William Faulkner's Light in August," Proof, 2 (1972): 175-181.

Comparison of two pages of a salesman's dummy of Light in August with the published novel reveals changes in structure that suggest "a good deal about the way Faulkner built the novel." Ficken also describes earlier manuscripts in which the focus in the opening of the novel is on Gail Hightower and on Joe Christmas, instead of Lena Grove. No quotations are offered for comparison.

Fadiman, Regina K. Faulkner's "Light in August": A Description and Interpretation of the Revisions. Charlottesville: The University Press of Virginia, 1975.

"In light of the disputes over the novel, a thorough analysis of the revisions is greatly needed." Fadiman employs "process criticism, which I define as interpretation of a completed work derived from an examination of the methods and stages of its revision.... I have tried whenever possible to find consistent patterns of change...." "Faulkner added many episodes and passages after he had written a nearly complete version of the novel." The documents examined include several pages of manuscript at the University of Texas, the 188 page manuscript and the 466 page typescript at the University of Virginia, corrected galleys, and pertinent manuscripts of other novels. Some of the kinds of revisions described are structural revisions within episodes, compression of episodes, reordering of episodes, addition of new material, and adjustments for consistent chronology. Fadiman concludes that (1) Faulkner was not a systematic writer; (2) he wrote in small independent units; (3) the final ordering of these units was of primary importance to the meaning of the book; and (4) the final order of the segments of _Light in August_ successfully expressed his intentions.

Faulkner, William. _Notes on a Horsethief._ Greenville, Mississippi: The Levee Press, 1950.

This original version of the story of the stolen racehorse, later rewritten and published as a part of _A Fable_, is a limited edition of 975 copies, signed by the author.

Izard, Barbara, and Clara Hieronymous. _Requiem for a Nun, On Stage and Off._ Nashville: Aurora Publishers, 1970.

This is not a scholarly work, but Ms. Izard, who played Temple Drake in a production of the play, and Ms. Hieronymous give a detailed account of the genesis, the various versions, and the various productions (American, French, Greek, British) of Faulkner's play. They offer photocopies of pages from the scripts of those productions, showing written-in changes, including Albert Camus'. The book is richly illustrated.

Polk, Noel. "The Textual History of Faulkner's _Requiem for a Nun_," _Proof_, 4 (1975): 109-128.

The typescript upon which this study focuses contains the first version and two versions of Act II. "Originally, everybody--Temple, Gavin, Gowan--changed for the better; in the first revision, they all changed for the worse. In the final version, they do not change at all--Stevens remains his harsh, implacable self; Temple, who has suffered much, is not purged and cannot cry, though she very much wants to...." Polk defends _Requiem for a Nun_ and William Faulkner's later work in general against criticism that he feels is unjust and unperceptive. Saxe Commins, Faulkner's Random House editor, is depicted as unsympathetic to his client's artistic aims.

Massey, Linton. "Notes on the Unrevised Galleys of Faulkner's _Sanctuary_," _Studies in Bibliography_, 8 (1956): 195-208.

"Faulkner altered the entire focus and meaning of the book; he simplified a too-complex structure; he excluded the irrelevant; he clarified the obscure passages where ambiguity was not an asset; he amplified those portions requiring emendation; he gave the novel a climax; and he freed it from its bonds of previous servitude to an earlier book." An appendix provides a key to comparisons of the galley proofs and the published book, but the article itself provides no line-by-line comparisons. This article should be read first, in conjunction with Langford's book, Faulkner's Revision of "Sanctuary." Their interpretations conflict; Langford, however, worked from more complete material.

Langford, Gerald. Faulkner's Revision of "Sanctuary": A Collation of the Unrevised Galleys and the Published Book. Austin: University of Texas Press, 1972.

This is an excellent example of columned comparison. Faulkner always disparaged this novel because he deliberately made it "the most horrific tale" he could imagine in order to make money. But when he saw the galleys, having published The Sound and the Fury and As I Lay Dying, he was appalled, so he rewrote the novel in galleys. "In the collation that follows, a reader with the published text before him can reconstruct the original version for himself, simultaneously noting the cancellations, the additions, and the rewritten passages." In his long introduction, Langford argues that the galley version is in some ways superior to the "rearranged" published version. The galley version attempts a fuller presentation of the character of Horace Benbow, but then abandons it; the published version simplifies Benbow's story to accommodate a new ending. "The revision turns out to consist most strikingly of omissions and of changes in the order of presenting events--in other words, an alteration of the narrative method.... Sanctuary was a turning point in his experimentation." Langford contends that Faulkner's revision did not reduce the lurid aspects of the novel, but shifted it into chronological order, stepped up its pace, and trimmed it for ready use as a Hollywood drama.

Faulkner, William. Sartoris. New York: Harcourt, Brace, 1929. SEE Faulkner, Flags in the Dust.

Meriwether, James B. "Notes on the Textual History of The Sound and the Fury," Papers of the Bibliographical Society of America, 56 (1962): 285-316.

Faulkner wrote The Sound and the Fury in six months of 1928. Meriwether describes the writing and relates the publishing history, displaying errors in three editions in three tables: Table A, Errors in the 1929 Edition; Table B, Errors in the First English Edition; and Table C, Errors in the Modern Library Edition. Meriwether contends that the Appendix-as-Foreword of the Modern Library edition should be relegated to the status of a true appendix in future editions. Meriwether describes the primary materials available for a study of Faulkner's revisions of The Sound and the Fury but does not include such an effort in this article. "In addition to a carbon of his final typescript, Faulkner preserved among his papers a manuscript, lacking only one page of being complete. As was his custom, he used thin sheets of legal-sized paper, leaving a wide left-hand margin for corrections. A page-by-page comparison, with spot collation, of manuscript, carbon typescript, and published book reveals that each version follows the previous one closely, though with a great deal of verbal polishing and minor revision from manuscript to typescript, and a certain amount of further polishing from typescript to published book. The manuscript itself gives evidence of very extensive rewriting, with many passages added, some canceled, and with its pagination revealing that many of the pages Faulkner preserved represent revisions and expansions of previous ones."

Izsak, Emily K. "The Manuscript of The Sound and the Fury: The Revisions in the First Section," Studies in Bibliography, 20 (1967): 189-202.

Izsak deals "with revisions in the first section, where the transformation of four stories into a novel is to be seen primarily and perhaps only.... One type of revision transformed the first section from an independent narration into one which precisely anticipates the third and fourth sections." Two major types of revision are the addition of the birthday passages, "relevant to the interpretation of the symbolic significance ... of the Christian aspects of the novel," and "all the passages having to do with the traveling show" to define Jason's character. Excellent direct comparisons are worked into the body of the essay.

Faulkner, William. "That Evening Sun," Collected Stories of William Faulkner. New York: Random House, 1934 (1950). Compare with earlier version called "That Evening Sun Go Down," The American Mercury, XXII, No. 87 (March 1931): 257-265.

Gregory, Nancy E. "A Study of the Early Versions of Faulkner's The Town and The Mansion," Dissertation Abstracts International, 36 (December 1975): 3686A-3687A.

"This study is largely based on an examination of typescript material for The Town and The Mansion in the Faulkner Collection at the University of Virginia. Existing are a nearly complete typescript of The Town, located among recto pages of an incomplete typescript (154 pages) of The Town and verso pages of an early typescript draft of The Mansion, and that early draft of The Mansion itself. This dissertation draws upon evidence from these early typescript versions of the two novels, from additional fragments of Town and Mansion material on versos of the two typescripts, and from early short stories incorporated into the novels, to explore the intent of the author as revealed in revision and alteration of material."

McHaney, Thomas L. William Faulkner's "The Wild Palms"; A Study. Jackson: University Press of Mississippi, 1975.

Faulkner, William. Uncollected Stories of William Faulkner. Joseph Blotner, ed. New York: Random House, 1979.

The volume contains three kinds of stories: those never reprinted in any of Faulkner's collections, those later revised to become parts of novels, and those that had remained unpublished. Twenty of the stories were revised to fit into The Unvanquished, The Hamlet, Go Down, Moses, Big Woods, and The Mansion. Blotner's notes to those stories give a good picture of Faulkner's habit of making multiple use of his material for both financial and artistic reasons. A bibliography directs the reader to numerous articles and books that describe and analyze Faulkner's revision process as he converted groups of stories into "anthology novels." Go Down, Moses has received the most attention. One may discern several areas in which further work is possible. "Taken together, these stories present a view of Faulkner's developing art over a span of more than thirty years. They embody a wide variety of styles and subject matter. His attitude toward them quite naturally varied too." "In the cases of stories which were further revised to become parts of books, I have tried to outline the process of growth from inception to completion."

Meriwether, James B. "The Short Fiction of William Faulkner: A Bibliography," Proof, 1 (1971): 293-329.

This is an excellent listing that gives all available information about revised versions of each piece. "This bibliography ... is offered as an aid to the further study of Faulkner's short fiction. It lists all textually significant forms known to me of all his works of fiction shorter than full-length novels. Locations are given for manuscript, typescript, and proof versions. In order to establish their relationships, all published versions listed have been collated.... The annotations provide discussion, where it seems necessary, of problems of dates, titles, and relationships." The bibliography is divided into three major sections with an introduction and a title index: stories, published, unpublished, or lost; excerpts from novels; collections. Faulkner's various versions of his short stories provide a major opportunity for studying the creative process through an examination of revisions.

Garrett, George P. "An Examination of the Poetry of William Faulkner," Princeton University Library Chronicle, 18 (1957): 124-135.

In addition to discussing Faulkner's verse in general, Garrett furnishes evidence of Faulkner's revision of his work, apparently to refute a mistaken view at the time that Faulkner did not revise. Two versions of a sonnet by Faulkner are presented, one that was published as "Spring" in Contempo, I, No. 17 (February 1, 1932), and as XXXVI in his volume A Green Bough (1933). The revisions include (1) dropping capitals as insignia of individual lines; (2) dividing the sestet into two three-line parts; and (3) clarifying the central metaphor by introducing the word stallion and capitalizing its opposite, Wind. Garrett also presents photographic representations, with Faulkner's revisions written on them, of (1) a page of manuscript from The Sound and the Fury; (2) a page of manuscript from Sanctuary; (3) a page of manuscript from As I Lay Dying; (4) a page of manuscript from The Hamlet; (5) a page of typescript from Intruder in the Dust; and (6) a page of galley proof from The Town.

Meriwether, James B. "William Faulkner: A Check List," Princeton University Library Chronicle, 18 (1957): 136-158.

This check list should constitute the starting point for students interested in locating revised versions of Faulkner's published work. Meriwether gives information about the extent of revision and about the manner in which certain pieces are combined to make longer works as well as about excerpts that are revised and published separately. In his first entry for Absalom, Absalom!, for example, Meriwether states that "Pp. 278-292 of Chapter VII incorporate, extensively revised, the short story 'Wash' (from Doctor Martino; reprinted in Collected Stories). Chapter I (pp. 7-30) had appeared, entitled 'Absalom, Absalom!' and with a number of minor changes, in American Mercury, August 1936, as one of a series of excerpts from work in progress by American authors."

Meriwether, James B. "The Literary Career of William Faulkner: Catalogue of an Exhibition in the Princeton University Library," Princeton University Library Chronicle, 21 (Spring 1960): 111-164.

The best parts of this complete account of MSS and editions of Faulkner at Princeton are 13 pages of photo-reproduced MSS and typescripts with Faulkner's revisions written in.

HENRY FIELDING

Hunting, Robert S. "Fielding's Revisions of David Simple," Boston University Studies in English, 3 (1957): 117-121.

Henry Fielding's revisions of his sister Sarah's The Adventures of David Simple are categorized and dealt with in short sections of this article: (1) The Use of Pronouns; (2) Tightened Sentence Construction; (3) Changes Actuated by Fielding's Knowledge of Law; (4) Elevation of Diction; (5) Correction or Qualification of Fact; and (6) The Insertion of Irony. Hunting states that "this brief study does certainly add to our knowledge of Fielding's concern for a clear, correct, and 'elegant,' style. It reaffirms, too, our judgement that--with some happy exceptions--the literary ladies of these times did not write very well."

Battestin, Martin C. "Fielding's Revisions of Joseph Andrews," Studies in Bibliography, 16 (1963): 81-117.

Battestin examines Henry Fielding's revisions as they show up among the first five editions of Joseph Andrews. Not counting changes in punctuation and paragraphing and all apparent printer's errors, 311 revisions are counted in the second edition, 163 in the third, 112 in the fourth, and 47 in the fifth. "Though it is ultimately the shape and spirit of the finished work that matter, an examination of the novel in process can tell us much about Fielding's craftmanship and his purpose. Analyzing the text at the point of revision, we come as close as possible to the writer at the moment of composition--smoothing or sharpening his style, breathing the breath of life into scene and character, whetting the edge of his satire." Battestin describes several categories of revision: (1) correcting errors caused by rapid original composition; (2) miscellaneous alterations, including name changes; (3) touching up for the improvement of style; (4) repairing weaknesses in the story; (5) striving for symmetry in the structure of the novel; (6) injecting more life and humor into the characters, the largest recipient being Parson Adams;

(7) changes in the satire of the novel; (8) strengthening the theme that attempted to "correct a prevalent contempt of the clergy"; and (9) changes that reflect Fielding's shifting political loyalties. One hundred twenty-eight textual notes represent all of the major revisions, with two or more versions being given in each note.

RONALD FIRBANK

Davis, Robert Murray. "Ronald Firbank's Notebooks: '... writing books was by no means easy'," Harvard Library Bulletin, 25 (April 1977): 172-192.

Davis examines Firbank's notebooks to obtain clues to the process of composition in such works as Vainglory, The Artificial Princess, Caprice, Valmouth, and Inclinations. "Even though the notebooks and variants among printed versions of the novels cannot reveal everything about Firbank's methods of composition, they do indicate several important features of his style and technique. In the first place, his stylistic effects depend upon achieving greater and greater complexity of structure, particularly elements that interrupt, often irrelevantly, the basic structure of the sentence. His plots and situations are developed in a way analogous to that of the sentences: a number of apparently disparate elements are placed in juxtaposition, qualifying and interrupting each other."

F. SCOTT FITZGERALD

White, William. "Two Versions of F. Scott Fitzgerald's 'Babylon Revisited': A Textual and Bibliographical Study," Papers of the Bibliographical Society of America, 60 (1966): 439-452.

William White compares the 1931 Saturday Evening Post version of "Babylon Revisited" with the 1935 version included in Taps at Reveille and displays the differences in seven pages of direct columned juxtapositions. "The basic story, of course, did not change at all, but it was considerably sharpened and every word was made to count more."

Fitzgerald, F. Scott. "The Great Gatsby": A Facsimile of the Manuscript. Edited and with an Introduction by Matthew J. Bruccoli. Washington, D. C.: Microcard Editions Books, 1973.

"The present edition is the first photographic facsimile of the manuscript of F. Scott Fitzgerald's The Great Gatsby--including rejected material, as well as the holograph and typescript drafts of later insertions.... Several examples of the author's revised galleys have also been included to show the reader how Fitzgerald continued to perfect the novel while it was in production. The introduction reconstructs the gestation and development of The Great Gatsby through Fitzgerald's revised galley proofs." Fitzgerald set out to achieve "something extraordinary and beautiful and simple and intricately patterned." After the first draft "the craftsman took over and sweated."

Bruccoli, Matthew J. The Last of the Novelists, F. Scott Fitzgerald and "The Last Tycoon." Carbondale: Southern Illinois University Press, 1977.

"Close examination of the manuscripts and notes for the unfinished novel known as The Last Tycoon allows us to gauge the state of F. Scott Fitzgerald's work-in-progress at the time of his death and thereby to re-assess this work properly. It is evident that in case of work-in-progress authorial intention is the crucial consideration for interpretation and evaluation. In such a work we must scrutinize the evidence for clues to its evolution; and it is obligatory that we determine how far the work had really progressed." Edmund Wilson's doctored text published decades ago "is misleading because it presents Fitzgerald's working drafts in a finished form.... Examination of Fitzgerald's drafts reveals that he regarded none of this material as finished. There are no final drafts--only latest working drafts.... The Last Tycoon is not really an 'unfinished novel,' if that term describes a work that is partly finished. The only way to regard it is as material toward a novel." Bruccoli sketches backgrounds for the novel and its composition, examines the drafts carefully, discusses the unwritten episodes, and examines the book Wilson prepared. In an appendix, he offers Fitzgerald's notes. An excellent example of the "in progress" genre.

Fitzgerald, F. Scott. Tender Is the Night, in Three Novels of F. Scott Fitzgerald. Edited with Introduction, Appendix, and Notes by Malcolm Cowley. New York: Charles Scribner's Sons, 1953.

Several years after it was published, Fitzgerald proposed to his editor Maxwell Perkins that Tender Is the Night be reissued with the novel rearranged in chronological order. "If pages 151-212 were taken from their present place and put at the start the improvement in appeal would be enormous." That was not done until Cowley himself prepared this revised edition in 1953. "The question remains whether the final version as Fitzgerald would like it is also the best version of the novel.... He sacrificed a brilliant beginning and all the element of mystery, but there is no escaping the judgment that he ended with a better constructed and more effective novel." The earlier version lacked focus. "We are certain in reading the final version that the novel is psychological, that it is about Dick Diver, and that its social meanings are obtained by" seeing Dick as a representative figure. The final revision brings the book even closer to the plan Fitzgerald made in 1932. "The Rosemary section of the novel no longer misleads our expectations; coming in the middle it simply adds fullness and relief to the story. Although the new beginning is less brilliant than the older one, it prepares us for the end and helps us to appreciate the last section of the novel as we had probably failed to do" on reading the first version. "That is the principal virtue of Fitzgerald's new arrangement." In "Appendix: The Manuscript of 'Tender'," Cowley describes the various drafts in Princeton University Library and reprints a section Fitzgerald omitted called "The World's Fair" (published earlier in The Kenyon Review), and a section called "Monsieur IV" appears for the first time in this appendix. Cowley also provides eight pages of notes, some of which describe other revisions.

Bruccoli, Matthew J. The Composition of "Tender Is the Night": A Study of the Manuscripts. Pittsburgh: University of Pittsburgh Press, 1963.

This complete account of the seventeen drafts of F. Scott Fitzgerald's Tender Is the Night begins with the Melarky holograph in 1925 and makes comparisons as it moves to the Melarky typescript, the Melarky-Narrator holograph (1926), the Melarky-Narrator typescript, the Kelly holograph (1929), the Melarky second holograph (1930), the Diver notes (1932), the Diver holograph, the Diver typescript, the Diver carbon, the Diver second carbon, the Diver second typescript, serial galleys and revises, serial page proof, Scribner's Magazine, book galleys, book page proof, and the book (1934). Revisions are presented by comparing versions in parallel columns, by displaying textual collations, by arraying books and chapters in structural comparisons, and by reproducing twenty-eight pages of manuscript facsimile. Two examples of major revisions by Fitzgerald are (1) the change from third person point of view to first person narrator and back to third person again, and (2) the shifting of flashbacks into chronological order in the plot line. Bruccoli defends Fitzgerald's structure of the novel and his characterization of Dick Diver against the adverse criticism of many early reviewers.

Higgins, Brian, and Hershel Parker. "Sober Second Thoughts: Fitzgerald's 'Final Version' of Tender Is the Night," Proof, 4 (1975): 129-152.

In 1951 Malcolm Cowley published a version of Tender Is the Night, which represents F. Scott Fitzgerald's apparent final wishes regarding that work and which involved a reordering of its parts into chronological sequence. After Higgins and Parker review the controversy that has resulted among critics and scholars as to whether the 1934 version or the 1951 version is better, they present a thoroughly documented argument for the superiority of the 1934 version. "Fitzgerald's later decision to switch the beginning and part of the middle of the book around, while it gave a more powerful focus to the opening, caused great damage, in the long run, to all parts of the novel. Rewriting, reshaping parts of Tender Is the Night might indeed have produced a better novel; reordering it caused far more problems than it solved."

Bruccoli, Matthew J. "A Collation of F. Scott Fitzgerald's This Side of Paradise," Studies in Bibliography, 9 (1957): 263-265.

The Hinman Collating Machine at the University of Virginia was used to compare the first edition of This Side of Paradise (1920) to a 1954 Scribner's reprint. "This collation revealed thirty-one changes which fall into six categories: corrections of misspelled references to books and authors (10); corrections of misspellings of names and places (5); other corrections of errors in spelling and usage (6); corrections of errors involving careless proof-reading (3); corrections of miscellaneous errors (3); and revisions of non-errors (4)." Bruccoli concludes that this first printing was not done well at all and that the publisher and author must share the blame. All thirty-one changes are presented at the end of the article along with a note from Fitzgerald in which he apologizes to the American Booksellers Association for this sloppiness.

Bronson, Dan E. "Vision and Revision: A Genetic Study of Scott Fitzgerald's Short Fiction with Some Excursions into His Novels," Dissertation Abstracts International, 33 (November 1972): 2362-A.

"The compositional history of 'The Debutante,' an exuberant tale from the early years, reveals the rapid growth of Fitzgerald's structural skills and his discovery of a major theme--the role of money in our lives. The revisions of 'Crazy Sunday,' a fine work from the middle period, show him working skillfully with problems of style, structure, and characterization in a successful attempt to dramatize his insight into the relationship of illusion, Hollywood, and the American Dream. The several versions of 'Author's House,' a sketch from the final phase, record his struggle to gain distance and detachment from his material."

GUSTAVE FLAUBERT

Steegmuller, Francis. Flaubert and Madame Bovary. Chicago: The University of Chicago Press, 1939. Revised edition, 1950. Second edition with corrections, 1968. Phoenix edition 1977, revised with new author's note, 1977.

A rare account of the genesis and development of a novel (best read along with Flaubert's letters). The appendix is a reproduction of the second scenario prepared by Flaubert. Steegmuller also discusses writing and rewriting of Flaubert's other fiction.

FORD MADOX FORD

MacShane, Frank. "A Conscious Craftsman: Ford Madox Ford's Manuscript Revisions," Boston University Studies in English, 5 (Autumn, 1961): 178-184.

"Ford is ... remembered ... as one of the few novelists of modern times who tried to explain why technical consciousness was necessary in writing." In many essays, he "hammered away at the perplexing problems of technique." With Conrad, he was very conscious of the importance of openings and endings. "... Four separate drafts of the opening of Ford's unfinished novel, Professor's Progress, have been preserved, and these provide an interesting study of the way in which Ford tried to bridge the gap between the dramatic opening and the reflective opening." All four opening paragraph versions are given. "The novelist who considers his work as a progression in which motives and actions will be made clear only at the very end, must therefore suppress strong scenes, for however attractive they may be in themselves, they will interfere with the final effect. Ford's unwillingness to obey this rigorous code in order to protect the architecture of his tetrology, Parade's End, is made clear in the suppression of the Some Do Not scene." McShane quotes the long scene that ends the book. "Those who consciously strive for an art that will seem artless will be appreciated by later generations for the efforts they have made."

E. M. FORSTER

Levine, J. P. "An Analysis of the Manuscripts of A Passage to India," Publications of the Modern Language Association, 85 (March 1970): 284-294.

E. M. Forster's holograph at the University of Texas Library consists of four stages: (1) MS. A, a complete draft; (2) MS. B, one fourth the length of A; (3) MS. C, eighteen pages of typescript; and (4) four pages of changes and additions on verso pages of A and B. Levine compares the drafts of the episodes about the festival of Gokul Ashtami and the visit to the caves in terms of method, theme, plot, and characterization. Stylistic revisions are also noted by direct comparisons of passages. "As for Forster's method, a comparison of drafts with the text reveals that his goal is to entertain the reader by means of contrast: personal and ideological conflicts are heightened in the published work; details are more sharply drawn. Finally, various changes in the characters indicate that some of them--Aziz and Mrs. Moore specifically--were gradually reshaped as Forster's theme of fissure and connection grew more prominent."

Ellem, Elizabeth. "E. M. Forster: The Lucy and New Lucy Novels. Fragments of Early Versions of 'A Room with a View'," Times Literary Supplement, May 28, 1971, pp. 623-625.

Ellem studies 117 sheets of Forster notes and manuscripts that contain tentative chapter titles, outline plans, and first draft sections of Forster's early attempts to write a novel, referred to successively as "The Concert," the "Lucy" novel, and the "New Lucy" novel. Ellem describes the differences between "Lucy" and "New Lucy" as being differences of mood and of the characters' personalities. "Phrases and ghosts of characters from 'Lucy' and 'New Lucy' appeared in Where Angels Fear to Tread (October, 1905), and The Longest Journey (April, 1907). And passing references in Forster's letters and notebooks from 1904 to 1907 show that Lucy was not forgotten. But it was not until after the publication of The Longest Journey that Forster seriously considered rewriting 'New Lucy'." In October 1908, Forster published A Room with a View.

JOHN FOWLES

Fowles, John. The Magus. Boston: Little, Brown & Co., 1965.

Compare with Fowles' revised edition, Little, Brown, 1977. "Though this is not, in any major thematic or narrative sense, a fresh version of The Magus, it is rather more than a stylistic revision. A number of scenes have been largely rewritten, and one or two new ones invented." He states that "the erotic element is stronger in two scenes," and that the ending is now clearer.

BENJAMIN FRANKLIN

Zall, P. M. "The Manuscript and Early Texts of Franklin's Autobiography," Huntington Library Quarterly, 39 (August 1976): 375-384.

Zall describes the stages by which the Autobiography was written over a period of nineteen years and the texts of the various published editions. "Changes in stroke, ink, and nib indicate that Franklin's practice was to compose one sheet as rapidly as possible, then review and revise what he had just written before going on to the next sheet of four pages. While he did enter revisions in the columns left blank to receive them, he also made corrections along the line as he wrote and between the lines both as he was writing and as he revised. In later pages he would provide a choice of words to be selected in some subsequent revision, but otherwise he took as much care in revising as in writing, so that the manuscript is a product of art rather than spontaneous composition."

ROBERT FROST

Crane, Joan St. C. "Robert Frost's 'Kitty Hawk'," Studies in Bibliography, 30 (1977): 241-249.

"Frost wrote three versions of 'Kitty Hawk' over a period of eight years. The first and shortest (128 lines) was used as the 1956 card; the second, much expanded (432 lines) was printed in The Atlantic Monthly (November 1957). A new poem of 64 lines with the title, 'The Great Event Is Science. The Great Misgiving, The Fear of God, Is That the Meaning of It Shall Be Lost,' was printed in The Saturday Review (21 March, 1959). This poem contained 33 lines excerpted from the second version and 31 new lines. The final version, having 471 lines, was printed in In the Clearing (1962). It incorporates the 64-line poem in its entirety, discards some sections of the second version and contains additional text." Crane presents a collation of the three versions.

JOHN GALSWORTHY

Scheick, William J. "Chance and Impartiality: A Study Based on the Manuscript of Galsworthy's Loyalties," Texas Studies in Literature and Language, 17 (Fall 1975): 653-672.

Scheick uses parallel columns to display differences between manuscript and published versions of John Galsworthy's play. "This article commences with a detailed discussion of the opening scene of Loyalties, particularly stressing those revisions which affect dialogue, dramatic tension, characterization, and structural detail. The subsequent discussion focuses on significant instances of these four concerns in other parts of the play and suggests the relation of these revisions to the meaning of the work, especially with regard to the motif of chance and to authorial impartiality."

GEORGE GISSING

Wolff, Joseph J. "Gissing's Revision of The Unclassed," Nineteenth-Century Fiction, 8 (June 1953): 42-52.

George Gissing revised his second novel, The Unclassed, for its second edition eleven years after the first edition (1884-1895). Wolff makes direct comparisons to illustrate the changes. "The first, representing a substantial fraction of the revised version, remains in his earlier mode, a specimen of the immature Gissing; the second, evidencing greater skill and fewer signs of the author's intrusion, stands in the manner of Gissing's riper endeavors.... "

ELLEN GLASGOW

Dillard, R. H. W. "The Writer's Best Solace: Textual Revisions in Ellen Glasgow's The Past," Studies in Bibliography, 19 (1966): 245-250.

Dillard compares the text of "The Past," a short story, in its Good Housekeeping version and the version included in book publication, The Shadowy Third, a collection of her stories. In two instances, parallel columns are used to compare versions of passages. One fairly lengthy passage that Glasgow deleted is shown, and two added passages are quoted. "Actually there are 190 changes in the story. Eighty-two of these are substantive, some as long as several paragraphs. The changes are of three general kinds: simple corrections and revisions of spelling and punctuation, single word changes for precision of meaning and texture, and larger revisions to heighten suspense and to increase the reader's awareness of the characters and the tensions between them."

Steele, Oliver. "Ellen Glasgow's Virginia: Preliminary Notes," Studies in Bibliography, 27 (1974): 265-289.

"Perhaps the most fascinating thing about the early drafts of a gifted writer is that they sometimes record the stages by which, for the writer, the hypothetical and abstract become concrete and actual." Two preliminary outlines for the novel Virginia are presented here in their entirety (12 pages). Steele points out how several characters are changed in the stages of composition represented by the two outlines and the published novel. A good example of these changes is Cyrus Treadwell, who was originally conceived in great detail as an arch-villain materialist but who was played down in the final version because his character would probably have drawn the focus away from Virginia. Nine separate versions of the opening scene are discernible in the notes.

EDWARD GIBBON

Craddock, Patricia B. "Gibbon's Revision of the Decline and Fall," Studies in Bibliography, 21 (1968): 191-204.

"Although these changes are few in comparison with the total bulk of the Decline and Fall, they provide valuable evidence of Gibbon's way of working.... " These revisions were made by Gibbon's hand in five of the six volumes of the British Museum copy (c. 60 m. 1). Most of the added material is in the first chapter of Volume I. It has never been incorporated in subsequent editions. Gibbon made tentative plans to do a complete and thorough revision but never followed through. Craddock categorizes several kinds of revisions by Gibbon: (1) to soften positives and reduce superlatives (advice from Hume); (2) to correct errors of fact or emphasis; (3) to supply new facts or reflections; (4) to make assertions more strongly or with more irony.

THOMAS GRAY

Gray, Thomas. "Elegy Written in a Country Churchyard," The Norton Anthology of English Literature, Vol. I, M. H. Abrams, et al., eds. New York: Norton, 1979, pp. 2514-17.

"Our transcriptions from the poets' drafts attempt to reproduce, as accurately as the change from script to print will allow, the appearance of the original manuscript page."

GRAHAM GREENE

Higdon, David L. "Graham Greene's Second Thoughts: The Text of The Heart of the Matter," Studies in Bibliography, 30 (1977): 249-256.

"The changes--158 in number--show Greene correcting facts, sharpening idiomatic phrasing, transposing order, and refocusing action and motivation. This cannot be claimed uniformly, for a number of changes, probably compositional in origin and overlooked in the proofing, result in demonstrably inferior readings or obvious grammatical and logical errors." "... By the time he completed the other revisions, many of them anything but minor as he claims, the novel had become strikingly new. As Greene wished, few readers will be able to respond to the 1971 Scobie as they did to the 1948 Scobie, for the rhetoric surrounding him is quite different."

THOMAS HARDY

Wright, Walter F. The Shaping of "The Dynasts": A Study in Thomas Hardy. Lincoln: University of Nebraska Press, 1967.

In Chapter 5, "The Text from Rough Draft to Book," Wright makes comparisons among the rough draft and the copy in the Memorial Library, the manuscript in the British Museum, and the printed text. Some of the kinds of changes Hardy makes include (1) the conversion of prose materials to verse; (2) identification of characters; (3) matters of historical accuracy; (4) revisualization of scenes; (5) new approaches to an action; (6) reassignment of speeches; (7) maintenance of consistency in philosophic terminology; and (8) the elimination of commonplace phrasing and the changing of lines to intensify emotion. "Indeed, to judge from his own practice in revising, the weaknesses which disturbed him were not at all the oddities which for his contemporary critics made him obtuse, but the occasional lapses into the tradition or commonplace. When he was at his best, the images forced themselves on his consciousness pell-mell, incongruously, defiant of logic; and if, having set them down on paper, he later struck them, the reason was usually that new images, fresher and more intense, had come into his imagined cosmos and demanded to be preserved. "

Schweik, Robert C. "The Early Development of Hardy's Far from the Madding Crowd," Texas Studies in Literature and Language, 9 (Autumn 1967): 415-428.

From a study of the fair copy manuscript of Far from the Madding Crowd that Thomas Hardy furnished to the Cornhill, Schweik infers an earlier version of nine initial chapters that were eventually revised and incorporated into Chapters I through XV of the serialized novel. "By adding the dramatizations of Fanny Robin's story and developing Boldwood as another major character, Hardy laid the groundwork for a broader treatment of human feeling than was possible within the conventional love triangle with which he had begun; and the particular emphasis of the scenes added indicates that he was interested not only in developing a more complex set of character relationships but in extending the scope of the novel by exploiting opportunities for portraying human loneliness and suffering in a wider range of social situations and emotional atmospheres. "

Schweik, Robert C. "A First Draft Chapter of Hardy's Far from the Madding Crowd," English Studies, 53 (1972): 344-349.

This first draft chapter, not utilized as a separate entity in the fair copy sent to Cornhill Magazine, shows Oak and Troy as very different characters from the way they are shown in the completed serial version. In this initial draft Oak's strength and integrity are contrasted to Troy's calculated guile; in the serial version Oak has become clever as well as strong and honest, while Troy has degenerated into an irresponsible and careless drunk. Hardy salvaged some passages that describe the swamp from this deleted chapter and used them in Chapter XLIV. Schweik presents the corresponding fragments for direct comparison and to support the statement that "we do learn from the evidence of Hardy's first draft that his initial purpose in describing the swamp was to emphasize its character as a 'nursery of pestilences' endangering the health of Bathsheba's sheep; and the continuation of the same language in the fair copy suggests an unchanged purpose--to emphasize that Bathsheba has slept near a very unhealthy place indeed. "

Slack, Robert C. "The Text of Hardy's Jude the Obscure," Nineteenth-Century Fiction, 11 (March 1957): 261-275.

Thomas Hardy's revisions of the 1895 first book edition of Jude the Obscure for the 1903 Macmillan edition reflect his response to the attacks against his "immorality." Slack presents both versions of the scene in which Arabella throws the pig's pizzle at Jude. In the 1903 revision, Hardy becomes much less definite in his references to the missile used and tones down the sensuality of the encounter. The 1912 Macmillan edition represents another revision. "There are 87 random stylistic changes, mostly of little importance. All the other 124 revisions are concerned with meaning: The author has made details more explicit; he has altered factual information; he has changed the effective meaning of details or passages. Hardy's intention in revision might thus be judged to be more concerned with meaning than with style."

Ingham, Patricia. "The Evolution of Jude the Obscure," The Review of English Studies, 27 (February 1976 and May 1976): 27-37 and 159-169.

This two-part article traces the growth of the novel by Thomas Hardy from manuscript to serial to book editions. "Thus the story from its earliest version is hardly the simple one that has sometimes been suggested. It sprang from an autobiographical description of Hardy's boyhood temperament. It grew into a consideration of what was by the 1890's his own deep concern: the relationship between the sexes as played out by a complex man who only partly understood himself and a woman ill at ease with her own sexuality."

Chase, Mary Ellen. Thomas Hardy from Serial to Novel. 1927: reprint, New York: Russell & Russell, 1964.

Chase compares the serial versions of The Mayor of Casterbridge, Tess of the D'Urbervilles, and Jude the Obscure to the book forms of the novels as published in America by Harper and Brothers. For each novel, she presents the major changes in: (1) incident and plot; (2) characterization; (3) setting; (4) literary atmosphere (addition and alterations); and (5) diction and sentence structure. Chase concludes that all changes except those in incident and plot were made to improve the novels before they were brought out in book form. The changes in incident and plot were made from the original versions to adapt the novels to the sensational tastes and Victorian inhibitions of magazine readers. The books, then, were reversions to the original plot, including incidents that had been felt too realistic for the mass reading public of popular periodicals.

Winfield, Christine. "The Manuscript of Hardy's Mayor of Casterbridge," Papers of the Bibliographical Society of America, 67 (1973): 33-58.

This manuscript was used as printer's copy for the serial publication of The Mayor of Casterbridge in The Graphic: An Illustrated Weekly Newspaper (January 2 to May 15, 1886) but contains deletions, interlinear substitutions, and interpolations. Additions have also been made on the verso of some leaves. "These revision groupings are worth noting, not only for the information they yield on the probable stage of composition at which certain amendments were made, but also for the illustration they afford of the frequency and thoroughness of Hardy's revision; for their distribution in the text suggests that Hardy reviewed his material after completing about two thirds of the novel, as well as subjecting it to a more extensive revision after completion of the entire work." Winfield describes those stages of composition in Chapter XII and concludes that the major plot revisions in this chapter were not made until over half of the novel was written. She also concludes that some of these changes were made in "deference to the prudery of the magazine-reading public."

Wheeler, Otis B. "Four Versions of The Return of the Native," Nineteenth-Century Fiction, 14 (June 1959): 27-44.

The four versions of The Return of the Native by Thomas Hardy are represented by seven texts published from 1878 to 1912. Although Wheeler places most emphasis on changes in action, character, and setting, he describes stylistic changes that involve deletions, combinations, and emendations for the purposes of greater exactness and economy and for making the novel faster moving and more colloquial in its language. "If critics of the 1870's and 1880's were slow to grant him a place in the first rank, there may be more justice in their verdicts than we have thought--apart from their moralistic objections. Certainly the story of Clym and Eustacia has a far greater impact on the imagination in the third or fourth version than it does in the first or second. The main characters are more full-bodied, more plausible; the conflicts are stronger, the plot more tightly knit. The realistic surface, despite minor flaws, is more elaborate and more convincing through his painstaking attention to details of setting, which fuse this novel into the imaginary Wessex, and to details of speech and mannerism in the minor characters who are responsible for so much of the local color."

Bebbington, W. G. The Original Manuscript of Thomas Hardy's "The Trumpet-Major." Windsor: Leift & Sons Ltd., no date.

The original manuscript is compared with the Macmillan book version edited by Mrs. F. S. Boas to determine: (1) the divisions for the twelve parts of the monthly serial in Good Words, January to December 1880; (2) the differences between the chapter headings in the manuscript and in the book; (3) the differences between the chapter divisions in the manuscript and in the book; (4) textual differences between the manuscript and the book (denoting deletions by italics and substitutions by parentheses); and (5) changes in the names of characters and places. Bebbington concludes that Hardy's revisions were not extensive.

Kramer, Dale. "Two 'New' Texts of Thomas Hardy's The Woodlanders," Studies in Bibliography, 20 (1967): 135-150.

The first two authorized American publications of The Woodlanders (the Harper's Bazaar serial and Harper & Brothers book version) prove to be earlier versions than the British serial or book edition. Kramer discusses revisions performed among the manuscript, the American serial, the American book, and the British serial. The revisions were all made on proof sheets and did not involve structural changes or lengthy additions; they rather consisted of deletions, substitutions, and emendations designed to promote consistency in characters and a high level of artistry in the figurative language employed. "Hardy was content with his work only after numerous rereadings and revisions that would have stultified the creativeness of a less dedicated writer. Indeed, Hardy was an inveterate reviser, given to making basically, nit-picking revisions as well as--if not more than--to making significant changes."

Kramer, Dale. "Revisions and Vision: Thomas Hardy's The Woodlanders," Bulletin of the New York Public Library, 75 (1971): 195-230; 248-282.

In Part I Kramer discusses the composition of the novel, the manuscript revisions, and the American texts; in Part II he deals with the variants in the English editions. Kramer makes comparisons among eight versions. "In The Woodlanders most of the major trends in revisions are caused primarily by external influences, but not merely censorship. Editors, reviewers, and readers informed Hardy where he had not made his meanings clear enough, and he clarified and emphasized those meanings in ensuing revisions; but at the same time he rejected many other suggestions. The expectations of magazine readers of a certain moral standard is also reflected both in the omission of overly direct statements and in the suppression of blasphemous curse words for the serial. Throughout the post-serial editions there is a steadily increasing frankness in the treatment of sex--a larger number of coarser curse words, a greater frankness and boldness of the sexual basis of the characters' motivations, and an indication of the happiness Hardy obviously feels Grace and Giles could find if their ability to act independently were not restricted by artificial mores."

Purdy, Richard Little. Thomas Hardy: A Bibliographical Study. London: Oxford University Press, 1954.

"My constant concern, in short, has been to show how Hardy's novels and poems got written and how they got published and by what stages they came to the form in which we now know them." An example of the kind of information and commentary by Purdy is furnished by Tess of the D'Urbervilles: (1) descriptions of serial issues; (2) descriptions of manuscripts; (3) "Notes on Composition and Publication"; (4) "Notes on Revision and Publication" (Second Impression Revised); (5) an account of the American edition; (6) accounts of subsequent editions; and (7) description of the dramatization.

NATHANIEL HAWTHORNE

Gross, Seymour L. "Hawthorne's Revision of 'The Gentle Boy'," American Literature, 26 (May 1954): 196-208.

After its initial appearance in the Token (1832), Nathaniel Hawthorne revised his tale "The Gentle Boy" for inclusion in Twice-Told Tales (1837) by deleting passages which seemed to diffuse the overall effect that he sought. For example, statements that tended to soften and make more human either the Puritans or the Quakers were excised. "And when these deletions are viewed in their totality, they exhibit how Hawthorne has managed to give his piece a firmer point of view through the solidifying of a remarkably perilous balance between Puritan and Quaker. In short, he has clarified the terms of his tragedy."

Gross, Seymour L., and Alfred J. Levy. "Some Remarks on the Extant Manuscripts of Hawthorne's Short Stories," Studies in Bibliography, 14 (1961): 254-257.

Gross and Levy compare four of Hawthorne's MSS of short

pieces with the published versions ('The Wedding Knell,' 'Earth's Holocaust,' 'The Snow Image,' and 'Feathertop'), primarily to check on high-handed editorial practices of the period, but some authorial revision shows up. "Occasionally, however, Hawthorne's revisions decidedly clarified his intentions. In 'The Wedding Knell,' Hawthorne altered his description of Mr. Ellenwood from diseased sensitiveness to diseased sensibility...." Eighteen of Hawthorne's revisions in his manuscripts are shown. Gross and Levy conclude that, despite Hawthorne's complaints, his editors made very few substantive changes in his work.

Miller, Harold P. "Hawthorne Surveys His Contemporaries," American Literature, 12 (May 1940): 228-235.

In the Pioneer of February, 1843, Nathaniel Hawthorne's tale "The Hall of Fantasy" first appeared with brief references to many of his contemporaries (Bronson Alcott, Washington Allston, Orestes Brownson, Bryant, Cooper, Emerson, O. W. Holmes, Irving, Longfellow, Lowell, Poe, and others) who were not mentioned in the revised version published three years later in Mosses from an Old Manse. Miller concludes that Hawthorne's unfavorable remarks about these figures in the periodical version were cut in order to smooth the way for a favorable reception of Mosses. "It is unlikely that any delicate esthetic motive influenced the revision, since Hawthorne did not take trouble to mend the gaps which were left by the omissions. As the narrative appears in Mosses, praise and disparagement of reformers and writers stand awkwardly side by side, because intervening paragraphs have been dropped."

Turner, Arlin. "A Note on Hawthorne's Revisions," Modern Language Notes, 51 (November 1936): 426-429.

Sophia Peabody Hawthorne's influence on her husband apparently caused him to delete certain passages from several tales between their publication in periodicals and their being gathered in book form. A reference to a scantily clad young woman in "The Seven Vagabonds" in its original version in The Token for 1833 was excised for the 1842 edition of Twice-Told Tales. Other tales that succumbed to her "purifying" influence were (1) "The Toll-Gatherer's Day," changed between The Democratic Review of 1837 and the 1842 Twice-Told Tales and (2) "Monsieur du Miroir," changed between The Token of 1837 and Mosses from an Old Manse (1846).

JOSEPH HELLER

Nagel, James. "Two Brief Manuscript Sketches: Heller's Catch-22," Modern Fiction Studies, 20 (1974): 221-224.

Heller revised and expanded Catch-22 over a decade. "It would seem that several basic changes in Heller's conception of his novel occurred between the time he wrote the first sketch and the time he wrote the second, despite the fact that they both appear on the same page.... The 'Hemingway' potential for this novel diminished into subtle parallels within a distinct difference of form.... And the hospital scene, here suggested for the first time, was ultimately developed into one of the most important in Catch-22." The sketches are published in full. See also "Catch-18," an early version of a chapter of the novel, published in New World Writing, 7 (1955): 204-214.

ERNEST HEMINGWAY

Reynolds, Michael S. Hemingway's First War: The Making of "A Farewell to Arms." Princeton: Princeton University Press, 1976.

Reynolds is as interested in reconstructing from an examination of versions of the novel the autobiographical and non-autobiographical sources as he is in examining revisions, but much of this study is devoted to showing the reader the various revisions. The appendices show a timetable for the writing of the first draft and "Rejected First Drafts, Sample Variant Endings, and Titles." Section One, "1928-1930: The Writer at Work," is the most useful. "I always rewrite each day up to the point where I stopped," said Hemingway. "When it is all finished, naturally you go over it. You get another chance to correct and rewrite when someone else types it, and you see it clean in type. The last chance is in the proofs. You're grateful for these different chances."

Wagner, Linda W. "The Marinating of For Whom the Bell Tolls," Journal of Modern Literature, 2 (November 1972): 533-546.

"No major Hemingway novel so well reveals this process of gradual mastery of possible materials as For Whom the Bell Tolls, the 1940 book which was written only after Hemingway had explored its themes, and established prototypes for many of its characters, in his NASA columns, five short stories, a movie scenario, and The Fifth Column (his only play).... It is plausible to consider this work--done from the fall of 1937 to the spring of 1939--as presaging For Whom the Bell Tolls." The stories are: "The Denunciations," "the Butterfly and the Tank," "Night Before Battle," "Under the Ridge" (all in The Fifth Column and Four Stories of the Spanish Civil War) and "Nobody Ever Dies." The movie is The Spanish Earth, a documentary. "Hemingway often praised himself for knowing when to revise and when to cut."

Hemingway, Ernest. The Nick Adams Stories. New York: Scribner's, 1972.

"Arranged in chronological sequence (1925-1933), the events of Nick's life make up a meaningful narrative in which a memorable character grows from child to adolescent to soldier, veteran, writer, and parent--a sequence closely paralleling the events of Hemingway's own life." There are eight new pieces, of which only "Summer People" is complete; "The Last Good Country" is 64 pages of good Hemingway writing, unfinished; "On Writing" is also well-done. "The only writing that was any good was what you made up, what you imagined. That made everything come true." Writing "was really more fun than anything. That was really why you did it. It wasn't conscience. It was simply that it was the greatest pleasure. It had more bite to it than anything else." "He knew just how Cezanne would paint this stretch of river.... Nick, seeing how Cezanne would do the stretch of river and the swamp, stood up and stepped down into the stream. The water was cold and actual. He waded across the stream, moving in the picture."

Howell, J. M., and C. A. Lawler. "From Ambercrombie & Fitch to The First Forty-nine Stories: The Text of Ernest Hemingway's 'Francis Macomber'," Proof, 2 (1972): 212-281.

Variants from four revisions of "The Short Happy Life of Francis Macomber" supply a view of magazine editing practice as well as insight into Ernest Hemingway's creative processes: Appendix II--All changes on the original typescript; Appendix III--Variants between the typescript and the September 1936 Cosmopolitan version; Appendix IV--Variants between the typescript and the version in Scribner's The Fifth Column and the First Forty-nine Stories (1938); Appendix V--Variants between the 1936 Cosmopolitan version and the October 1947 Cosmopolitan version. "Hemingway's intentions in 'The Short Happy Life of Francis Macomber' are approached best through an examination of the typescript before it was edited by the Cosmopolitan people." For example, Hemingway added phrases to make it clear that Macomber had been a coward for a long time, not just since he had run from the lion. Four pages of the typescript with Hemingway's revisions upon them are presented in legible facsimile.

GERARD MANLEY HOPKINS

Hopkins, Gerard Manley. "Thou Art Indeed Just, Lord," The Norton Anthology of English Literature, Vol. II, M. H. Abrams, et al., eds. New York: Norton, 1979, pp. 2527-28.

"Our transcriptions from the poets' drafts attempt to reproduce, as accurately as the change from script to print will allow, the appearance of the original manuscript page."

A. E. HOUSMAN

Haber, Tom Burns. The Making of "A Shropshire Lad": A Manuscript Variorum. Seattle: University of Washington Press, 1966.

A. E. Housman's poetry notebooks in the Library of Congress contain developmental versions of 60 of the 63 poems in A Shropshire Lad. "All final entries of poems that approximate fair copy I have collated with the manuscript Housman sent to his publisher and have where possible noted all significant variations introduced between the time the poems left his desk and their appearance in print." Each poem is presented in its first edition published form, followed by the drafts in order of their composition from earliest to latest. Haber generalizes that the appeal of the individual poems and not their sequential organization gives the book its quality as literature.

ALDOUS HUXLEY

Wilson, R. H. "Versions of Brave New World," Library Chronicle of the University of Texas, 8 (Spring 1968): 28-41.

The typescript, with Aldous Huxley's revisions penned in, and the galley proofs are examined and compared. Wilson concludes that "Huxley did not work by producing successive versions of the whole novel, but by constant piecemeal revision." Huxley rarely cancelled material without replacing it. "Typically, cancelled words are rearranged or replaced in stylistic revision, sometimes literary in motive, at others minutely 'editorial'." Self-censorship, both sexual and religious, accounts for some changes. Additions, however, are stressed by Wilson as being the most significant kind of revision performed by Huxley.

HENRIK IBSEN

Gassner, John, and Ralph G. Allen. Theatre and Drama in the Making. Boston: Houghton Mifflin Company, 1964.

Henrik Ibsen's notes for A Doll's House and Ghosts are presented with an introduction that explains steps of composition that were typical of him. "The first drafts of these plays were composed in a great rush, presumably while the iconoclastic spirit still possessed Ibsen, while he was still under the influence of the angry thesis which had prompted him to write. Then came the slow, painful process of revision, a process which sometimes produced seven or eight drafts and which often lasted more than a year and a half." Gassner and Allen also include Eugene O'Neill's working notes for Mourning Becomes Electra and Tennessee Williams' short story "Portrait of a Girl in Glass," upon which he based The Glass Menagerie.

HENRY JAMES

Humphreys, Susan M. "Henry James's Revisions for 'The Ambassadors'," Notes and Queries, n. s. 1 (1954): 397-399.

In comparing the 1903 North American Review serialized version of The Ambassadors by Henry James to the version in the New York Edition of his works (1907-1909), Humphreys discovers that one whole interpolated section seems to have been inserted in the wrong place. This conclusion has been based entirely on internal evidence. "Had James placed this new section before the previous one, either at the end of Book X, or the beginning of Book XI, such inconsistencies would have been avoided, but at the same time the ironical effect for which James was striving would have been diminished." For the resolution of this question, see Edel, "The Text of The Ambassadors."

Edel, Leon. "The Text of The Ambassadors," Harvard Library Bulletin, 14 (1960): 453-460.

Henry James withheld three and one-half chapters of The

Ambassadors from the 1903 serial version in the North American Review but inserted them in the first English book edition (Methuen) and the first American book edition (Harper), both published in the fall of 1903. Transitional passages were added to the inserted sections in the Methuen edition but not in the Harper edition. One chapter was inserted out of proper order in the Harper edition, and this error has been propagated down to some editions currently in print. James chose the less prolix Harper version upon which to base his New York Edition of 1907-1909, apparently still unaware of the misplaced chapter. Edel makes available the "connective tissue" that James added to the Methuen edition. For an earlier attempt to resolve this question of the misplaced chapter with internal evidence alone, see Humphreys' "Henry James's Revisions for 'The Ambassadors'."

Gettmann, Royal A. "Henry James's Revision of The American," American Literature, 16 (1945): 279-295.

The differences between the 1877 edition of The American and the 1907 version in the New York Edition reveal Henry James's practice as a reviser of his work. Arraying corresponding passages in parallel columns, Gettmann demonstrates stylistic changes: (1) to more precise and specific words; (2) to concrete imagery; (3) to additional adjectival and adverbial modifiers; (4) to more appropriate stage directions in dialogue; and (5) to more figures of speech. Changes in characterization give more depth, credibility, and human detail to the people in the novel; but James has made no fundamental alterations in the characters. Although Gettmann does not see a set theory of revision guiding James in his work, he ventures a description of re-writing, something that James avoided doing, as "compressing or extending the time covered in a novel; omitting, adding, or redisposing episodes; altering the situation which sets the plot in motion; changing the forces which bring about the resolutions; omitting or adding characters or changing their traits and motives."

Traschen, Isadore. "Henry James: The Art of Revision. A Comparison of the Original and Revised Versions of The American," Dissertation Abstracts, 12 (1952): 623-624.

"The American, reissued in 1907, underwent the most extensive revisions. While most changes involved a word, phrase, or sentence, James frequently rewrote several paragraphs in sequence, and once added two pages. There were occasional deletions, usually of a sentence or two, rarely a paragraph, though in three instances somewhat less than a page was cut."

Schulz, Max F. "The Bellegardes' Feud with Christopher Newman: A Study of Henry James's Revision of The American," American Literature, 27 (March 1955): 42-55.

When James revised The American for the New York Edition (1907-1909), he sought to make more believable the Bellegardes' rejection of Newman by altering both this aristocratic French family and Newman himself. In the course of his revisions, James increased the antiquity of the Bellegardes, their passionate natures, their association with the imagery of castles and wine, and their overt hatred of Newman. The characterization of Newman was given more depth by increasing his pride in his commercial past, his enjoyment of crude Western humour, the stress on his friendship with Valentin, his stature as an equal to Mme de Cintre, his formal knowledge, his wealth, and the height of his consciousness. "James put the Bellegardes' dislike for Newman on a more personal footing. This basic revision gives greater credence to the Bellegardes' final refusal to accept Newman as a son-in-law. Any more drastic revision in an attempt to efface the implausible denouement would have required a complete alteration of the story's structure."

Traschen, Isadore. "Henry James and the Art of Revision," Philological Quarterly, 35 (1956): 39-47.

Traschen compares the original published version of The American to the revised version in the New York Edition, placing corresponding passages in parallel columns in order to demonstrate revisions. Traschen focusses on revisions that introduce or increase certain kinds of imagery for the purpose of communicating specific meaning: (1) circus images with Newman as the performer; (2) property or business images centered in Claire; (3) wine images involving the Bellegardes; and (4) animal images that successfully characterize Urbain de Bellegarde. "He sought to unify his material, to have it exert a maximum pressure of meaning at all points. But this was only to be expected of a writer who believed that reality was to be understood through form. Yet we may regard James as he sat down before the great labor of the revisions from still another point of view. For James, revision was not a matter of choice, but of immediate and absolute necessity. That is, it was a moral act of the highest kind."

Traschen, Isadore. "James's Revisions of the Love Affair in The American," The New England Quarterly, 29 (1956): 43-62.

Henry James's original version of The American is compared to the revised version in the New York Edition to investigate the changes that intensified the love relationship between Newman and Claire. "In seeking the answer, it must be remembered that James limited himself to revisions which seldom exceeded three or four consecutive paragraphs. He had no intention of violating the structure of the book." Newman's conscious actions as a lover toward Claire are made to seem more aggressive, even violent; but his unconscious responses are passive, waiting for Claire to act. Traschen attributes this pattern to James's personal celibacy and his ignorance of many of the normal feelings of lovers. "It is still true, nevertheless, that the revisions reveal the later James to be more deeply aware of the sexual aspect of love."

Tartella, Vincent. "James's 'Four Meetings'; Two Texts Compared," Nineteenth Century Fiction, 15 (June 1960): 17-28.

Direct columned comparisons between 1877 version and 1909 version. "The frequency with which James republished the story implies something of his opinion of it.... Although the plot and the natures and relationships of the several characters remain in every essential as they were in the original story, the revision, totaling approximately twelve thousand words, runs very nearly two thousand words longer.... James restyled every paragraph--some, of course, more extensively than others. A study of the changes James made in his story after years of writing experience will perhaps prove interesting to students of James and also of some value to the novice in creative writing." "The important revisions James made in the story reveal his anxiety to realize all the possibilities latent in character and situation."

Vandersee, Charles. "James's 'Pandora': The Mixed Consequences of Revision," Studies in Bibliography, 21 (1968): 93-108.

Vandersee compares the New York Edition text of Henry James's "Pandora" (1907-1909) with the texts of the most recent prior editions: London, 1885 and Boston, 1885. Three examples of broad changes are: (1) Mrs. Bonnycastle, based on Marian Adams (wife of Henry Adams), who had committed suicide, was not changed from a sharp-tongued character to spare Adams' feelings; rather, she was made more deliberate in her ridicule of others; (2) the now expatriated James intensified his disparagement of America, but with the motive of making Vogelstein seem more of an alien who is unable to understand America and Americans; and (3) "The tone is more overtly comic--a shift from discreet satire into broad burlesque." Six kinds of revisions effect small verbal changes: (1) revision of single words for no observable reason; (2) revision of single words with noticeable effect, one of which is in formality; (3) "Brighter details"--expansion of thought that works; (4) duller details--expansion of thought that is awkward; (5) excision of significant detail; and (6) addition of significant detail. "... The net result is neither striking improvement nor fatal tampering. The story is better in some ways, worse in others. But it is different...."

Gegenheimer, Albert F. "Early and Late, Revisions in Henry James's 'A Passionate Pilgrim'," American Literature, 23 (May 1951): 233-242.

Three stages of revision among four publications of "A Passionate Pilgrim" (Atlantic Monthly, 1871; A Passionate Pilgrim and Other Tales, 1875; Stories, revised, 1885; the New York Edition, 1908) furnish evidence that James grew as an artist and improved his work with every opportunity for revision. "The majority of changes in each revision (and for James it was a literal reseeing of his material) are distinct improvements. In general, passages become shorter, excess descriptions are dropped, ornate and flowery language becomes considerably plainer and more precise, and ambiguities are carefully but quietly eliminated." Gegenheimer illustrates these improvements with excellent comparative examples from the texts.

Matthiessen, F. O. Henry James: The Major Phase. 1944; reprint, New York: Oxford University Press, 1963.

The Appendix, "The Painter's Sponge and Varnish Bottle," which also appears as an article in The American Bookman (Winter 1944), contains Matthiessen's responses to the revisions of The

Portrait of a Lady as encountered in James's personal copy, written in longhand in the margins and inserted as pages of typescript. James made several kinds of changes: (1) deleting the word picturesque in several cases and substituting romantic; (2) increasing the use of the word vulgar and terms of the intellect such as contemplation, mind, intelligence, and consciousness; (3) using more colloquialisms; (4) using more imaginative forms for "he said-she said"; (5) moving from the abstract to the more concretely imagistic; (6) increasing deliberate ambiguity in characters; and (7) changing to "a more high-keyed emotional register." James extensively rewrote two scenes so as to realize more of their dramatic potential: the scene when the Countess Gemini substantiates Isabel's suspicions and the scene with Caspar when he presses Isabel not to return to Osmond.

Krause, Sydney J. "Henry James's Revisions of The Portrait of a Lady: A Study of Literary Portraiture and Perfectionism," Dissertation Abstracts, 16 (May-September 1956): 1256-1257.

"As revision for James meant nothing less than the complete reactivation of the work in his imagination, his intentions in revising become clear only when each revision is projected against the background of his method and themes. That is the analysis proposed in this dissertation with the aim of gaining an intimate view of James's art as the pursuit of perfectionism."

Mazzella, Anthony J. "The Revised Portrait of a Lady: Text and Commentary," Dissertation Abstracts International, 33 (February 1973): 4424A-4425A.

The dissertation from which this abstract was taken includes the entire text of the novel in six volumes, 1,300 pages. "Closely considered, the revised Portrait reveals that the 1881 American Edition and the 1908 version that appears in the New York Edition are two different works. Source material for this thesis is the complete Text of the works in their differing states prepared as one part of this study. The Commentary, in addition to describing and analyzing the changes documented in the Text, contains appendices that reveal how much even James's marked copy differs from the final version, and the degree to which the poor quality of his copy affected final punctuation so that, for example, the apparent deletion of commas is actually due to a faulty late impression."

Baym, Nina. "Revision and Thematic Change in The Portrait of a Lady," Modern Fiction Studies, 22 (Summer 1976): 183-200.

"The text of 1908 is not sufficiently revised to transform the work into a late James piece, but is enough changed to cloud the original dynamics of the story. It is a baffling and problematical work, much more so than the text of 1881. The changes created many of the problems. They override the social theme of the work and partly erase it. The matrix of values which radiates out from 'independence' in 1881 centers in 'awareness' in 1908, with attendant dislocations of emphasis."

Durkin, Sister Mary Brian. "Henry James' Revisions of The Reverberator," American Literature, 33 (November 1961): 330-349.

The 1908 New York Edition version of The Reverberator proves to be a considerable improvement over the 1888 Macmillan edition. Directly quoted passages from both versions are compared in parallel columns to show how James made changes that provided "concrete nouns, specific adjectives, and image-creating metaphors. Far from complicating his style, his emendations improved The Reverberator; heightened dialogue, expanded stage directions, and increased informality in tone and diction aided dramatic effectiveness, thematic clarity, and character portrayal."

Harvitt, Helene. "How Henry James Revised Roderick Hudson: A Study in Style," Publications of the Modern Language Association, 39 (1924): 203-227.

In this seminal study of authorial revision, Harvitt compares the first edition of Roderick Hudson (1883) to the Macmillan edition (1921), supplying evidence for her conclusions by positioning corresponding direct quotations in parallel columns. Almost every sentence was changed, but the order of the paragraphs was maintained. The kinds of changes discussed are (1) description; (2) addition of phrases indicative of learning; (3) increased use of figures of speech; (4) additions of "forced or unnatural" expressions; (5) substitution of concrete expressions; and (6) alterations that seem completely unimportant. "The effect of that introspective, analytical trait is an obscuring of spontaneous, natural passages, making them labored, heavy, ambiguous, and sometimes almost impenetrable. There is a feeling of effort, of deliberate striving for effect which spoils the youthful production and robs it of what was fresh and easy and sincerely unaffected."

Bercovitch, Sacvan. "The Revision of Rowland Mallet," Nineteenth-Century Fiction, 24 (September 1969): 210-221.

This comparison of the first edition of Roderick Hudson (1875) with the New York Edition (1907) concentrates on the characterization of Rowland Mallet. The revisions reveal "unmistakably that James meant to draw attention to Rowland's perverse willfulness, to the self-deluding rationality and narrow self-involvement that underlie his 'solemnity' and circumscribe his intelligence." Corresponding passages from both versions are compared directly in parallel columns and in following order to demonstrate some of the kinds of revision employed by James: (1) more emphasis on the dramatic; (2) greater stress on the emotions; (3) an increasing concreteness; (4) more psychological complexity; and (5) elaborate imagery.

Rosenbaum, S. P. "The Spoils of Poynton: Revisions and Editions," Studies in Bibliography, 19 (1966): 161-174.

Rosenbaum compares The Atlantic Monthly serialization (first printed version), the first American edition (second printed version), the first British edition (third printed version), and the New York Edition (fourth printed version). When Henry James revised the serial version for the first American edition, he made over fourteen hundred changes: reducing punctuation, tightening sentence structure, and correcting awkward statements; but his most important change was the title: from "The Old Things" to The Spoils of Poynton. Revisions for the first British edition were made on the sheets of the first American edition and involved removing commas and improving syntax as well as moving toward more specificity and greater accuracy. Specific descriptive details account for the most significant additions made for the New York Edition. "The only responsible alternative to the New York Edition of the novel is the first English edition. 'The Old Things' is the most inaccurate and badly written of the four texts, and the first American edition is not a completely consistent revision of these faults."

McElderry, B. R., Jr. "Henry James's Revision of Watch and Ward," Modern Language Notes, 67 (November 1952): 457-461.

Henry James revised Watch and Ward, originally published as a serial in the Atlantic Monthly (August through December 1871), for the 1878 publication in book form. He excised a superfluity of rhetorical jewels, corrected wordiness, removed bookish words, reduced the number of contractions, and decreased the workload of some paragraphs. "Revision of the text was an attempt to polish and refine a mediocre story. The changes are effective as far as they go, and they demonstrate a sharpening sense of style and workmanship, but they did not alter the fundamental situations or characterizations. What the novel lacked no merely literary labor could supply."

Fish, Charles. "Form and Revision: The Example of Watch and Ward," Nineteenth Century Fiction, 22 (1967): 173-190.

The 1871 version of Henry James' Watch and Ward, serialized in the Atlantic Monthly, is compared to the revised 1878 book publication. One of the problems that James tried to deal with in his revision was the problem of points of view or "alternating centers of interest." Some of the purposes of the revisions were (1) to lessen the distance between character and author; (2) to remove an intruding character or author when the point of view began to become ambiguous; (3) to imply more and make more demands on the reader's imagination; (4) to give the character of Roger more credibility; and (5) to change Fenton so that he is not an American stereotype. "The alternating centers of Watch and Ward provided a 'certain form,' but tentative as they were, they could not achieve the finished structure of the later novels. He could not completely recast the story, but here and there he could make changes. Therefore the author's voice sometimes disappears, leaving the reader closer to the thoughts and words of the characters. Occasionally James strikes out a passage that violates the general pattern of point of view and center of interest."

Vincec, Sister Stephanie. "'Poor Flopping Wings': The Making of Henry James's The Wings of the Dove," Harvard Library Bulletin, 24 (January 1976): 60-93.

Vincec writes a detailed account of the composition of The Wings of the Dove, finding it to lack necessary unity as a result of a dual focus that is never resolved. "Finally, James's failure to re-read the entire novel before publication or to apply that effective antidote, compression, left on his hands a too-lengthy novel with structural imbalances that no mere verbal revision could correct. One thing is clear. The author's subtlety has no bearing on the structure of this novel." In a short section of the article on revision, Vincec finds three dozen authorial variants between the 1902 Scribner (American) edition and 1902 Constable (English) edition, but a much more thorough revision is indicated for the 1909 New York edition. "Collation of the two American editions, Scribner's of 1902 and the New York edition of 1909, reveals that James introduced over a thousand variants into the later one. They range in nature from changes in the order of words to the alteration of significant details of characterization."

James, Henry. Lady Barberina and Other Tales: Benvolio, Glasses and Three Essays. With Variants, Notes, Introduction and Bibliography by Herbert Ruhm. New York: The Vanguard Press, 1961.

This volume makes available three pieces of fiction by Henry James with the variants that resulted from his revisions of successive editions, from the earlier editions up through the New York Edition of 1907-1909. Lady Barbarino and Glasses are preceded by the notes James made as he originally conceived of these tales, but no such notes have been located for Benvolio. Variants are indicated by bracketed text, which denotes changes, and by free-standing numbers, which point out additions. "As the revisions reveal in this volume, points of salience have been excised in favor of a more gradual, more rounded presentation."

"Henry James Reprints." Times Literary Supplement, 5 February 1949, p. 96.

This unsigned article describes the controversy over Henry James's revisions; whether his work was improved or made worse by the changes he wrought in successive editions. Quoting from different versions of Owen Wingrove, Roderick Hudson, and Four Meetings, the article concludes that the earlier James was less prolix, clearer, and easier to read than the later one and that "whatever he may himself have thought about the matter in this old age, it was in the unsophisticated texts that the early novels and stories brought him the only wide popularity he ever enjoyed." A spate of letters in response to this article followed in later issues of the Times Literary Supplement from February 12 to March 19.

ROBINSON JEFFERS

Shebl, James. In This Wild Water: The Suppressed Poems of Robinson Jeffers. Pasadena, California: Ward Ritchie Press, 1976.

Shebl examines here an interesting case of a major, individualistic poet succumbing to censorship by his own publisher. "Random House assumed the role of guardian-censor for postwar America and removed ten poems from the original manuscript" of The Double Axe, "making a number of changes in the remaining poems as well." In Chapter 5, Shebl "discusses why Jeffers deferred to editorial opinion and allowed the poems to be excised.

Curiously, Jeffers reworked two of the poems that ultimately appeared.... My reading of them points up the artistic possibilities of the expunged poems."

SAMUEL JOHNSON

Moody, A. D. "The Creative Critic: Johnson's Revision of London and The Vanity of Human Wishes," Review of English Studies, n. s., 22 (1971): 137-150.

Moody discusses the substantive variants among three versions of The Vanity of Human Wishes: a manuscript draft (November 1748), the first edition (January 1749), and Dodsley's Collection (1755). Four versions of London are compared: a manuscript draft, the first edition (May 1738), the second edition (May 1738), and Dodsley's Collection (1748). The Vanity of Human Wishes was revised in over 120 of its lines, London in 35. "Most of the revisions show Johnson strengthening his writing by enforcing finer discriminations of sense and feeling in both word and rhythm." Moody concludes that Samuel Johnson the critic, as revealed in his revisions of his own poetry, is not nearly as profound as Samuel Johnson the poet.

Johnson, Samuel. "The Vanity of Human Wishes," The Norton Anthology of English Literature, Vol. I, M. H. Abrams, et al., eds. New York: Norton, 1979, pp. 2512-14.

"Our transcriptions from the poets' drafts attempt to reproduce, as accurately as the change from script to print will allow, the appearance of the original manuscript page."

Smith, David Nichol, R. W. Chapman, and L. F. Powell. Johnson and Boswell Revised by Themselves and Others: Three Essays. Oxford: Oxford University Press, 1928.

The three essays are "Johnson's Revision of His Publications, especially The Rambler, Rasselas, and The Idler" by D. N. Smith; "Boswell's Revises of The Life of Johnson" by R. W. Chapman; and "The Revision of Dr. Birkbeck Hill's Boswell" by L. F. Powell. D. N. Smith estimates that Johnson may have made as many as 25,000 changes in the various issues of The Rambler. Parallel columns display examples of revisions in Rasselas. Smith states that "those who think that the essence of Johnson's style consists in amplification, in making a little go a long way with the help of a Latinized vocabulary, in using a Latin word in preference to an English one--these people *might* profit from a study of Johnson's revisions."

BEN JONSON

Dutton, A. Richard. "The Significance of Jonson's Revision of 'Every Man in His Humour'," Modern Language Review, 69 (1974): 241-249.

Dutton compares the revised version of Every Man in His

Humour in the 1616 Folio with the earlier Quarto version. The revisions seem characteristic of the middle period when Jonson began setting most of his plays in London. Some of the kinds of revisions described are (1) fewer references to poets and poetry; (2) more use of colloquial idiom; (3) changing the setting from Florence to London; (4) excision of stilted forms; and (5) making the speech more appropriate to the character. "By almost every criterion, in fact, the revised Every Man in His Humour is an improvement on the original; the diffuse plot is made slightly clearer, the denouement is shortened, made more straightforward and intelligible, while the characterization and the setting are more fully realized."

JAMES JOYCE

Scholes, Robert E. "Some Observations on the Text of Dubliners: 'The Dead'," Studies in Bibliography, 15 (1962): 191-205.

Two publishers balked at bringing out Dubliners without being able to censor it, even after type had been set up and galley proofs had been printed of either part or all of the work. Consequently, some of the corrections and revisions made by Joyce at two stages have never been incorporated in these stories as we know them. "The relationships among the various texts can be illustrated most clearly by tracing one passage through all its stages." Scholes does that, with very interesting results. He then quotes ten improvements Joyce made which are not to be found in the published version. Scholes provides an appendix in which he shows Joyce's list of corrections. SEE Scholes' following entry, "Further Observations on the Text of Dubliners." Scholes also points out Joyce's reluctance to use commas and his frustrated attempts to avoid the conventional punctuation of direct discourse in this book of stories. "But a textual study of 'The Dead' alone is enough to establish the fact that we are reading one of our most precise and careful writers in editions which can be greatly improved, which can be made both more correct and more Joycean."

Scholes, Robert E. "Further Observations on the Text of Dubliners," Studies in Bibliography, 17 (1964): 107-122.

Although existing materials are insufficient to enable scholars to arrive at a definitive text, many of the corrections and revisions Joyce made that were not incorporated into the first edition can be restored; in some instances, however, at the risk of error of judgment. Scholes reviews the problems posed by the materials, then examines changes in each story, except "The Dead" (SEE the preceding entry by Scholes on that story), in most cases providing some comparisons of phrases, lines, short passages, in the early versions and the first edition. Scholes has "examined and collated all the available manuscript and proof versions of all the stories," except "The Dead." "Joyce was given to continual revising in proof." See especially Joyce's notes on "Eveline," "The Boarding House," "Clay," "Counterparts," and "Ivy Day in the Committee Room."

Adams, Robert M. "Light on Joyce's Exiles?: A New MS, a

Curious Analogue, and Some Speculations," *Studies in Bibliography*, 17 (1964): 83-105.

"... A curious manuscript containing dialogue for Joyce's only surviving play, *Exiles*," which was "never incorporated in the printed version" exists at Cornell and has been studied by Adams, who reprints, with keys relating it to the published play, the fragments in eight pages. He also traces similarities with Scribe's libretto for Meyerbeer's opera, *Robert Le Diable*. He argues that "the remarkable cleanness of the script ... suggests that we have, not a primitive version of the play, but a set of relatively late variations on its themes"; that we might think of two versions: "one is a public, the other a private version of the same play. On these terms, would not the 'private' version have special authority as a gloss on the 'public' one?... On these terms, *Exiles* is a drama written for two stages simultaneously, and so compromised *ab ovo* ... for this mode of understanding we shall always and inevitably lack essential materials."

Higginson, Fred H. "James Joyce's Revisions of *Finnegans Wake*: A Study of the Published Versions," *Dissertation Abstracts*, 14 (January-June 1954): 525.

"Examinations of the revisions of 'The Sisters' (a short story from *Dubliners*), of *Stephen Hero* (an early version of the *Portrait*) and of *Ulysses* show that by revision Joyce attains, by varying means and to varying degrees, the goals of economy, precision, and sharpness of focus. Economy predominates as a goal of the revisions of *Ulysses*. Vico's influence on *Finnegans Wake* is threefold: it affects the form (epical), the structure, and the language. The revisions of *Finnegans Wake* are directed principally toward sharpening the focus of the language so that the reader is forced into a realization of the Vichian continuity of history, myth, and languages."

Hart, Clive. "Notes on the Text of *Finnegans Wake*," *Journal of English and Germanic Philology*, 59 (1960): 229-239.

Hart details changes Joyce made on proofs. A copy of *Finnegans Wake* in hand would facilitate the usefulness of this information. "A very large number of alterations and additions to proofs and typescripts never reached the printing stage, due largely to the extreme untidiness of the material the printers and typists had to work from."

Hayman, David. "From *Finnegans Wake*: A Sentence in Progress," *Publications of the Modern Language Association*, 73 (1958): 136-154.

Hayman studies thirteen stages of the development of one sentence in Book III of *Finnegans Wake*, a sentence that James Joyce worked on for fourteen years, starting in 1924. "Built, literally constructed, within a tactile framework of the established mysteries, myths, and symbols, the finished piece revolves like a carved bead about the central axis or universally accepted situation. While maintaining a static-kinetic balance through thirteen successive changes, while placing all movement in the future, while making it all tentative and equivocal, Joyce nevertheless suggests an infinite variety of actions and provides for a delicate variation in mood. Working under self-imposed restrictions, he produces skillfully manipulated paradoxes from which arise the synthetic experience of the reader."

Joyce, James. Scribbledehobble: The Ur-Workbook for "Finnegans Wake." Edited, with notes and introduction, by Thomas E. Connolly. Chicago: Northwestern University Press, 1961.

Connolly presents this notebook with entries that were used in Finnegans Wake followed by page and line numbers indicating where the notebook entries were used in the final composition. To demonstrate how the Scribbledehobble notebook can be used, Connolly cites an entry, then gives its elaboration in a notebook in the British Museum, follows up with another entry that develops it further, and finally gives the ultimate version, indicating deletions, substitutions, and, most importantly, additions. "Certainly, when he began to work on Finnegans Wake, he had completely reversed the method of writing from that used in the Portrait. Now his method resembled that of an expert Japanese lacquerer who begins with a basic coat and then, layer upon layer, builds up his medium so that the final product is a highly polished surface that reveals a warm and rich depth down to the basic wood."

Hayman, David. A First-Draft Version of "Finnegans Wake." Austin: University of Texas Press, 1963.

"... The present volume represents an attempt to expose within the artificial unity of a liberally defined first-draft version as many as possible of the salient aspects and peculiarities of that collection [all of the available Joyce MSS.]. It is my experience that the complex and almost illegible first-draft versions of the basic chapters, when combined with the first drafts of later interpolation and important additions, can serve more than adequately as a guide to the runes of the creative process." Revisions indicated are additions, additions to additions, cancellations, substitutions, substitutions within substitutions, substitutions within additions, and additions within substitutions. Hayman lists and explains six methods of composition that he discerns in Finnegans Wake: (1) straight composition; (2) revise-and-complete; (3) episodic; (4) episodic fusion; (5) piecemeal or mosaic; and (6) framing.

Joyce, James. A Portrait of the Artist as a Young Man. Text, Criticism, and Notes, edited by Chester G. Anderson. New York: The Viking Press, 1968.

SEE Section II "Related Texts by Joyce," especially "The Trieste Notebook." SEE entry on Stephen Hero. Compare with Stephen Hero.

Scholes, Robert, and Richard M. Kain, Editors. The Workshop of Daedalus: James Joyce and the Raw Materials for "A Portrait of the Artist as a Young Man." Evanston, Illinois: Northwestern University Press, 1965.

Part II of this book presents biographical materials (including sketches by writers such as W. B. Yeats and Padraic Colum). Part III includes literary materials external to Joyce that furnished fuel for his functioning as an artist (Pater, Yeats, Swinburne, Aquinas, Shelley, Flaubert, Wilde, Ovid). Part I makes available manuscript materials that give insight into the development of Stephen Hero, A Portrait, and Critical Writings: (1) The Epiphanies; (2) The Paris Notebook; (3) The First Version of "A Portrait" (and notes for "Stephen Hero"); (4) Sparks from a Whetstone (Stanislaus Joyce's Diary); (5) The Pola Notebook; (6) The Trieste Notebook; and (7) Fragments from a Late "Portrait" Manuscript. "... One inescapable conclusion derived from these labors demands a statement. It becomes increasingly apparent that Joyce had either an actual or a literary source in mind for almost every passage in A Portrait."

Gabler, Hans Walter. "Towards a Critical Text of James Joyce's A Portrait of the Artist as a Young Man," Studies in Bibliography, 27 (1974): 1-53.

Gabler is more concerned with textual validity than with comparisons of authorial versions, but some useful information about authorial revision is included. D = holograph MS; T = typescript; E = Egoist serialization; H, B, J = book edition. "Authorial correction and revision intervened at each stage of transmission between D and J, thus conferring secondary authority on each of the textual witnesses T, H, B, and J." Gabler outlines "a comprehensive editorial hypothesis on the basis of which a critical edition could be envisioned." A few corrections and variants are quoted and compared.

Levin, Harry. James Joyce: A Critical Introduction. New York: New Directions, 1941.

Levin compares Stephen Hero, an early version of A Portrait of the Artist as a Young Man, with the finished work.

Joyce, James. Stephen Hero. Edited by Theodore Spencer, John J. Slocum, and Herbert Cahoon. New York: New Directions, 1963.

The early incomplete draft of A Portrait of the Artist as a Young Man. Edited from the manuscript in the Harvard College Library by Theodore Spencer. A new edition, incorporating the additional manuscript pages in the Yale University Library and the Cornell University Library, edited by John J. Slocum and Herbert Cahoon. A page of Joyce's notes and a page of Stephen Hero in manuscript are reproduced. "It can be seen at a glance," says Spencer, "that this early version is very different from the version eventually published as A Portrait of the Artist as a Young Man. The period covered by the 383 pages of the manuscript occupies only the last 93 pages of the published version.... Every reader of the present text will want to make his own comparisons between its picture of Stephen Daedalus and the picture given by the final version," but Spencer outlines some of the major differences, one of which is that the early version is loaded with the kind of additive detail one does not find in the much more economical and selective Portrait. Spencer notes two kinds of revisions in Stephen Hero itself as copied from earlier drafts by Joyce: words deleted and changed, and long passages cut.

Litz, A. Walton. "Joyce's Notes for the Last Episodes of *Ulysses*," *Modern Fiction Studies*, 4 (Spring, 1958): 3-20.

Litz gives examples of notes from the note-sheets used in the later episodes alongside the passages in which they were used and contends that these particular notes were put together and used in the later stages of revision. "It was the function of the note-sheets to assure that patterns and relationships already visualized by Joyce reached their foreordained positions in the text. Like the mosaic worker, he was continuously sorting and re-grouping his raw materials, assigning each fragment to its proper place in the general design. The mechanical nature of this process emphasizes the mechanical nature of those ordering principles which give *Ulysses* its superficial unity, and which sometimes obscure the deeper unity of the novel."

Prescott, Joseph. "Stylistic Realism in Joyce's *Ulysses*," in *A James Joyce Miscellany, Second Series*. Edited by Marvin Magalaner. Carbondale: Southern Illinois University Press, 1959, pp. 15-66.

Prescott uses manuscript notebooks and sheets from the University of Buffalo Library, a manuscript of *Ulysses* from the collection of A. S. W. Rosenbach, a number of typescript sheets, and the serial version in the *Little Review* to discuss Joyce's use of revision in heightening and intensifying the realism in his style. "No one ... has yet analyzed the materials of *Ulysses* as they were going through the creative process in Joyce's now widely scattered manuscripts, typescripts, proof sheets, and other preliminary drafts. The purpose of this study is to analyze the technique of *Ulysses* as it is revealed by the growth of the text through the innumerable, extensive, and significant changes which the author made in various stages in the writing of the book. The revisions constitute an enormous body of material which yields much new light on Joyce's intentions and methods. Joyce's revisions represent almost exclusively a process of elaboration." In his style, he strives for "precision in the use of words, specification, vividness, dramatization, onomatopoeia, and rhythms."

Litz, A. Walton. *The Art of James Joyce: Method and Design in "Ulysses" and "Finnegans Wake."* London: Oxford University Press, 1961.

"It was my intention to write a 'biography' of *Ulysses* and *Finnegans Wake*, tracing the growth of each work and using this evidence to document Joyce's shifting artistic ideals. My main interest was in technique, and I sought to discover how the methods of the *Wake* developed out of those of *Ulysses*.... Joyce's techniques underwent radical changes," through a "gradual evolution in method and design" that one can see only in the manuscripts. "In a sense the process of composition parallels the process we follow as readers: a gradual accretion of details which finally form themselves into related patterns. To trace the evolution of an episode is to re-enact our own gradual apprehension of the work." See especially Chapter One. Litz provides an appendix dealing with "early vestiges of *Ulysses*," and another showing the "chronology of Joyce's Work in Progress, 1914-1939." Litz uses note-sheets, manuscripts, galley proofs, serial publications, and book versions to study Joyce's revisions in Ulysses and Finnegans Wake. Earlier and later versions are arrayed in sequence and in parallel columns to exemplify Joyce's basic approach to revisions as expansion and elaboration. Joyce rewrote all of the earlier sections of Ulysses that had appeared in the Little Review. "The early episodes of Ulysses were drafted in a style not far from that of A Portrait; but when Joyce returned to them in 1920 and 1921 he attempted radical alterations in their style and structure." (1) The original versions function as outlines for the expanded final versions; (2) The original versions contain the seeds for every major element of the final versions; and (3) The formal correspondences between the Homeric epic and the episodes of Ulysses were produced in late revision. Litz contends that "It is a damning commentary on Joyce's method [in writing Finnegans Wake] that a study of earlier versions provides important clues to the meaning of a passage in the final text."

Adams, Robert M. Surface and Symbol: The Consistency of James Joyce's Ulysses. New York: Oxford University Press, 1962.

The process of composition of Ulysses is discussed in a section entitled "Prudence and Vision" in Chapter 5, "Scholar, Poet, Wit." "In making these late additions, Joyce seems frequently concerned to exercise the full range of his reference, and to dot the novel with rocky little crystals of impenetrably private fact. But I think the work which he did on early versions of the book rose from a more intense and fusing vision, to which the conscious display of erudition was largely irrelevant."

Madtes, Richard E. "Joyce and the Building of 'Ithaca'," English Literary History, 31 (December 1964): 443-459.

In order to exemplify his contention that James Joyce's revisions involved few deletions and substitutions but a large quantity of additions, Madtes examines nine stages of the composition of the seventeenth chapter of Ulysses, "Ithaca": (1) Collection of notes; (2) Composition of rough draft; (3) Completion of fair copy; (4) Revision of fair copy; (5) Revision of first typescript; (6) Revision of second typescript; (7) Revision of first galley proof; (8) Revision of second galley proof; (9) Revision of final page proof. "But 'revision' is a misleading word; 'expansion' would be more accurate. After completing the basic draft and making a fair copy, Joyce worked through the episode from beginning to end six different times, incorporating a new set of additions each time. Forty-two per cent of the episode (9,380 words out of the final 22,421) was composed in these additions. How many words did he change, substituting others in their place? Only 348. And how many words did he delete entirely? An almost negligible 79."

Herring, Phillip F. "Ulysses Notebook VIII. A. 5 at Buffalo," Studies in Bibliography, 22 (1969): 287-310.

The notebook is published here in full, preceded by six pages of introductory observations by Herring. "In Ulysses Joyce's creative process was one of continual accretion, expansion and elaboration of verbal and thematic material relevant to a particular episode." "It is hoped that this introduction and edition will open the way for a more thorough critical evaluation of notebook VIII. A. 5 as one of the designs woven into the tapestry of Ulysses." SEE Herring, Joyce's Ulysses Notesheets.

Herring, Phillip F. Joyce's "Ulysses" Notesheets in the British Museum. Charlottesville: For the Bibliographical Society of the University of Virginia by the University Press of Virginia, 1972.

"The publication of the Ulysses notesheets constitutes a kind of invasion of privacy, a forbidden view revealing the secret manipulations of the on-stage magician, but it is hoped that it will lead to clarification of Joyce's method and intent rather than to ridicule of a practice we were never meant to see." Joyce described himself as a "mosaic craftsman.... each of the eighteen episodes was continually revised and expanded (almost never condensed) from early sketches right up to a few days before the date of publication.... The novel was literally an organically evolving book. Joyce's method was meticulous and exacting; he could never be completely satisfied with anything he wrote. The piecing together of ideas and phrases through the various drafts of Ulysses, though his goal was always to give both unity and depth to his mosaic design, resulted from an almost psychotic compulsion.... The Ulysses notesheets in the British Museum ... comprise one of the most important sources of information on Joyce's creative techniques." These notesheets for the last seven episodes of Ulysses (Cyclops, Nausicaa, Oxen of the Sun, Circe, Eumaeus, Ithaca, and Penelope) form the second stage of composition of the novel. The notesheets are all reproduced, preceded by essays on all seven episodes.

JOHN KEATS

Stillinger, Jack. "The Text of 'The Eve of St. Agnes'," Studies in Bibliography, 16 (1963): 207-212.

"Employing the principle that a proper text of the poem will embody the latest readings intended by the poet, including those that there is good reason to think were rejected by the publishers against the poet's wishes, future editors of Keats' poem, whether making a scholarly text or putting together selections for an anthology, should restore" lines 314-322 and the additional stanza between VI and VII in the original manuscript. Stillinger quotes and discusses those passages to show that their omission has led to misinterpretations of the poem.

Keats, John. "To Autumn," "The Eve of St. Agnes," The Norton Anthology of English Literature, Vol. II, M. H. Abrams, et al., eds. New York: Norton, 1979, pp. 2522-23, 2521-22.

"Our transcriptions from the poets' drafts attempt to reproduce, as accurately as the change from script to print will allow, the appearance of the original manuscript page."

Lyon, Harvey T. Keats' Well-Read Urn: An Introduction to Literary Method. New York: Henry Holt, 1958.

Chapter One: The Poem--an introduction and the texts of the ode. Chapter Two: The Letters--from Keats. Chapter Three: The Commentators--criticism. Lyon offers textual, scholarly, critical material covering 135 years as a way of examining a single work, "Ode on a Grecian Urn." Also included are the odes "To a Nightingale," "To Melancholy," "To Autumn," and "To Indolence." "I have shown all the variant readings among the versions printed during Keats's life and among the longhand copies made by his friends." Passages from Keats' letters that pertain to the odes are presented. Passages from critical commentaries by numerous critics follow.

Gittings, Robert. The Odes of Keats and Their Earliest Known Manuscripts. Kent, Ohio: Kent State University Press, 1970.

The manuscripts in Keats' handwriting (except for "Grecian Urn" in George Keats' handwriting) appear photographically reproduced on recto pages, with corresponding printed versions (also marked with the revisions of the manuscripts in order to assure legibility) appearing on verso pages. An introduction entitled "How the Odes Were Written April to September 1819" precedes the printed texts of the 1820 edition of all five odes. Notes on the odes and their manuscripts, with each ode treated separately, constitute the last fifteen pages of the volume. "Keats's revisions on this manuscript ["Ode on Melancholy"] distinctly confirm a movement in his mind towards a philosophy of stoic acceptance...."

RUDYARD KIPLING

Ponton, Dorothy. Rudyard Kipling at Home and at Work. Published by the author at Poole, 1953.

Dorothy Ponton, Kiplings's secretary for many years, describes, among other things, his working habits.

D. H. LAWRENCE

Jarvis, F. P. "A Textual Comparison of the First British and American Editions of D. H. Lawrence's Kangaroo," Papers of the Bibliographical Society of America, 59 (1965): 400-424.

An examination of the first British (Secker) and the first American (Seltzer) editions of Kangaroo, published within two weeks of each other in 1923, proves the American edition to be the more elaborately revised of the two and, according to Jarvis, the superior version. A table of substantive and semi-substantive variants between these versions is presented in parallel columns. Some of the kinds of changes that Lawrence made for the American edition are grammatical changes, changes to more effective synonyms, and changes in "objectionable" passages. "In the end, then, though the Seltzer edition has its peculiar weaknesses as a text, a comparison with the British text establishes it as the more reliable of the two, and though Seltzer somehow 'lost' Lawrence's 'last page,' the American edition as it now stands, even without the appended conclusion, is by far the more artistically satisfying of the two."

Gingher, Robert S. "The Three Versions of Lady Chatterley's Lover," Dissertation Abstracts International, 39 (July 1978): 294A-295A.

"From 1926 to 1929 D. H. Lawrence wrote three separate versions of Lady Chatterley's Lover. The changes he made in revising a very short first manuscript into a much longer second and third illustrate his own shifting interests with certain issues and themes in his last full-length novel. Lawrence's variations on the theme of counterfeit love and tenderness inform all three versions."

Cushman, Keith. "D. H. Lawrence at Work: The Making of 'Odour of Chrysanthemums'," Journal of Modern Literature, 2 (1971-1972): 367-392.

Cushman studies the development of Lawrence as a man and as an artist by comparing successive versions of the scene in which a wife and/or mother view the bringing in of the corpse of the husband/father and proceed to wash it in preparation for burial. The versions examined are from: (1) "The Father," Part 1, Chapter IV, The Peacock (1908); (2) "Odour of Chrysanthemums," English Review proofs (1910); (3) "Odour of Chrysanthemums," English Review text (1911); (4) The Widowing of Mrs. Holroyd, Act III (1913); (5) "Odour of Chrysanthemums," The Prussian Officer and Other Stories (1914); (6) The "Marsh and the Flood" chapter, The Rainbow (1914). One of Cushman's main points is that Lawrence grew to understand that his mother was at least as responsible as his father for the failure of their marriage and that this knowledge is reflected in the changing treatments of the body-washing scene.

Boulton, James T. "D. H. Lawrence's 'Odour of Chrysanthemums': An Early Version," Renaissance and Modern Studies, 13 (1969): 5-48.

Boulton provides the complete English Review proof sheet version of this short story, the revisions made by Lawrence as changes on and additions to the proof sheets, and the additional variants as they appeared in the English Review of June 1911. In addition to cutting at least five pages (particularly the paragraphs that describe the children at play), Lawrence made a fundamental change in the basic emphasis of the story. "In the published story, the focus of the writer's attention has notably shifted from the beginning to the end; from, that is, the evolving situation in the Bates's house in which the circumstantial details of the mother and children awaiting Bates's return are central, to the adult emotions associated with the preparation of the dead man's body for burial. Lawrence's relative immaturity in the story printed here is manifest; the revisions recorded in the textual apparatus equally testify to his growth in self-criticism."

Farmer, David. "An Unpublished Version of D. H. Lawrence's Introduction to Pansies," Review of English Studies, n. s., 21 (1970): 181-184.

This 600-word introduction, dated Christmas 1928, is about half the length of the published version, which is dated January 1929. "A comparison of this text with the introduction published in the unexpurgated edition shows how Lawrence used this version as a basis for expanding his ideas." The reader must furnish his own copy of the latter introduction and draw his own conclusions.

Cushman, Keith. D. H. Lawrence at Work, The Emergence of "The Prussian Officer" Stories. Charlottesville: University of Virginia Press, 1978.

Revised extensively just after he had finished the third draft of The Rainbow, the stories in The Prussian Officer and Other Stories, written early in Lawrence's career, are among his best early fiction, Cushman declares. "They achieved their final form only after a lengthy and complicated process of revision.... Lawrence recast these stories so extensively ... because his fundamental conception of their material had changed so radically.... The Prussian Officer revisions allow us to examine in detail the crucial turning point in the work of a major twentieth-century writer." The stories examined are: "Odour of Chrysanthemums," "Daughters of the Vicar," "The Shades of Spring," "The White Stocking," "The Prussian Officer," and "The Thorn in the Flesh." Also included are appendices examining "The Prussian Officer" texts, the origins of "The Christening." "A Prussian Officer Calendar" "provides a chronological history of all the ... stories, along with the major dates pertaining to the novels Lawrence wrote in the same years and some key dates from his biography."

Finney, Brian H. "D. H. Lawrence's Progress to Maturity: From Holograph Manuscript to Final Publication of The Prussian Officer and Other Stories," Studies in Bibliography, 28 (1975): 321-332.

Finney compares the first holograph manuscript versions, the periodical versions (The Smart Set) and the collected versions (The Prussian Officer and Other Stories) of "The White Stocking" and "The Shadow in the Rose Garden." The revisions of "Daughters of the Vicar" are discussed in terms of the 1911 manuscript, the 1913 manuscript, and the collected version in The Prussian Officer and Other Stories. "It is in 1913 and 1914 that Lawrence learnt to replace a reliance on plotted events by an emphasis on internal feelings, an appeal to sentimentality by a sterner regard for psychological realism, and an intrusive use of autobiographical material by narrative objectivity. What was explicit before 1912 becomes implicit after that date. The successive revisions Lawrence made to his first collection of short stories provide an illuminating glimpse into the making of one of this century's foremost writers."

Ross, Charles L. "The Revisions of the Second Generation in The Rainbow," The Review of English Studies, 27 (August 1976): 277-295.

Ross examines the holograph version, the typescript version, and proofs of D. H. Lawrence's novel. "One might reasonably expect a 'Branwensaga' to present its most complex thematic and formal substance in the last generation. But the revisions show that Lawrence's last energies were spent on the second, so that his most exploratory thinking centres there rather than, as one might have anticipated, on the third. It is a matter of critical debate whether the new thematic and formal advances of the revisions outweigh the undeniable aesthetic imbalance. That they are a tribute to Lawrence's resourceful and exploratory artistry is beyond doubt."

Branda, Eldon S. "Textual Changes in Women in Love," Texas Studies in Literature and Language, 6 (Autumn 1964): 306-321.

Several direct columned comparisons. "The two currently published American editions of D. H. Lawrence's Women in Love--Modern Library from Random House and Compass Books from the Viking Press--contain important textual differences, the reason for which is nowhere explained.... It is the intention here to show when and how and, as far as possible, why these changes came about." Branda refutes the often repeated charge that Lawrence "did not revise, only rewrote his work." He especially tried to control his inclination to editorialize, another major charge often made against him.

Ross, Charles L. The Composition of "The Rainbow" and "Women in Love." Charlottesville: University of Virginia Press, 1979.

"Ross provides a precise chronology of all the manuscripts of The Rainbow and Women in Love, as well as a detailed examination of the physical states of the manuscripts where they yield important information about the sequence of writing and revision. He includes a history of Lawrence's involvement with the various drafts and assesses the impact of literary agents and publishers on the growth of the novels." Ross disproves the claim that Lawrence wrote as a form of therapy, as a romantic artist too possessed by inspiration to work consciously at his craft. Ross argues that Lawrence "evolved habits of rewriting that often improved his work. His skills at revision were especially called upon when he was forced by prudish publishers to alter The Rainbow. In the same way, he undertook a full-scale rewriting of Women in Love when he knew its outspokenness had made it unpublishable. Lawrence made emendations that strengthened the texture and structure of both novels. Ross compares the unpublished versions of numerous passages with those in the printed novels to reveal Lawrence's complicated revision techniques. There is, as well, a compelling argument for a new critical edition of The Rainbow that provides specific suggestions to restore Lawrence's final intentions in the text."

SINCLAIR LEWIS

Richardson, Lyon N. "Arrowsmith: Genesis, Development, Versions," American Literature, 27 (May 1955): 225-244.

Sinclair Lewis revised his unfinished manuscript of Arrowsmith for serial publication in the Designer and the Woman's Magazine (June 1924 to April 1925) and made further revisions for the book edition (Harcourt, Brace, 1925). In the book version 336 complete paragraphs appear that are not in the serial version. These deletions include expletives, anti-clerical remarks, criticism of certain types of medical professionals, sexual references, certain medical references, and passages excised simply for the purpose of shortening the installments. The passages that appear in the Designer but not in the book have (1) been added for transition where excisions have been made and (2) been cut before book publication in a later stage of revision. "Although the many climaxes that Lewis contrived for his effects are more conspicuous in the Designer than in the book, and although the few paragraphs deleted from the Designer revisions are to the advantage of the book, most of the many deletions made for the Designer removed irritating blemishes."

Richardson, Lyon N. "Revision in Sinclair Lewis's The Man Who Knew Coolidge," American Literature, 25 (1953): 326-333.

"A comparison of the text of the first monologue of the series as printed in the American Mercury for January, 1928, with the text as it appears in the volume [New York, 1928], reveals that Lewis made about 175 alterations and additions for the book, not counting changes in paragraphing, capitalization, and punctuation." Richardson presents and discusses Lewis's revisions in two categories: additions and alterations. The additions are largely elaborations of Lowell Schmaltz's hymns of praise for his Rectophone, radio, and electric refrigerator. The alterations increase the incidence of banalities and ungrammatical expressions.

JAMES RUSSELL LOWELL

Tanselle, G. T. "The Craftsmanship of Lowell: Revisions in The Cathedral," Bulletin of the New York Public Library, 70 (1966): 50-63.

Tanselle presents lines from The Cathedral that differ among four editions: A. Atlantic Monthly, XXV (January 1870); B. The Cathedral (Fields, Osgood 1870); C. The Cathedral and the Harvard Commemoration Ode (Fields, Osgood 1877); D. Riverside Edition (Houghton, Mifflin 1890). Most of the revisions were made for the Fields, Osgood 1870 edition and included the addition of sixty-seven lines, primarily for the purpose of philosophic elaboration. Twenty-four verbal revisions were almost all single word changes rather than alterations in syntax. "... Lowell's revisions in The Cathedral reveal certain aspects of his poetic personality--the inability to be severely critical of a passage and banish it for long, the capacity for insight into subtle changes of sound and connotation, the minute attention to the word and phrase but not to the larger structure, the sensitivity to outside criticism."

Bail, Hamilton Vaughan. "James Russell Lowell's Ode," Papers of the Bibliographical Society of America, 37 (1943): 169-202.

This account of the composition, recitation, and various published versions of Lowell's Ode Recited at the Commemoration of the Living and Dead Soldiers of Harvard University, July 21, 1865 presents the variations among five editions. Although the Atlantic Monthly version appeared first, the private printing was written first and changed for the Atlantic, mostly by alterations in punctuation. Lowell requested proofs for the Memorial Biographies editions and made several insertions. To the version in Under The Willows and Other Poems Lowell added a new stanza, the ninth.

LOUIS MACNEICE

Brennan, Moya. "A Poet's Revisions: A Consideration of MacNeice's Blind Fireworks," Western Humanities Review, 23 (1969): 159-171.

The title of this article may mislead the reader who wishes to study Louis MacNeice's revisions of individual poems, for Brennan is actually concerned with the fact that thirty whole poems originally published in Blind Fireworks (1929) were left out of Collected Poems 1925-1948 and only thirteen from that first volume were included. "In considering the entire body of selected poems as against those rejected it will be seen that theme as well as unity of form has been the criterion in retaining some and discarding others. Only those poems have been chosen which transmit an objective viewpoint or world-view showing how man may integrate himself into a hostile universe."

THOMAS MANN

Schiffer, Eva. "Changes in an Episode: A Note on [Thomas Mann's] Felix Krull," Modern Language Quarterly, 24 (1963): 257-262.

Schiffer compares a 1937 early fragment version with Mann's revision of it in the 1954 book version, showing a strengthening of three major themes and an improvement in style. "The above comparisons will suffice to show Mann's skillful integration of usable segments of the 1937 fragment in the stylistically much-improved final version, which he has tightened thematically and expanded in relevant detail." The columned comparisons are in German, but those who don't read German may benefit from the points Schiffer makes.

ANDREW MARVELL

Kelliker, W. H. "A New Text of Marvell's 'To His Coy Mistress'," Notes and Queries, n. s., 17 (1970): 254-256.

What has been thought to be a corrupt copy of "To His Coy Mistress" is supported by Kelliker as an early version. "The text of To His Coy Mistress is, of course, incomplete and corrupt, containing clear indications that it was patched up from imagination where memory failed. Careful examination, however, suggests that the version is not simply a bad text of the poem as we know it from the Folio. There are hints that it belongs to an earlier stage of composition." This article contains the version in question in its entirety.

HERMAN MELVILLE

Stewart, George R. "The Two Moby Dicks," American Literature, 25 (January 1954): 417-448.

Relying mostly on internal evidence, Stewart concludes that

Moby Dick may be viewed as having three stages of composition related to three parts of the novel: (1) the original story, somewhat revised (Chapters I-XV); (2) the original story, significantly revised (Chapters XVI-XXII); and (3) a reconception of the original story (Chapters XXIII-Epilogue). "If there is one thing that seems certain about Melville as a writer, it is that he did not plan a book carefully to begin with or even think it through in his mind. In addition to Moby Dick, others of his books start in one direction and then shift, so that the reader who likes the first part of the book is likely to be disappointed in the last part, and vice versa."

Barbour, James. "The Composition of Moby Dick," American Literature, 47 (November 1975): 343-360.

Using extant letters descriptive of the stages of writing, chapters dated by external evidence, and other source material, Barbour draws several conclusions. (1) There were three well-defined stages in Herman Melville's composition of Moby Dick: (a) an early novel about whaling (February to August of 1850); (b) chapters on cetology (August 1850 to early 1851); (c) Ahab chapters and revisions of the earlier story (early 1851 to autumn 1851). (2) The cetological chapters were written for the early novel. (3) The original story was revised in two stages. (4) "The Castaway" furnishes the first evidence of a revised conclusion. (5) Melville utilized large sections from the two stories when he joined them.

Vincent, H. P. The Tailoring of Melville's "White-Jacket." Evanston: Northern University Press, 1970.

This study of the genesis of Herman Melville's White-Jacket has more to do with sources, themes, and biographical information than with the actual composition of the book. Direct columned comparisons are made between passages written by Melville and passages contained in the following five books: (1) William McNally, Evils and Abuses in the Naval and Merchant Service Exposed ... (Boston: 1839); (2) Samuel Leech, Thirty Years from Home, or a Voice from the Main Deck ... (Boston: Charles Tappan, 1843); (3) Nathaniel Ames, A Mariner's Sketches (Providence: 1831); (4) A British Seaman, Life on Board a Man-of-War (Glasgow: Blackie, Fullarton, & Co., 1829); (5) Henry James Mercier and William Gallop, Life in a Man-of-War ... (Philadelphia: Lydia R. Bailey, 1841). "White-Jacket trained Melville in literary appropriation. His procedure was the practice of Shakespeare, freely to take, significantly to alter...."

GEORGE MEREDITH

Measures, Joyce E. "Meredith's Diana of the Crossways: Revisions and Reconsiderations," Dissertation Abstracts, 28 (July-August 1967): 637-A.

"The study of the manuscripts reveals that Meredith's dominant concern is with the nuances of emotional and psychological response of his characters. Consistent and deliberate use of repetitive structuring in the scenes of the novel suggests Meredith's skill in construction. A consistent pattern of insertion of visual detail after the first draft reveals an attempt to make the novel more concrete and vivid. The comparison also suggests that, contrary to the opinion of several Meredith scholars, the source of Meredith's stylistic complexity is not his practice of revision."

Cotton, Jo Ray. "Evan Harrington: An Analysis of George Meredith's Revisions," Dissertation Abstracts, 29 (September-October 1968): 895A-896A.

"Now he is more interested in preserving the dramatic moment, in keeping the characters consistent, and in perfecting his style. Thus the main thrust of the revisions is to delete extravagant behavior in certain characters (especially John Raikes), to tone down the style in a number of passages for the sake of clarity and simplicity, to lessen sentimentality as well as burlesque, and to tighten the whole narrative structure by cutting out over-lengthy digressions."

Hergenhan, L. T. "Meredith's Revisions of Harry Richmond," Review of English Studies, 14 (1963): 24-32.

George Meredith excised four chapters, three of them consecutive, from The Adventures of Harry Richmond (1871) when he revised it for the 1886 edition. Hergenhan suggests that these chapters may have been removed in response to adversely critical comments by several reviewers and to a general feeling that Harry was not a very sympathetic character. Hergenhan contends that the novel is better in its original version and calls for the issuance of a popular reprint in that form. "The suppressed passages may show Harry behaving in much the same way as he had done on previous occasions, but nevertheless their removal is a loss to the novel. They heighten the effect of painful tortuosity which makes the account of Harry's growth so comprehensive and convincing, and which thus justifies Meredith's close workmanship."

Thomson, Fred C. "Stylistic Revisions of One of Our Conquerors," Yale University Library Gazette, 36 (October 1961): 62-74.

A comparison of two manuscript drafts of George Meredith's One of Our Conquerors, the later one containing the author's marginal and interlinear revisions, reveals that Meredith's changes made the novel scarcely better and much more difficult to read because of an increased metaphorical and syntactical intricacy. "Metaphor becomes less a delicate instrument of perception than a flaunted credential of literary and intellectual status. If the novel does in the last analysis misfire, the revisions show that it does so because Meredith tried to compensate through sheer force of style for a work not fully matured on the deeper levels of conception."

Hergenhan, L. T. "Meredith's Use of Revision: A Consideration of the Revisions of Richard Feverel and Evan Harrington," Modern Language Review, 59 (1964): 539-544.

The Ordeal of Richard Feverel, first published in 1859, was revised for the 1875 second edition and for the 1896 de luxe edition of George Meredith's works. Both revisions are characterized by deletions of passages involving Sir Austin's "system" and of exaggeratedly satirical figures, scenes, and behavior. Expression is simplified in both cases. "To sum up, I consider that the final version of Richard Feverel is on the whole better than the original novel, better in its form, characterization and style. Yet, while one may be sensible of the improvements Meredith made, one may also feel that besides encountering some resultant difficulty and incompleteness in certain places, one misses the comic inventiveness and witty exuberance that burgeoned more freely in the original novel." Evan Harrington is discussed in terms of the Once a Week serial (February-October 1860), the January 1861 first English edition, and the de luxe 1896 edition. Condensation, clarification, and simplification are the accomplished aims of these revisions.

Sacco, Lillian. "The Significance of George Meredith's Revisions of The Ordeal of Richard Feverel," Dissertation Abstracts, 28 (July-August 1967): 242-A.

"Because of the importance of accurate textual information as the basis for sound criticism, I have collated the three versions of The Ordeal (1859, 1875, and 1896), to determine the extent and significance of the textual variations. My analysis suggests that 'excision' is a more precise term than 'revision' for describing Meredith's method of alteration because the most extensive changes consisted of the wholesale omission of sequential passages."

Meredith, George. Selected Poems of George Meredith. Edited with an introduction by Graham Hough. London: Oxford University Press, 1962.

Compare the first published version of "Love in the Valley" (1851) with a later revised version. Both are presented here. "When Meredith re-wrote and expanded 'Love in the Valley,' long after the only begetter of the poem was dead, the significant additions were those in which the figure of the girl is mingled with the natural scene and comes almost to seem its perfect flowering and expression. This corresponds with the general direction of Meredith's thought."

Beer, Gillian. "Meredith's Revisions of The Tragic Comedians," Review of English Studies, 14 (1963): 33-53.

Eight pages of direct columned comparisons between the manuscript and the first edition are presented. "This article examines the revisions and emendations he made to the manuscript and in proof ... and through them explores the problems with which Meredith was faced in writing The Tragic Comedians and the ways in which he attempted to solve them."

Harris, Margaret. "George Meredith's Notes and Notebooks," The Yale University Library Gazette, 52 (October 1977): 53-65.

Harris compares passages as originally written into the notebooks and as they appear in published form. "The main conclusions to be drawn from a study of Meredith's notebooks relate to the long gestation of much of his fiction, and his constant preoccupation both in published works and manuscript memoranda with bizarre situations, witty characters, and themes like egotism and marriage."

JOHN MILTON

Heyworth, P. L. "The Composition of Milton's *At a Solemn Musick*," *Bulletin of the New York Public Library*, 70 (1966): 450-458.

John Milton's manuscript notebook in Trinity College library, Oxford, contains four drafts of "At a Solemn Musick." A comparison of these versions shows Milton making changes to (1) achieve euphony; (2) maintain poetic decorum; (3) avoid unintentional ambiguities; and (4) accomplish economy and simplicity of structure. "From the first draft it is clear that before he wrote it down the limits of the poem were fixed in his mind...." "Page 4 shows that Milton was first concerned to get his individual images and lines 'right,' to find the exact word or phrase and the one appropriate in the context. This done, he turned to the task of making his poem into a coherent whole...."

Milton, John. "Lycidas," *The Norton Anthology of English Literature*, Vol. I, M. H. Abrams, et al., eds. New York: Norton, 1979, pp. 2508-10.

"Our transcriptions from the poets' drafts attempt to reproduce, as accurately as the change from script to print will allow, the appearance of the original manuscript page."

GEORGE MOORE

Moore, George. *Confessions of a Young Man*. Edited by Susan Dick. Montreal: McGill-Queens University Press, 1972.

"The text used for this edition of *Confessions of a Young Man* is that of the first edition.... The writing of *Confessions* began in 1887 and did not end until 1923." Nine versions span those years. Ms. Dick provides 38 pages of variorum notes. In the first of three different prefaces, Moore wrote: "St. Augustine... wrote the story of a God-tortured soul; would it not be interesting to write the story of an art-tortured soul?"

Davis, W. Eugene, and Mark J. Lidman. "'I am still a young man': George Moore's Last Revisions of *Confessions of a Young Man*," *Bulletin of the New York Public Library*, 79 (Autumn 1975): 83-95.

Davis and Lidman examine a recently discovered copy of the 1926 Heinemann edition of *Confessions of a Young Man* in which George Moore wrote revisions of the text that apparently constitute his last intentions in this regard. All of these revisions are transcribed and presented in this article along with two facsimile pages with revisions penned upon them. Davis and Lidman see these changes as having to do mainly with style. "The kinds of changes Moore made can be grouped as follows: (1) deletions of words and punctuation marks; (2) substitutions for cancelled passages; (3) changes in paragraphing; (4) annotations; and (5) check-marks."

Gettman, Royal A. "George Moore's Revisions of *The Lake*, *The Wild Goose*, and *Esther Waters*," *Publications of the Modern Language Association*, 59 (June 1944): 553-554.

"My purpose in this study of George Moore's revisions is (1) to venture a few generalizations with respect to the dates, the number, and extent of the revisions and his motives in rewriting and (2) to compare closely the first and final texts of The Lake, The Wild Goose, and Esther Waters." After publication, "Moore revised all of his novels except Mike Fletcher, and he twice revised eight of them." "Moore's revision of The Lake ... is not a mere retouching of sentences but a reshaping of the novel." "The effect of the revision is to make The Wild Goose 'oral and continuous,' particular and dramatic." Moore revised Esther Waters three times. "One way in which Moore sought greater 'finish' was to fuse descriptive details and facts by presenting them through the eyes of Esther." "Occasionally Moore recast exposition into dialogue." Gettmann offers columned comparisons to show that "the prose style of the original is often wretched."

Jernigan, E. Jay. "The Forgotten Serial Version of George Moore's Esther Waters," Nineteenth Century Fiction, 23 (June 1968): 99-103.

Entitled "'Pages from the Life of a Workgirl,' this 'short story' was actually ten chapters from the manuscript version of his nearly completed novel Esther Waters." Moore extensively revised the proof sheets of the novel, "a practice normal for him; consequently, the 'piece' cut from the 'picture' changed considerably between its appearance as serial and as book." Jernigan demonstrates the extent of the revision with a tabular collation of chapter distribution. "Including two new chapters, Moore added approximately fifteen pages to the serialized text and deleted about four. Basically, the added material develops five significant situations..... Omissions from the serial version are much less important.... Also omitted from the book version were a number of intrusive authorial comments describing Esther's thoughts and motives which, considered together, presented her much less sympathetically." Jernigan quotes the passages omitted. "Moore made a number of minor textual repairs. For example, he occasionally altered paragraph divisions, diction, and word order in what seems a general attempt to achieve a more idiomatic style.... Moore revised the serial portion ... to develop his characterization of Esther...."

Jernigan, E. Jay. "George Moore's 'Re-tying of Bows': A Critical Study of the Eight Early Novels and Their Revisions," Dissertation Abstracts, 27 (November-December 1966): 1339-A.

"Counting all significant revisions, a total of twenty-five published textual versions exist of the eight early novels; they are distributed by date as follows: A Modern Lover, 1883, 1885, 1917, 1917; A Mummer's Wife, 1885, 1886, 1917; A Drama in Muslin, 1886 (serial), 1886 (book), 1915; A Mere Accident, 1887, 1895, 1922; Spring Days, 1888 (serial), 1888 (book), 1912; Mike Fletcher, 1889; Vain Fortune, 1891 (serial), 1891 (book), 1892, 1895; Esther Waters, 1893 (serial), 1894, 1899, 1920. As a whole, the seventeen revisions listed above reflect Moore's active pursuit of narrative concentration in accordance with his gradually changing critical convictions. Considered by type or method, three generally cohesive groupings emerge. The first consists of Moore's minor technical and stylistic revisions of his earliest work, effected within a year or two of original publication. The second comprises his revisions during the 1890's, which, while they sometimes comprehend the very fundamentals of narration, are concerned primarily with thematic structure. The third reflects his later approach to narration as embodied in his well-known 'melodic line,' an attempt to realize a 'rhythmical sequence of events described with rhythmical sequence of phrase'."

WRIGHT MORRIS

Morris, Wright. Man and Boy. New York: Knopf, 1951 (University of Nebraska reprint, 1978).

SEE note on "The Ram in the Thicket."

Morris, Wright. "The Ram in the Thicket," Wright Morris: A Reader. New York: Harper, 1970, pp. 587-609.

This story originally appeared in Harper's Bazaar, 1948. Compare with the first 82 pages of Man and Boy (Knopf, 1951; University of Nebraska reprint, 1978).

WILLARD MOTLEY

Klinkowitz, Jerome, and Karen Wood. "The Making and Unmaking of Knock on Any Door," Proof, 3 (1973): 121-137.

The original novel by Willard Motley, Leave Without Illusions, was a million words long but was cut radically to make Knock on Any Door "acceptable" to the public at the time--1947. This article includes "Motley's unpublished preface to his novel. It reveals his intentions in the book, which were obscured and then suppressed during the interminable stages of cutting." The uncut versions of the novel reveal a much more experimental, bolder technique. Klinkowitz and Wood also include several of Motley's long letters to his editor.

IRIS MURDOCH

Batchelor, Billie. "Revisions in Iris Murdoch's Under the Net," Books at Iowa, No. 8 (April 1968): 30-36.

Batchelor studies the holograph manuscript of Under the Net, compares it with the first edition (1954), and concludes that there were three stages in the growth of the novel: the first draft of the entire novel, the revisions made upon the first draft, and the revisions made between the manuscript and the published book. The first revision included dialogue changes, changes in incident that affect the plot, a name change, and stylistic changes for the purposes of clarity, precision, and richer texture. The second revision focused on economy and tightening up by deletions of passages such as elaborations of Hugo's thoughts, dialogue about politics, and description of the hospital and activities there. "The result of these revisions was twofold: on the one hand, added compression, economy, and concentration, on the other hand, richness and density of texture and an overall stylistic excellence."

FRANK NORRIS

Katz, Joseph, and J. J. Manning. "Notes on Frank Norris's Revisions of Two Novels," Papers of the Bibliographical Society of America, 62 (1968): 256-259.

Frank Norris revised both McTeague and A Man's Woman in response to criticism that they contained objectionable material. The revisions were accomplished in both cases so that the new passages fitted into the space of the old and could be patched into existing plates. In McTeague a scene involving August Sieppe's wetting his pants was replaced; and in A Man's Woman the graphic description of a surgical amputation is softened. The original and the revision of the amputation scene are arrayed in parallel columns in this article.

SEAN O'CASEY

Ayling, Ronald. "A Note on Sean O'Casey's Manuscripts and His Working Methods," Bulletin of the New York Public Library, 73 (1969): 359-367.

Ayling describes the O'Casey manuscripts in the Berg Collection of the New York Public Library and points out that O'Casey retained these materials during his lifetime as reference materials for new compositions. Red Roses for Me (1942) is based on notes about O'Casey's railway work experience that he wrote down in the 1920's. O'Casey is quoted from a 1952 New York Herald Tribune interview about his working procedure. "All [my] work is first written down in longhand, then a rough script is typed from this, changing, adding, and taking away (making the script better, and sometimes making it worse), till the whole work is roughly done; a second draft is then done, changing, adding, and removing again, and from this what is thought to be a final copy is typed, which as the days pass, and new thoughts come, proves to be unsatisfactory in many places, for a lot of changes are made in the galley-proofs, and some even in the page-proofs, before they are passed for printing. Work? Ay, manalive, it is, and I don't like it, and never shall!"

FLANNERY O'CONNOR

Harrison, Margaret. "Hazel Motes in Transit: A Comparison of Two Versions of Flannery O'Connor's 'The Train' with Chapter 1 of 'Wise Blood'," Studies in Short Fiction, 8 (1971): 287-293.

The short story "The Train" is "notable not so much for high literary quality as for the fact that it quite obviously formed the nucleus of the first chapter of 'Wise Blood.' ... To note the differences (as opposed to the similarities) between story and chapter is to note changes consciously made and therefore reasonably attributable to Miss O'Connor's growing awareness of her own peculiar thematic and technical aims." "Analysis ... should only deepen respect for those mysteries known as artistic development and the creative process." Direct columned comparisons are made, and a diagram shows how O'Connor rearranged blocks of action.

O'Connor, Flannery. The Complete Stories. New York: Farrar, Straus and Giroux, 1971.

O'Connor's first story, "The Geranium," was rewritten as her last, "Judgment Day." A comparison of the two can be very instructive.

EUGENE O'NEILL

Gassner, John, and Ralph G. Allen. Theatre and Drama in the Making. Boston: Houghton Mifflin Company, 1964.

Gassner and Allen offer O'Neill's working notes for Mourning Becomes Electra.

Tinsley, Mary A. "Two Biographical Plays by Eugene O'Neill: The Drafts and the Final Versions," Dissertation Abstracts International, 31 (September 1970): 1297-A.

"I have tried to provide the reader who is interested in Eugene O'Neill, in his last two full-length plays, and in the nature of the creative process, with a general account of O'Neill's work habits during the 'late period,' with a specific account of the composition of Long Day's Journey Into Night and A Moon for the Misbegotten, and with an analysis of the differences between the drafts and the final versions of these two plays."

WILFRED OWEN

Welland, D. S. R. "Wilfred Owen's Manuscripts," Times Literary Supplement, June 15, 1956 (p. 368) and June 22, 1956 (p. 384).

Welland describes the manuscripts of Wilfred Owen's poetry in the British Museum and comments tangentially about the revisions in poems such as "Strange Meeting" and "Dulce et Decorum Est," but he does not systematically discuss the revisions of any single poem. Owen is described as expunging the over-done Romantic rhetoric of early versions and replacing it with language more suitable to the context. "Time and again successive drafts of a poem will show a progressive movement towards the superb impersonality that characterizes his best work by the gradual elimination of pronouns in the first and second person in favour of less personal constructions...." This article is followed by letters of response from Edith Sitwell (p. 377) and Joseph Cohen (p. 475). Cohen's letter attacks Welland's article.

COUNTESS OF PEMBROKE (MARY SIDNEY)

Waller, G. F. "The Text and Manuscript Variants of the Countess of Pembroke's Psalms," Review of English Studies, 26 (February 1975): 1-18.

Waller studies the revisions made by Mary Sidney, Countess of Pembroke, upon psalms originally cast in English verse by her brother, Sir Philip Sidney. "Certainly, between Sidney's versions and the Countess's latest revisions lie a great many variants and independent or parallel versions, all making up a rich and fascinating story of nothing less than the growth of the Countess of Pembroke's literary vocation and poetical skills."

FRANCESCO PETRARCH

Dutschke, Dennis John. "A Study of Petrarch's Canzone XXIII from First to Final Version (Codice Vaticano latino 3196-Codice Vaticano latino 3195)," Dissertation Abstracts International, 37 (September 1976): 1537A.

"The present study is an analysis of one of Petrarch's earliest vernacular poems, Canzone XXIII, according to the autograph manuscript Codice Vaticano latino 3196 and Codice Vaticano latino 3195. The former contains an early rough draft copy of the canzone, including corrections, variants and personal interventions by the author. The latter constitutes the final version of the poem. In total, they document the twenty-year evolution of the poem from the beginning idea to finished composition, from ca. 1333-34 to 1356."

EDGAR ALLAN POE

Broderick, John C. "Poe's Revisions of 'Lenore'," American Literature, 35 (January 1964): 504-510.

Properly, there are two totally different versions of the poem: "A Paean," a grief-stricken lover's dramatic monologue, and "Lenore," a dramatic dialogue between the lover and some friends, published in Graham's Magazine. An intermediate version published in the Pioneer has been claimed by some critics to be the best version, but Broderick contradicts this contention. "Far from being superior, the intermediate version is important chiefly for its evidence that Poe is moving from a somewhat strained lyrical subjectivity to the firmness of dramatic dialogue. Almost all the changes in style, diction, and arrangement are made for dramatic strengthening."

Gross, Seymour L. "Poe's Revision of 'The Oval Portrait'," Modern Language Notes, 74 (1959): 16-20.

Edgar Allan Poe revised "The Oval Portrait," which was first published in the April 1842 Graham's Magazine, for its appearance in the Broadway Journal (26 April 1845). The revisions include a de-emphasis of the narrator and excision of all references to him as a user of opiates. Additionally, the wife of the artist is changed to a loving and obedient spouse, without the original hint of wildness and the supernatural. "Since all of Poe's revisions tighten up the moral framework of the tale and clarify its theme by the removal of irrelevant Gothicism, it was inevitable that he should change the title from the sensational "Life in Death" to the more neutral "The Oval Portrait."

Evans, Walter. "Poe's Revisions in His Reviews of Hawthorne's Twice Told Tales," Papers of the Bibliographical Society of America, 66 (1972): 407-419.

A comparison of Edgar Allan Poe's May 1842 review of Hawthorne's Twice Told Tales in Graham's Magazine with his November 1847 essay on the subject in Godey's reveals a shift in Poe's style as a writer, but also his valuing of the literary concepts involved. Some of the changes made were (1) replacing the imperial "we" with the personal "I"; (2) moving toward a manner that is less assertive; (3) attempting to be less pompous; (4) attempting to express himself with greater precision; and (5) smoothing his style. "These reworkings of parallel passages in the two essays indicate a shift in Poe's emphasis from a broad consideration of tales to focus on skillful construction; there is a consequent revaluation of several writers which includes a movement from nearly unrestrained commendation of Hawthorne to heightened criticism of his allegorical tendencies and lack of true originality."

ALEXANDER POPE

Hoilman, Dennis R. "Alexander Pope's Revisions of An Essay on Man," Dissertation Abstracts, 29 (September-October 1968): 1209A.

"Most of Pope's revisions were aimed at clarifying and tightening the poem's expression. He sought compactness, not by reducing the number of lines, but by increasing the number of ideas per line, achieving in this way the terse, concise, and epigrammatic qualities for which the Essay is noted. In addition, he gave the most careful attention to details of parallelism and antithesis, varying the textural patterns of balance to avoid monotony and sharpening the similarities and contrasts between parallel and antithetical terms to gain precision and increased ironic and satiric intensity."

Pope, Alexander. "An Essay on Man," "The Rape of the Lock," The Norton Anthology of English Literature, Vol. I, M. H. Abrams, et al., eds. New York: Norton, 1979, pp. 2511-12, 2510-11.

"Our transcriptions from the poets' drafts attempt to reproduce, as accurately as the change from script to print will allow, the appearance of the original manuscript page."

Griffin, Dustin. "Revisions in Pope's 'Ode on Solitude'," Modern Language Quarterly, 36 (September 1975): 369-375.

Griffin arrays several versions of lines in the first stanza. "Pope's revisions, even in the first stanza, are in fact minimal, but taken together they make significant difference, less in conception (which *may* have shifted slightly) than in quality. The poem is richer, more complex, yet more coherent, quieter (more precise, more understated, more economical) and more powerful, more English, and at the same time closer to its Latin originals."

T. F. POWYS

Boulton, J. A. "The Mood of God: An Early Version of Mr. Tasker's Gods," Notes and Queries, n. s., 19 (1972): 56-59.

The first seventy-six pages of T. F. Powys' Mr. Tasker's Gods are discussed in terms of an earlier manuscript version. The kinds of revisions observed are minor additions of words and phrases, major additions, and substantial deletions. Boulton would have preferred for the deleted material to remain a part of the novel. "In this first novel--first to be composed but not first to be published--where allegory and fantasy intrude uneasily into the mainly realistic substance one feels the need, I think, of the overt statement that the deleted passages gave. The novel would have become less a thing of shreds and patches."

JOHN CROWE RANSOM

Mann, David, and S. H. Woods, Jr. "John Crowe Ransom's Poetic Revisions," Publications of the Modern Language Association, 83 (March 1968): 15-21.

Mann and Woods compare Ransom's Selected Poems, 1963, to earlier versions, arraying corresponding passages in parallel columns. The better-known poems were little revised, but the lesser-known ones have been reworked significantly. The revisions are divided into two large groups--minor changes and major changes--and six descriptive categories: (1) changes in individual words; (2) punctuation adjustment; (3) changes of whole lines; (4) excisions or additions longer than a line; (5) rewriting of some entire poems; and (6) including poems not reprinted before. "Many of the poems have, in our opinion, been improved by the changes he has made, some of them strikingly so. The alterations often show shifts toward simpler diction, smoother meter, and greater clarity, which might have been predicted from Ransom's practice in his better-known work."

SAMUEL RICHARDSON

Pierson, Robert Craig. "The Revisions of Richardson's Sir Charles Grandison," Studies in Bibliography, 21 (1968): 163-189.

Pierson describes some of the kinds of changes made by Samuel Richardson in five editions, from 1754 to 1810: (1) italicizing words; (2) adding parentheses and brackets; (3) grammatical corrections; (4) single word changes; (5) from informal to less informal expressions; (6) adding phrases or clauses for clarification; (7) rewording or shifting clauses and sentences for greater clarity, for emphasis, or for logical comparison; (8) adjusting characters' speech to make it more consistent with their stations; (9) changing dates; (10) adding footnotes; (11) dropping paragraphs unkind to the ancients; (12) propriety: less affected titles or forms of address; in personal references to servants; deletion of affected repetition; deletion or modification of indelicate or affected words, phrases, and clauses; and a reduction of immoderate praise; and (13) an increase in the number of paragraph divisions to make the page more appealing to the eye. Richardson encouraged suggestions for changes written in the margins by friends and sponsors and made many of these changes in following editions. "In general the changes in Sir Charles Grandison, though slight, are improvements. Some of them remove inconsistencies and improbabilities; others remove some (though not enough) of the affected and excessive behavior; still others tend to elevate the language and to remove improprieties."

Harris, Jocelyn. "The Reviser Observed: The Last Volume of Sir Charles Grandison," Studies in Bibliography, 29 (1976): 1-31.

Samuel Richardson responded to the wishes of friends such as Lady Bradshaigh in revising his work. Harris uses circumstantial evidence to infer probable revisions in Volume VII of Sir Charles Grandison. "Longing to be considered a serious writer, he sought the approbation of reasonable people, the educated elite who could recognize the loveliness of truth naked, and agree with him about it. By energetically sending proofs or complimentary copies to friends and literary figures he tried to enlist a community of understanding worthies for his book, but even they saw different draperies."

Kinkhead-Weekes, M. "Clarissa Restored?" Review of English Studies, ns 10 (1959): 156-171.

Since the third edition of Clarissa contained over 200 pages of text and notes not in the first edition, Samuel Richardson published a volume Letters and Passages Restored from the Original Manuscripts of the History of Clarissa to enable purchasers of the first two editions to have more or less complete versions of the novel. Kinkhead-Weekes contends that most of the changes were made by Richardson, not to restore previously deleted matter, but to accommodate the novel to the misreadings and objections of the public after the first and second editions. These changes establish a pattern: (1) an emphasis on the darker side of Lovelace; (2) an elucidation of the problem of Clarissa's "delicacy"; and (3) a reinforcement of the moral teaching of the novel. Kinkhead-Weekes suggests that the first edition might be a better choice than the third edition, which is presently accepted as standard.

Eaves, T. C. D., and B. D. Kimpel. "The Composition of Clarissa and Its Revision before Publication," Publications of the Modern Language Association, 83 (1968): 416-428.

Samuel Richardson carried on a lively correspondence with a large number of acquaintances while he was writing Clarissa, asking for and receiving suggestions for improving the novel through revision. Eaves and Kimpel have used the correspondence to develop a picture of the revisions that took place before the first edition. Three of the purposes accomplished by these revisions were (1) to cut the length by eliminating letters by different characters that covered the same ground; (2) to make Lovelace more obviously evil except as he is perceived early on by Clarissa; and (3) to make the language more elegant by eliminating colloquialisms. "Richardson asked a good many people for advice, but the advice he took was on minor matters. He evidently had the general course of the novel firmly fixed in his mind before he showed it to Hill for the first time, as well as his own conception of the characters, and in spite of his pleas for help he never paid much attention to what his friends said on these matters--luckily, since the conception of Clarissa's tragedy is his own creation."

Warde, William B., Jr. "Revisions in the Published Texts of Clarissa," Dissertation Abstracts International, 31 (September 1970): 1243-A.

"Major changes, ranging from revisions of entire letters to additions of well over two hundred pages, develop more clearly and fully psychology of character and the high moral purposes of the novel. In the four volumes of the second edition Richardson makes major changes primarily to counteract misreading of character and to emphasize dramatic conflict; in the third edition he follows the patterns of changes in the second edition but becomes more concerned with emphasizing morality and instruction."

Van Marter, Shirley. "Richardson's Revisions of Clarissa in the Second Edition," Studies in Bibliography, 26 (1973): 107-132.

Van Marter presents her findings on Samuel Richardson's revisions of Clarissa as discerned in the second edition of 1749. "The majority of smaller revisions are designed to correct and elevate the text in tone, as well as to render it more concrete and vivid. Syntax becomes smoother; grammar is corrected; diction is elevated; thousands of contractions are expanded; abbreviations and numbers are spelled out." Examples of larger revisions are: (1) changes to support Clarissa's innocence and virtue; (2) changes to point up the Harlowes' evil; (3) changes to enhance Hickman's character; (4) changes of indirect discourse to direct speech; (5) change of a dramatic scene into play form by prefacing spoken lines with the name of the speaker. "... Richardson's changes taken as a whole are not uniformly successful, but they do reveal, as his novel does too, both his considerable strengths and his particular weaknesses as an artist."

Van Marter, Shirley. "Richardson's Revisions of Clarissa in the Third and Fourth Editions," Studies in Bibliography, 28 (1975): 119-152.

"... I will again present a varied sampling of Richardson's changes, emphasizing those which most fundamentally affect certain features of Clarissa, such as character, narrative method, style, etc...." Van Marter gives a complete account of additions, deletions, substitutions, and expansions in the third edition. Some examples follow: (1) two new paragraphs clarify the motives of Lovelace; (2) three additional pages disclose Lovelace's plans to obtain and furnish a house for Clarissa; (3) Lovelace's plan to rape several women is elaborated; (4) four added passages amplify Lovelace's irreverence and cruelty; (5) lines that stress Lovelace's remorse are eliminated; (6) over one hundred miscellaneous revisions develop no pattern; (7) passages are altered from indirect to direct discourse; (8) adjectives, verbs, and adverbs are changed to make the language more intense; (9) many expressions are revised to make them more concrete and pointed; and (10) colloquialisms are dropped to effect a more noble tone.

Eaves, T. C. D., and B. D. Kimpel. "Richardson's Revisions of Pamela," Studies in Bibliography, 20 (1967): 61-88.

Eaves and Kimpel describe the revisions made by Samuel Richardson in all of the many editions of Pamela, but their main emphasis is the 1801 edition based on Richardson's last intentions regarding the work, which includes over 8400 changes in Volumes I and II. Some of the kinds of changes are: (1) expansion of verb contractions; (2) correction of grammatical errors; (3) substitution of elegant expressions for more vulgar ones; (4) substitution of other expressions for "said" in dialogue; (5) decrease in religious references; (6) de-emphasis of sexual references; (7) excision of fulsome praise for Pamela; and (8) increase in the amount of dialogue. "Both texts [first edition and 1801 edition] should be made available for anyone who wants to study Pamela in her country habit and in her country-gentry habit, but for anyone who simply wants to read Pamela for enjoyment, we believe that the text of the first edition should be the one reprinted. It is closer to the Pamela whom Richardson actually imagined, whereas all succeeding texts try to approach the Pamela he thought he should have imagined."

EDWIN ARLINGTON ROBINSON

Dauner, Louise. "Two Robinson Revisions: 'Mr. Flood's Party' and 'The Dark Hills'," Colby Library Quarterly, Series 8 (June 1969): 309-316.

The last stanza of a manuscript version of "Mr. Flood's Party" is compared to its revised counterpart in a published edition, and the last four lines of "The Dark Hills" are given the same treatment. Dauner concludes that, although Edwin Arlington Robinson did not usually revise his works extensively, the revisions studied here reveal that "when Robinson does make changes, he characteristically moves toward greater logical and metaphorical unity, a more sensuous and flexible rhythmic movement, and greater universality. In a character portrayal, details tend to become more tightly integrated, to create a stronger confirmation of the character."

DANTE GABRIEL ROSSETTI

Peterson, Carl A. "The Pierpont Morgan Manuscript of Rossetti's 'The Blessed Damozel': Dating, Authenticity, Significance," Papers of the Bibliographical Society of America, 67 (1973): 401-429.

A main purpose of this study is to refute positions of other scholars in regard to this poem and to defend Rossetti's integrity as an artist. In the process, six versions of the seventh stanza are presented (1850, 1856, 1869, 1870, 1872, 1881); and Peterson concludes that the reasons for almost all of the revisions were artistic. "... A number [of changes] are introduced to clarify an image or to improve the movement or rhythm of a line, and most of the remainder are efforts to get rid of a vague word or a vacuous phrase or to play down some of the stylistic mannerisms of the 1850 version (chiefly those depending upon adverbial and participial constructions). All constitute, to paraphrase Rossetti, part of that polishing and burnishing process that for him followed the 'fundamental brainwork'."

Keane, R. N. "D. G. Rossetti's Poems, 1870: A Study in Craftmanship," Princeton University Library Chronicle, 33 (Spring 1972): 193-209.

Using the Troxell Collection in the Princeton University Library, Keane describes the progress through eight proof stages and trial books of Rossetti's Poems of 1870. Four pages of facsimiles of proofs with Rossetti's revisions penned upon them are included, and some specific examples of the poet's changes are given, along with information about the help he received from friends such as Swinburne in reading proof and making improvements. The facsimile pages display part or all of "Love's Nocturn," "A Last Confession," "Jenny," and "Song of the Bower." "One can see him involved in every facet of the book: adding and removing poems, rearranging the order of the poems, revising and re-revising the text--literally composing in the margins--and giving attention to type size, margins, punctuation, arrangement of headlines, pagination, and finally, binding and endpapers."

JOHN RUSKIN

Landow, G. P. "Ruskin's Revisions of the Third Edition of Modern Painters, Volume I," Victorian Newsletter, No. 33 (Spring 1968): 12-16.

When John Ruskin began writing what became Volume I of Modern Painters, his purpose was to defend J. M. W. Turner's painting against critics who wrote for several periodicals. His pamphleteering tone and manner, therefore, became inappropriate for the serious extended work that Modern Painters became. Landow points out how the changes Ruskin made for the September 1846 revised edition of Volume I are indicative of his response to critics, his desire to make Modern Painters have broader application, and the need to make Volume I lead into Volume II. Although a considerable amount of deletion was necessary, Ruskin's normal practice "was not to delete but to add notes, and his additions indicate the changes in his attitude and interests.... Throughout his career he continued to add notes to earlier works until, like a medieval palimpsest, a particular work, such as Modern Painters, would contain layers, occasionally contradictory, that had been deposited at different times. In the third edition he frequently supplied new notes, clarifying his earlier statements, qualifying them, or adding later commentary or praise."

JOHN SEELYE

Seelye, John. The True Adventures of Huckleberry Finn. Evanston: Northwestern University Press, 1970.

This book is not a revision, of course, but Seelye's retelling offers a unique and fascinating opportunity for comparative study. Seelye "has diligently and faithfully recorded the full account of Huck's epic journey the way Huck himself would have told it," declares the dust jacket, "--unvarnished, unbowdlerized, and unexpurgated. Curiously enough," the book "answers all the critical and scholarly objections to Mark Twain's version.... the boy's salty humanness, his realistic depiction of sin, sex, slavery, and salvation ... comes through unfiltered by Victorian prudery. New light is also thrown on such hitherto suppressed episodes as Huck's early romance and what really happened to Jim."

WILLIAM SHAKESPEARE

Stirling, Brents. "Julius Caesar in Revision," Shakespeare Quarterly, 13 (1962): 187-205.

Two areas of revision in Julius Caesar, inferred from internal evidence in Acts II and IV, are proposed: an interpolation in Act IV when Brutus learns of Portia's death and a combination of two scenes when the conspirators meet at Brutus's house in Act II. "Although the details of revision must remain uncertain, we can be fairly sure of two general characteristics of it both in Act II and in Act IV: if it occurred it was Shakespeare's, and it took place at some time after a prompt copy or fair copy of the play had been completed."

Engler, Balz. "How Shakespeare Revised Othello," English Studies, 57 (December 1976): 515-521.

"There are signs that the text had not quite reached its final shape when rehearsing began. Shakespeare seems to have added to the text still during preparations for the first night. In part at least these additions seem to be the result of testing the text on stage and of listening to the criticism and the suggestions of the actors."

Adams, John Cranford. "Shakespeare's Revisions in Titus Andronicus," Shakespeare Quarterly, 15 (1964): 177-190.

Adams contends that the Titus Andronicus, produced on January 23, 1594, was an extensively revised version of an earlier play and supports his position with evidence of redundancies, additions, contradictions, differences, and omissions that are related to the new use of the inner stage. "In short, the original Titus appears to have been written for a stage of two units (the Platform and Gallery), whereas the revised Titus was written for three (Platform, Gallery, and Inner Stage). As a consequence three scenes were radically recast and others modified to take advantage of improved stage resources."

GEORGE BERNARD SHAW

Leary, D. J. "A Deleted Passage from Shaw's John Bull's Other Island," Bulletin of the New York Public Library, 74 (1970): 598-606.

The carbon copy of a typescript that G. B. Shaw sent to Lady Gregory contains an exchange between Broadbent and Doyle that is much longer than it is in the Complete Plays (1963). The corresponding parts are presented here in detail. Leary suggests that John Bull's Other Island should be considered for revival production with this extended section reinstated. "Though there are sound dramatic reasons for this cut, reasons other than length, the passage is valuable for three reasons: (1) it clarifies the character of Tom Broadbent; (2) it anticipates developments of the plot; and (3) it establishes quite early in the play the conflict between dreaming or enthusiasm and efficiency or exploitation, a conflict which provides the dialectic tension in most of Shaw's major plays and in this play is represented in the contrast of Irish and English temperament."

Knepper, B. G. "Shaw Rewriting Shaw: a Fragment," Shaw Review, 12 (1969): 104-110.

George Bernard Shaw rewrote the close of Act III of Mrs. Warren's Profession in the same notebook in which he had written the original. Knepper presents these two versions of the end of the act, along with the version published in the Constable standard edition, in parallel columns. In the first version, Vivie succumbs to Frank's insistence that they play babes-in-the-wood and let themselves be covered with leaves; in the second version, Vivie refuses his suggestion with an extended emotional outburst; in the third version, she cuts him off with very few words as she quickly departs the scene. "In short, the first version is little more than unrelieved melodramatic mawkishness; the second moves far toward genuine dramatic force; the third achieves it."

MARY SHELLEY

Shelley, Mary. The Annotated Frankenstein. With an introduction and Notes by Leonard Wolf. New York: Clarkson N. Potter, 1977.

Comparison of the 1818 text of this novel with the much revised (and best-known) 1831 edition illustrates a classic instance of an author revising an earlier work to conform to various nonliterary considerations after a lapse of more than a decade. Wolf's note on the text succinctly describes in general terms the kinds of revisions Mary Shelley made. He reprints the first edition, while noting all the changes in marginalia.

PERCY BYSSHE SHELLEY

Smith, Paul. "Restless Casuistry: Shelley's Composition of The Cenci," Keats-Shelley Journal, 13 (Winter 1964): 77-85.

Shelley created his play The Cenci in three major stages: he translated "The Relation of the Death of the Family of the Cenci" in May 1818; he wrote the "Memorandum about the Cenci Case" in his Notebooks between May 1818 and May 1819; and he wrote the play between May 1819 and August 1819. As he translated "The Relation," Shelley left out inappropriate material; as he wrote the "Memorandum," he began to work out his characters and the outline of his narrative; as he wrote the play, he made changes that were "relevant to the problems of dramaturgy: compression, credibility, motivation, character delineation."

Curran, Stuart. "Shelley's Emendations to the Hymn to Intellectual Beauty," English Language Notes, 7 (June 1970): 270-273.

Curran reports two changes made in Shelley's handwriting on a copy of Hymn to Intellectual Beauty cut from the pages of the Examiner (January 1817). In one instance, Shelley changes "the names of Demon, Ghost, and Heaven" to "the name of God & ghosts and Heaven." In the other, he changes "birds and blossoming" to "buds and blossoming." "Minor though these emendations are, they suggest once again the minute care and critical intelligence Shelley brought to his art."

Shelley, Percy Bysshe. "O World, O Life, O Time," The Norton Anthology of English Literature, Vol. II, M. H. Abrams, et al., eds. New York: Norton, 1979, pp. 2518-21.

"Our transcriptions from the poets' drafts attempt to reproduce, as accurately as the change from script to print will allow, the appearance of the original manuscript page."

Zillman, Lawrence John. Shelley's "Prometheus Unbound": A Variorum Edition. Seattle: University of Washington Press, 1959.

In the Introduction to this volume, Zillman outlines the present knowledge of the text of the poem, discusses its principal editions, and surveys the body of critical opinion. The basic text presented is the 1820 first edition, with variant readings from other major editions, draft abstracts, and the Bodleian manuscript. Of the Critical Notes, Zillman says, "I have tried to choose wisely from that extensive body of writing that has accrued to the poem since its first publication in 1820, and to correlate the material in such a way that critical emphases and trends may be discernible." Shelley's drafts of Prometheus Unbound are made available in Appendix A. "It is impossible to know in what order the drafts were written, and for ease of reference they have therefore been arranged in text sequence."

JAMES SHIRLEY

Riemer, A. P. "Shirley's Revisions and the Date of The Constant Maid," Review of English Studies, n.s., 17 (1966): 141-148.

Comparing the first quarto (1640) of The Constant Maid by James Shirley and the second quarto (1661), Riemer argues that Q_2 was actually written earlier than Q_1. A speech from Act I, Scene ii, of Q_2 is considerably longer than its counterpart in Q_1, both of which are presented on page 143 of this article. Assuming that Riemer's contention about the order of composition is correct, this quoted material furnishes an interesting example of excision in James Shirley's practice of revision. "The next event was the revision of Love Will Find Out the Way, which probably took place in Dublin, and during the course of this the references to Lambert Simnel were replaced by allusions to Ford's play, the passage used in The Lady of Pleasure as well as some other material was deleted, the play was generally tidied and the title changed to The Constant Maid."

MARY SIDNEY

SEE under COUNTESS OF PEMBROKE (Mary Sidney).

SIR PHILIP SIDNEY

Godshalk, William Leigh. "Sidney's Revision of the Arcadia, Books III-IV," Philological Quarterly, 43 (1964): 171-184.

Godshalk describes Sir Philip Sidney's revisions in the last books of the Arcadia by comparing the Old Arcadia and the New Arcadia and suggests that Sidney followed some sort of topical order in making the changes. "The revisions fall into four broad categories: (a) changes in the love stories of Pyrocles and Philoclea, and Musidorus and Pamela; (b) links with the new narrative which precedes the last books; (c) deletion of the first person and apostrophes to the audience; and (d) changes of names and titles to fit the new narrative."

Lindheim, Nancy R. "Vision, Revision, and the 1593 Text of the Arcadia," English Literary Renaissance, 2 (1972): 136-147.

Sir Philip revised the Old Arcadia, which was modeled on classical drama, by working into it many additional episodes to make the New Arcadia. The composite text of 1593, read alone, might mislead the student. "For unconsidered use of the 1593 text necessarily makes one blind to developments in Sidney's understanding of the complexity of heroic and moral experience. It is not he who is to blame if critics fault him for writing as though he already knew all the answers, when, in fact, the alterations in vision between the Old and New Arcadia are significant enough to make us wonder whether the reason for Sidney's failure to complete the New Arcadia was not that his original plan was no longer workable."

WILLIAM GILMORE SIMMS

Lane, Thomas D. "Two Versions of Simms' Guy Rivers: A Record of Artistic Development in Changing Times," Dissertation Abstracts International, 33 (January 1973): 3654A-3655A.

"William Gilmore Simms' first novel, Guy Rivers: A Tale of Georgia (1834), offers a unique opportunity for tracing the author's development as an artist because Simms revised the novel for the Redfield 'Uniform Edition' some twenty years later." "Chapter V classifies the alterations Simms made in his revision of Guy Rivers as 1) technical alterations, i.e., revisions in the basic form of the novel and correction of mechanical errors; 2) verbal and phrasal alterations, consisting of Simms' additions, deletions, and substitutions of words and phrases in order to gain clarity, simplicity, and modernity and to soften the artificial Gothic tone of the novel; 3) alteration of narrative devices, specifically the enlargement of dramatic scenes, the substitution of specific scenes for generalized narrative, and the deletion of many authorial intrusions; and 4) changes in thematic emphasis, evident in the author's re-evaluation of several characters and scenes."

Dean, Paula D. F. "Revisions in the Revolutionary War Novels of William Gilmore Simms," Dissertation Abstracts International, 32 (April 1972): 5781-A.

"Simms also revised stylistically in various ways from individual word choices to longer passages. In conversations, Simms generally improved the passages by making them more natural to the speaker, more exactly a reproduction of dialect, or more efficient through carrying a larger portion of the exposition. His use of figurative language increased in revision, usually intensifying the episode."

TOBIAS SMOLLETT

Brack, O. M., Jr., and J. B. Davis. "Smollett's Revisions of Roderick Random," Papers of the Bibliographical Society of America, 64 (1970): 295-311.

Four editions of Roderick Random are compared: the first edition (January 1748), the second (April 1748), the third (1750), and the fourth (1755). "Smollett made fewer revisions in his second edition than in the other two editions he later revised. However, these revisions of 1748 are perhaps more interesting than the others to a student of Smollett's art, as he seems concerned here with completing and polishing character and with force of style. Later, his primary concern seems to have been smoothness, clarity, and grammatical fine points." Some of the changes Smollett made were for the purposes of (1) getting rid of evidence of haste, (2) polishing his style, (3) working toward precise expression, (4) correcting obvious mistakes in fact, (5) effecting smooth transitions, (6) eliminating verbosity, and (7) improving stilted language. Seventy-three examples of substantive revisions are given in the concluding section of this article.

GERTRUDE STEIN

Katz, Leon. "The First Making of The Making of Americans: A Study Based on Gertrude Stein's Notebooks and Early Versions of Her Novel (1902-1908)," Dissertation Abstracts, 27 (May-June 1967): 4255-A.

"With the aid of Gertrude Stein's notebooks, writing notes and early drafts, which provide source and hint for explication of many of her texts (and which further provide reason for redating much of her early writing), this study examines the first significant phase of Miss Stein's career, and traces the steps that led from the writing of the first draft of The Making of Americans in 1902, to the unique and maddening craft of the finished work."

JAMES STEPHENS

McFate, Patricia A. "James Stephens' Prose Inventions: Revisions in the Manuscripts of The Charwoman's Daughter, The Crock of Gold, and The Demi-Gods," Dissertation Abstracts, 27 (September-October 1966): 778A-779A.

"Analysis of the changes indicates that although Stephens has occasionally reformed his syntax or corrected a grammatical error, he has more often concentrated upon his choice of words; his most frequent revision is substitution, the replacement of neutral verbs, nouns, and adjectives by more lively or surprising ones. Stephens' extensive manuscript additions provide concrete or unusual details for his descriptive sections and serious or whimsical remarks for his narrative portions. While there are many substitutions and additions on the notebook pages, words and phrases have been excised from other sections in order to tighten narration, avoid redundancies, or eliminate the irrelevant."

McFate, Patricia A. "James Stephens' Verso Additions to the Manuscripts of The Crock of Gold," Bulletin of the New York Public Library, 73 (1969): 328-344.

The first draft of The Crock of Gold was written on the recto pages of six notebooks. Stephens' revisions include over 3000 changes on these recto pages and 132 additions made on the verso pages. McFate discusses the contributions made by the verso additions to the structure of the novel and the influence of the work of William Blake as demonstrated by these additions. "The verso additions were needed to delineate the characters more precisely and make their actions more comprehensible and to more carefully balance a variety of subjects and moods ranging from the whimsical to the solemn."

LAURENCE STERNE

Sterne, Laurence. A Sentimental Journey Through France and Italy by Mr. Yorick. Edited by Gardner D. Stout, Jr. Berkeley: University of California Press, 1967.

"This is the first full, scholarly edition of A Sentimental Journey. It provides an authoritative text based on the first edition, presents a collation of the first edition with the extant manuscripts, and records the extensive revisions Sterne made in the holograph manuscript used as the printer's copy for volume I." (Jacket copy)

BRAM STOKER

Stoker, Bram. The Annotated Dracula. With Maps, Drawings, and Photographs. Introduction, Notes, and Bibliography by Leonard Wolf. New York: Clarkson N. Potter, Inc. / Publisher, 1975.

This volume furnishes insights into the making of an international popular masterpiece in the horror genre. Interestingly, Wolf is a poet, fiction writer, and scholar, whose ancestors came from Transylvania.

HARRIET BEECHER STOWE

Stowe, Harriet Beecher. The Annotated Uncle Tom's Cabin. Edited with an Introduction by Philip Van Doren Stern. New York: P. S. Eriksson, 1964.

Stern deals very little with revision, but the information he does provide should be of use to readers studying other works on Stowe's revisions.

ALGERNON C. SWINBURNE

Peters, Robert. "A. C. Swinburne's 'Hymn to Proserpine': The Work Sheets," Publications of the Modern Language Association, 83 (October 1968): 1400-1406.

The "wave passage" from "Hymn to Proserpine" is made available to the reader of this study in three forms: photographic reproductions of Swinburne's work sheets, a diplomatic printing of the work sheets with cancellations and additions indicated, and the published passage in print (Poems and Ballads: First Series). Peters comments upon the revisions in a line-by-line discussion of the work sheets. Some of Swinburne's changes deal with problems in alliteration, imagery, and figures of speech. "What these sheets prove is that Swinburne was not the automatic writer, the gushing verse geyser, of legend. He was capable of employing the chisel assiduously, and far more often than is generally supposed."

Powell, E. G. "The Manuscript of Swinburne's 'Off Shore'," Library Chronicle of the University of Texas, 8 (Spring 1966): 9-22.

The earliest drafts of Swinburne's "Off Shore" are presented in diplomatic format, giving cancellations in parentheses to reveal the author's creative process and marginal variants to show the differences between the printed version and the manuscript. Powell has included detailed notes on the revisions as well as a commentary that points out the kinds of changes Swinburne made: an increase of alliteration and assonance, the avoidance of undesirable ambiguity, and the salvaging of rejected lines. "This manuscript is particularly valuable for one interested in the creative process involved, for Swinburne was apparently attempting to produce as quickly and efficiently as possible a fair copy from which type could be set. The first thirty-one stanzas are written in a neat hand and are in an orderly arrangement on the leaves. The remaining stanzas, since the poet begins to have second thoughts on wording and arrangement of stanzas, appear in rough draft and fair copy."

ALLEN TATE

Tate, Allen. "Ode to the Confederate Dead," Collected Poems, 1919-1976. New York: Farrar, Straus, & Giroux, 1977.

Compare this later revised version with the first published version in Mr. Pope and Other Poems.

EDWARD TAYLOR

Junkins, Donald. "Edward Taylor's Revisions," American Literature, 37 (May 1965): 135-152.

An examination of Taylor's manuscripts (Poetical Works and Manuscript Book) produces evidence that the poet was a conscientious reviser and furnishes a defense against critics who feel that Taylor was not enough concerned with means and method and, therefore, not an important poet. The revisions support a view of Taylor as a craftsman concerned with increased dramatic expression, simpler syntax, clearer images, and smoother rhythms. "All the evidence shows that he wrote, re-wrote, revised, crossed out, and incorporated, that he revised painstakingly, and that his process was artistically sound."

ALFRED LORD TENNYSON

Pfordresher, John. "A Bibliographic History of Alfred Tennyson's Idylls of the King," Studies in Bibliography, 26 (1973): 193-218.

"Tennyson began thinking about his Arthurian 'epic' when he was still a young man--we have notes for several different Arthurian projects sketched in the 1830's--and in 1833 he began with the end, composing his 'Morte d'Arthur' which was later integrated into 'The Passing of Arthur.' 'Morte d'Arthur' was published in 1842, but it took until 1885 for the last substantial portion of the poem to appear, the idyll 'Balin and Balan'." Pfordresher includes a bibliography of Idylls of the King divided into Manuscripts and Printer's Proofs (identifying the repositories of these items) and Published Editions (examined in the British Museum Library). Tennyson's method of composition is generally described: (1) In the early years he roughed out the entire pattern for a poem in his head before putting pen to paper. (2) In later years he wrote prose versions before beginning versification. (3) He revised heavily in the proof stage, one poem going through five different versions of proof. (4) He made revisions before every new edition of a previously published work. A detailed chronological description is given of the writing and publishing of all the parts of Idylls of the King.

Staines, David. "The Prose Drafts of Tennyson's Idylls of the King," Harvard Library Bulletin, 22 (1974): 280-308.

Tennyson wrote the early sections of Idylls of the King in poetic form from the first draft (Morte d'Arthur, Enid, Vivien, Elaine, and Guinevere); many of the sections composed later were written out first in prose form. This article presents transcriptions of the prose drafts of The Holy Grail, The Passing of Arthur, Gareth and Lynette, and Balin and Balan. "The prose drafts offer an important perspective on the poet's method of composition. They reveal the central ideas that form the nucleus of the idyll; they exhibit a closer dependence upon source material than the final poetic form suggests; they present the poet experimenting with different approaches to the stories he selects."

Tennyson, Alfred Lord. "The Lady of Shalott," "Tithonus," The Norton Anthology of English Literature, Vol. II, M. H. Abrams, et al., eds. New York: Norton, 1979, pp. 2523-26, 2526-27.

"Our transcriptions from the poets' drafts attempt to reproduce, as accurately as the change from script to print will allow, the appearance of the original manuscript page."

Shannon, Edgar F., Jr. "The History of a Poem: Tennyson's Ode on the Death of the Duke of Wellington," Studies in Bibliography, 13 (1960): 149-177.

Tennyson wrote the first version of this poem during the two months between the duke's death and his interment in St. Paul's. A comprehensive summary of the critical reviews of the poem indicates that the reviews were mixed and underlines the kind of pressure Tennyson was under to revise and improve. Even some of his revisions in the second edition were reviewed, demonstrating the intensity of the public scrutiny under which the poet had to work. Shannon works with six published editions, corrected proofs, manuscripts, and autograph alterations on published copies to write 278 variorum notes appended to this article. A copy of the poem in the hands of the reader would facilitate the usefulness of this study. "As a discussion of the revisions indicates and scrutiny of the text confirms, the Ode on the Death of the Duke of Wellington is far from a perfunctory funeral panegyric. It is a diligently wrought piece of artistry and, Janus-like, facing both Tennyson's poetical past and future, is an epitome of his mature thought."

Fuller, Gerry William. "The Aesthetic Significance of Tennyson's Revisions for the 1842 Poems." Dissertation Abstracts International, 37 (September 1976): 1562A-1563A.

Tennyson revised six major poems for the 1842 Poems: "The Lady of Shalott," "Mariana in the South," "The Miller's Daughter," "Oenone," "The Palace of Art," and "The Lotos-Eaters." "First in the six major poems, Tennyson improved the structural control by excising irrelevant material, focusing on key elements, and underscoring organizational patterns. Second, he made technical refinements in such elements as rhythm, diction, syntax, alliteration, and imagery. Rather than innovations, however, these improvements excise or ameliorate faulty passages in the original versions. (Most changes in the poems of minor revisions fit in this category, although these minor revisions, because they are so scattered, are not always obvious or consistent emendations). The third main area of change is an infusion of human interest through domestic detail, sympathetic characterization, and vivid depictions of the human condition."

WILLIAM MAKEPEACE THACKERAY

Harden, Edgar F. "The Growth of a Serial Novel: Five Installments of The Newcomes," Huntington Library Quarterly, 39 (February 1976): 203-218.

Harden studies the development of Thackeray's The Newcomes in the Charterhouse manuscript and collates the manuscript's final form with the first book issue (Bradbury and Evans, 1854-55). "Both in the manuscript stage and in press we can see how the need to create copy sufficient to fill a monthly number stimulated his inventiveness to extended achievements that develop possibilities latent within the framework of what was already set down and that significantly enrich his novel's texture--typically by clarifying relationships within his narrative, creating further links between portions of it, adding resonant allusions, and bringing out the emblematic potential of persons, places, and objects already created. Confronted with the necessity of reducing the length of his text, he was led to identify and cut weaker passages but also to delete material that need not otherwise have been canceled."

Shillingsburg, Peter L. "Thackeray's Pendennis: A Rejected Page of Manuscript," Huntington Library Quarterly, 38 (February 1975): 189-195.

Passages corresponding to this rejected sheet of manuscript are found in Chapters XXXIV and XXXVI of the 1849-50 first edition of The History of Pendennis. Thackeray probably began this version in order to fill out enough copy for a 32-page number, but it finally resulted in altering the characterization of John Finucane from unsympathetic to sympathetic. The change in the text, however, was not accompanied by a change in Thackeray's illustration of Finucane, which is presented here. The two versions of the text are presented in parallel columns. "Of course, Thackeray may not have remembered the illustration when he was revising, but even had there been time it would have been uneconomical to prepare another woodcut which would more accurately represent the revised concept of Finucane."

Sutherland, John. "The Composition of Thackeray's Philip," Yale University Library Gazette, 48 (January 1974): 195-199.

Sutherland presents a diplomatic rendering of a short section of the manuscript of Chapter XXI of Thackeray's Philip apparently used as setting copy for the Cornhill Magazine publication. Sutherland concludes from the revisions that Thackeray wrote his later novels "offhand," with many fewer changes than can be seen in his earlier work. "The small corrections speak for themselves, both as to the scrupulosity of the stylist and to his spontaneity of method. The finished passage has that casual, glinting superficiality which we recognize as typically Thackerayan."

Thackeray, William Makepeace. Vanity Fair. Geoffrey and Kathleen Tillotson, editors. Boston: Houghton Mifflin, 1913.

In the long introduction, the editors make many observations on differences between early manuscript versions and the first edition, and between the first edition and subsequent editions. In "Note on the Text," they list word changes between the manuscript and the "Cheap edition of 1853, which contains Thackeray's latest revisions," and in several instances they restore words and phrases from the first edition. "Appendix A" provides a further "Note on the Manuscript," indicating changes, and provides a facsimile of a page of manuscript from Chapter 9. In "Appendix B," the editors reprint a long passage omitted from Chapter 6, and show two manuscript versions. In "Appendix C," they offer "passages not in the printed text."

Thackeray, William Makepeace. Vanity Fair. Introduction by Joseph Warren Beach. New York: Modern Library, 1950.

In his "Note on the Text," Beach comments on Thackeray's revisions, presenting several pages of broad parody that Thackeray excised after the second paragraph of Chapter VI.

Sutherland, John. "A Plan for Vanity Fair," Princeton University Library Chronicle, 34 (Autumn 1972): 27-32.

In order to determine whether Thackeray, in writing Vanity Fair, was a careful planner or a brilliant improviser, Sutherland examines some very brief notes in the author's hand, presented in their entirety in this article. "This set of thumbnail and probably incomplete notes for the Waterloo chapters is uniquely informative about Thackeray's methods. Their uniqueness lies in that they show Thackeray inventing, outlining, measuring, altering, experimenting--going through all the functions we normally associate with 'planning'."

HENRY DAVID THOREAU

Cosbey, Robert C. "Thoreau at Work: The Writing of 'Ktaadn'," Bulletin of the New York Public Library, 65 (1961): 21-30.

A comparison of the first working draft, the first published version (1848), and the final published version (1864) reveals the skill and care Henry D. Thoreau employed in revising his essay "Ktaadn." "But the striking change from this first draft to the first published version is the achievement of a simple, dramatic, unified narrative and a fitting consistent tone. What may seem an unstudied simplicity in the published version is, in short, a deliberately and painstakingly achieved simplicity." The stylistic changes between the first published version and the final posthumous one include the excision of a large number of adverbs, the clarification of passages of description and exposition, and changes to increase the precision with which some passages are expressive of Thoreau's meaning.

Howarth, William L. "Successor to Walden? Thoreau's 'Moonlight--An Intended Course of Lectures'," Proof, 2 (1972): 89-115.

After the publication of Walden, Henry David Thoreau began again to mine his journal. He listed references to descriptions of moonlit nights, organized by months of the year, and transcribed these sections, revising as he copied. These transcriptions were used in the composition of a lecture, "Moonlight," which was ineptly cut and compressed by his sister Sophia and William Ellery Channing for posthumous publication as an essay in a volume, Excursions, and in the Atlantic Monthly. Howarth presents a journal entry in direct comparison to its transcribed version and also two corresponding passages from Thoreau's efforts to put together an essay on moonlight, one in present tense and the other in past tense.

Shanley, J. Lyndon. The Making of "Walden," with the Text of the First Version. Chicago: University of Chicago Press, 1957.

Shanley discerns seven groups of leaves among the Walden manuscripts that represent seven major stages in its composition: a first version from 1846-47 and six sets of additions, excisions, and other changes made between 1848 and 1854. Shanley's chapter titles suggest the manner of his dealing with Thoreau's creative procedure: I. The Walden Manuscript; II. The Successive Versions of Walden; III. Perfecting the Style; IV. Completing the Story; V. Developing the Structure. Chapter III, "Perfecting the Style," presents up to four different versions of certain segments, displayed across facing pages in four columns. The entire first version of Walden occupies the last 104 pages of this volume. "Although the journals made it clear that Thoreau added to Walden between 1847 and 1854, and especially after 1850, only the manuscript could reveal to how great an extent Walden is the result of a gradual re-creation of his experience rather than simply a recounting of that experience as he had entered it in his journal when it happened." This study offers an excellent opportunity for comparing early and finished drafts.

Lane, Lauriat, Jr. "Thoreau at Work: Four Versions of 'A Walk to Wachusett'," Bulletin of the New York Public Library, 69 (1965): 3-16.

Lane compares four versions of this essay: (1) a first manuscript version (half the length of the second); (2) a second manuscript version (equivalent in length to the printed versions); (3) the first published version in the Boston Miscellany (January 1843); and (4) the posthumously published Excursions (1863). The revisions are discussed in three sections: I Changes in Wording, II Changes in Content, and III Changes in Order. Changes in wording include permanent stylistic changes and stylistic changes reversed in later versions. Three versions of one long paragraph are presented in sequence. Changes in content are primarily the addition of physical detail to communicate a more vivid reality, and changes in order take place at the beginning and at the end of the essay, with three versions of the beginning being presented. "By his revisions he also tried to enlarge his experience so that, as he moved westward to the wilder and the less familiar and upward to the higher and the purer, he and his journey would become emblems of two kinds of transcendental aspiration, two 'walks' of the body and of the soul, that Thoreau was to take and to value and write about all his life."

Thoreau, Henry David. The Annotated Walden. Edited, with an Introduction, Notes and Bibliography by Philip Van Doren Stern. New York: Bramwell House, 1970.

Stern says little about revision but the information about the writing of the book provides valuable background for other studies of revision.

DALTON TRUMBO

Trumbo, Dalton. Night of the Aurochs. New York: Viking, 1979.

Robert Kirsch has combined Trumbo's unfinished novel and his notes.

ISAAK WALTON

Fehner, Richard E. "Izaak Walton's Life of Sir Henry Wotton, 1651, 1654, 1670, 1672, 1675: A Study of Sources, Revisions, and Chronology," Dissertation Abstracts, 22 (July-September 1961): 246.

"As a reviser, Walton's typical practice was to amplify and embellish his sentences, frequently revealing new information. He also corrected previous mistakes, kept the Life up to date, clarified obscure comments, introduced qualifying expressions, and reworked portions of the biography so as to make them more credible."

EVELYN WAUGH

Davis, R. M. "Textual Problems in the Novels of Evelyn Waugh," Papers of the Bibliographical Society of America, 63 (1969): 41-46.

Davis argues for a detailed bibliography of editions of Evelyn Waugh's works so as to make readers and critics aware of relevant revisions. In reference to Work Suspended, "Waugh seems to have discovered by the time of revision that the first-person narrator did not permit him as much latitude to present blocks of expository comments as he had thought. Other cuts are made either because they give a false emphasis to certain lines of action or because the events which they were originally intended to foreshadow never came to pass. Most notable is the excision of a long passage of dialogue between Plant and the art dealer who had commissioned Plant senior's surreptitious reproduction of old masters." Other novels by Waugh referred to in this article are Decline and Fall, Brideshead Revisited, Vile Bodies, and The Ordeal of Gilbert Pinfold.

NATHANAEL WEST

Daniel, Carter A. "West's Revisions of Miss Lonelyhearts," Studies in Bibliography, 16 (1963): 232-243.

Daniel offers direct columned comparisons. "Before Nathanael West's Miss Lonelyhearts was published in April, 1933, early versions of five chapters had appeared separately in periodicals. A comparison of these early chapters with the versions in the book shows that West made revisions of varying significance on all levels, some throwing light on the basic conception and meaning of the book, and some revealing ... West's personal preferences in diction and phrasing. An analysis of the revisions is highly rewarding because it helps to clarify the author's aims, some features of his thought, and the technical means by which he solved certain problems of style and structure." West experimented with a first person narration but discovered it to be "largely unsuitable in a novel which derives most of its impact from the author's implied ironical judgments of the main character." An attempt at interior monologue also proved disruptive. The columned comparisons show many kinds of revision, very clearly indicated.

EDITH WHARTON

Wharton, Edith. The House of Mirth. Edited by R. W. B. Lewis. New York: New York University, 1963.

Besides an illuminating critical introduction, Professor Lewis provides an appendix which reproduces seven pages of manuscript and typescript with accompanying commentary giving new insight into Wharton's developing conception of the novel. The result of her revisions "is a definite rhetorical and dramatic lightening.... The good example of Henry James (who urged himself and other novelists to 'dramatize, dramatize!') can be felt in the development."

WALT WHITMAN

Bowers, Fredson. "The Manuscript of Walt Whitman's 'A Carol of Harvest, for 1867'," Modern Philology, 52 (August 1954): 29-51.

Bowers here provides a diplomatic printing of the manuscript of "A Carol of Harvest, for 1867" that was probably the basis for the fair copy used in setting type for the Galaxy magazine publication (IV [1867], 605-9). Detailed notes explain the revisions discernible, a collation list of the 1871 Leaves of Grass and the Galaxy text variants follows, and the notes recording Whitman's impressions of a parade in 1865 are given in the appendix. "Its chief interest lies, of course, in the mass of revisions which show Whitman as a careful, conscious artist building up a poem of considerable power and felicity."

White, William. "An Unpublished Whitman Notebook for 'Lilacs'," Modern Language Quarterly, 24 (1963): 177-180.

Whitman apparently took notes as John Burroughs told him

about the hermit thrust, and he used this information in the composition of certain passages in "When Lilacs Last in the Dooryard Bloom'd." The notes are reproduced in their entirety along with the corresponding passages in the poem. "We have known that Burroughs had an influence on 'When Lilacs Last.' With the discovery of this notebook and a comparison of its contents with the naturalist's remark to Benton, we know exactly what Walt Whitman got from John Burroughs."

Bowers, Fredson. "The Manuscript of Whitman's 'Passage to India'," Modern Philology, 51 (November 1953): 102-117.

An autograph manuscript of "Passage to India," with Whitman's revisions written and pasted on it, is presented in diplomatic reprint, followed by Bowers' notes on the revisions, a collation of the manuscript with proof sheets, and a collation of the proof sheets with the 1871 edition. Bowers does not make critical generalizations about the revisions, but he makes them easily accessible to those who would.

Bowers, Fredson. "The Earliest Manuscript of Whitman's 'Passage to India' and Its Notebook," Bulletin of the New York Public Library, 61 (1957): 319-352.

Bowers presents the earliest known manuscript of Walt Whitman's "Passage to India" and the notebook with the plans and some trial lines for the poem in a diplomatic printing, accompanied by a detailed explanation of how Bowers reached the conclusions he did about the order in which parts of the work were accomplished. "This present article does not propose to engage in literary criticism, but I should remark that the transcendental note so strongly struck in the 'O Soul' insertion in contrast to the earlier part of the poem is a prominent part of the subsequent verses as we now have them, although it had been adumbrated in earlier lines and appears in draft in the original Notebook." The insertion of "O Soul" into "Passage to India" seems to have required extensive revision of following lines.

Bowers, Fredson. "The Manuscripts of Whitman's 'Song of the Redwood-Tree'," Papers of the Bibliographical Society of America, 50 (1956): 53-85.

Bowers provides two autograph manuscripts of Walt Whitman's "Song of the Redwood-Tree" in diplomatic reprints with copious notes explaining excisions, emendations, and substitutions in terms of colors of ink, kinds of paper, and sections that have been cut and pasted. "The first manuscript represents what may be the earliest semi-connected form of the poem, although doubtless verses from these sections had, as usual, been written out previously in miscellaneous papers now lost or scattered." The second manuscript was written immediately following the first and contains many revisions. This version was probably used to make the fair copy to send to Harper's Magazine, which paid Whitman $100.00 for first serial rights. Bowers does not judge critically the texts he has made available; his comments are all textual.

Taylor, E. W. "Analysis and Comparison of the 1855 and 1891 Versions of Whitman's 'To Think of Time'," Walt Whitman Review, 13 (1967): 107-122.

Both the entire 1855 first edition version and the entire 1891 final version of "To Think of Time" are arrayed in parallel columns and the revisions discussed, section by section. "When one compares the final version (1891) of the poem with the 1855 version, he becomes aware that Whitman did not arrive by chance at this unity of structure or his conclusion of faith in the eternal cyclic scheme of things. One becomes aware, too, that he was a conscious artist who through inserting and omitting words and phrases and by shifting the order of ideas arrived at a more precise conceptual and structural pattern in keeping with his vision of a 'spiritual law' for all."

Whitman, Walt. Whitman's Manuscripts: Leaves of Grass (1860): A Parallel Text. Edited with Notes and Introduction by Fredson Bowers. Chicago: The University of Chicago Press, 1955.

The holograph manuscripts of the Valentine-Barrett collection (transformed into conventional type, spacing, and lining), are presented on facing pages with the parallel text of the first printed versions of these poems in the third edition of Leaves of Grass, 1860. "The prime purpose of this volume, indeed, has been only to offer full texts for this unique collection of manuscripts, in combination with an analytical study of the history of the documents in which these texts have been preserved. In my own view, the critical possibilities which these manuscripts open up for the study of Whitman as a conscious artist and of his methods of composition and revision are so remarkable that for an editor in his necessarily brief space to attempt any summary evaluation would be an act of supererogation."

Whitman, Walt. Walt Whitman's Blue Book: The 1860-61 "Leaves of Grass" Containing His Manuscript Additions and Revisions. Edited by Arthur Golden. 2 volumes. New York: The New York Public Library, 1968.

Volume I is a facsimile reproduction of the copy of the 1860-61 Leaves of Grass in which Whitman made revisions in different colored pencil and in ink, by erasing, and by pasting in additional slips of paper with lines of verse written on them in order to prepare the printer's copy for the 1867 edition. Volume II, the textual analysis by Arthur Golden, presents all of Whitman's revisions and additions in the Blue Book with explanatory notes and references to the line numbers in Volume I. "A century after the Blue Book gained notoriety it has been made available to the public. One can now follow Whitman's advice to Traubel and take a glimpse into this workshop without being put off by the myths that have obscured its importance over the years."

Whitman, Walt. Complete Poetry and Selected Prose. Edited with an Introduction and Glossary by James E. Miller, Jr. Boston: Houghton, Mifflin, 1959.

This volume contains the 1891-1892 "Camden" text of the poems and is, therefore, useful in making comparisons with earlier editions (see *Whitman's Manuscripts: Leaves of Grass* (1860): *A Parallel Text*). In "Revision: Control of Abandon," a section of the Introduction, Miller compares two versions of "A Noiseless Patient Spider." "The revisions generally reveal a poet moving with some assurance toward a more concrete, vivid diction and a less halting but purely felt rhythm."

OSCAR WILDE

Lawler, Donald L. "Oscar Wilde's First Manuscript of *The Picture of Dorian Gray*," *Studies in Bibliography*, 25 (1972): 125-135.

"There is an interval of eleven months between the appearance of *Dorian Gray* in *Lippincott's* (*Magazine*) and the publication of *Dorian Gray* as a book by Ward, Lock & Co. During that period, Wilde made his final revisions of the novel, and they are the most extensive of all. He added five new chapters, introducing many new characters and continuing with the alterations he had made earlier in atmosphere, theme, and action." A study of his revisions reveals "a consistent program to expand the characterization of Lord Henry and to reduce the influence of Basil Hallward in the story." "Four full revisions of *Dorian Gray* before the novel took its final form suggest that the stereotyped view of Wilde as a careless and hasty writer may need reassessment." The main burden of the article is to prove by detection the existence of an earlier manuscript, now lost. Actual revisions are studied in the author's unpublished doctoral dissertation for the University of Chicago, "An Enquiry into Oscar Wilde's Revisions of *The Picture of Dorian Gray*," 1969.

TENNESSEE WILLIAMS

Gassner and Allen, *Theatre and Drama*. SEE entry under Henrick Ibsen.

Beaurline, Lester A. "*The Glass Menagerie*: From Story to Play." *Modern Drama*, 8 (September 1965): 142-149.

"Evidence survives for at least four stages in the composition of *The Glass Menagerie*: (1) The sixteen-page story entitled 'Portrait of a Girl in Glass' (written before 1943 and published in *One Arm and other Stories*, 1948) ... (2) A sixty-page one-act play in five scenes, of which twenty-one pages survive ... (3) A 105-page play manuscript.... It may represent about eight to ten layers of revision ... (4) The acting version, published by the Dramatics Play Service in 1948 (and revised again sometime in the mid-fifties)." Beaurline examines Tom's last speech and changes in stage directions, and the shifts in focus from Laura in the story to Tom in the play.

WILLIAM CARLOS WILLIAMS

Williams, William Carlos. *I Wanted to Write a Poem: The Auto-*

biography of the Works of a Poet. Reported and Edited by Edith Heal. Boston: Beacon Press, 1958.

This bibliography of Williams' book publications contains the poet's directly quoted comments about each volume, supplemented by his wife's remarks and noted down by the editor after a lengthy series of interviews in the poet's seventy-third year. Williams says very little about his revision process, but the prose and poetry versions of "The Last Words of My English Grandmother" are presented, and the original and revised versions of "The Nightingales" are placed side by side.

THOMAS WOLFE

Miehe, Patrick. "The Outline of Thomas Wolfe's Last Book," Harvard Library Bulletin, 21 (1973): 400-401.

Miehe argues convincingly that the outline for The Web and the Rock usually attributed to Wolfe is really the work of his editor at Harper, Edward Aswell, who "extensively revised, cut, and reordered the work to form what are now three novels: The Web and the Rock, You Can't Go Home Again, and The Hills Beyond." Aswell's efforts fall into what might be called the genre of editor-as-co-author. The outline is published in full. SEE Richard S. Kennedy's rebuttal in the next entry, "Thomas Wolfe's Last Manuscript."

Kennedy, Richard S. "Thomas Wolfe's Last Manuscript," Harvard Library Bulletin, 23 (1975): 203-211.

In reply to Miehe (HLB, 21: 400-401), Kennedy defends Wolfe's authorship of the outline of The Web and the Rock and presents four facsimile pages of typescript.

Kennedy, Richard S. The Window of Memory: The Literary Career of Thomas Wolfe. Chapel Hill: The University of North Carolina Press, 1962.

Kennedy describes how the cutting of Look Homeward, Angel as directed by Maxwell Perkins "made the difference between a loose, uneven piece of work that sacrificed effectiveness to digression, and a full, varied representation of life that gathered power as Eugene and the Gants lived out their days. For in making the revision, Wolfe quickened the narrative flow and centered attention on the main characters. He was forced to curb his tendency to step before the curtain with distracting comment." When Perkins first read the manuscript of Of Time and the River, it was told in first person from the viewpoint of John Hawkes. Perkins convinced Wolfe to rewrite it in third person as a continuation of the story of Eugene Gant. Edward Aswell's revised version of the "What Is Man?" passage is displayed in parallel columns with Wolfe's original on pages 404 and 405, and the Appendix is entitled "Thomas Wolfe's Rough Outline of His Last Book."

Kennedy, Richard S., and Paschal Reaves. The Notebooks of Thomas Wolfe. 2 volumes. Chapel Hill: The University of North Carolina Press, 1970.

These two volumes contain nine-tenths of the matter in the thirty-five pocket notebooks Wolfe carried between 1926 and 1938. Notes from six other sources are also included. A chronology of Wolfe's life in Volume One and the extensive and thorough index in Volume Two make it possible to locate specific information easily. For example, ninety-two page references are given under the heading of Eugene Gant, twelve under Helen Gant, and eighteen under Esther Jack. "When submitted to Scribner's, the manuscript [of Look Homeward Angel] was 1, 114 pages long and contained approximately 330, 000 words. In the process of revision it was reduced by about 95, 000 words, but Wolfe added some 5000 more, mostly for new transitions, so that the net reduction was roughly 90, 000 words. This compression was achieved by 147 cuts in the manuscript, two-thirds of which are listed in the latter part of this notebook and indicate how the reduction was accomplished."

VIRGINIA WOOLF

Latham, Jacqueline. "The Origin of 'Mrs. Dalloway'," Notes and Queries, 211 (March 1966): 98-99.

Latham notes that the relation between the short story "Mrs. Dalloway in Bond Street" and the novel Mrs. Dalloway has received little or no attention. She argues that "references in the Diary and the unpublished notebooks show it to be an integral part of the novel." Woolf was "particularly concerned with her style; 'too jerky and minute' she comments." The usefulness of this article is relatively minor.

Hoffman, C. G. "From Short Story to Novel: The Manuscript Revisions of Virginia Woolf's Mrs. Dalloway," Modern Fiction Studies, 14 (1968): 171-186.

A study of Virginia Woolf's notebooks reveals her plans for revision. "We come full circle to the short story. After Virginia Woolf completed the ending of the novel, she returned to the beginning and ... revised the short story."

Shields, E. F. "The American Edition of Mrs. Dalloway," Studies in Bibliography, 27 (1974): 157-175.

Shields compares the English and American first editions of Virginia Woolf's Mrs. Dalloway and the revised English proof sheets, which were used by the American publisher in setting type. Variants are revealed among all three sources, which Shields presents both in parallel columns and in following order. The thrust of this article is to evaluate the relative authenticity of the two editions (both are of equal value, but different) rather than to generalize about the revisions as they reveal Woolf's creative process. A large amount of specifically quoted material that illustrates Woolf's revisions, however, is available in this article for those who wish to make use of it. "Many of Virginia Woolf's revisions are very minor, involving polishing the style, correcting the punctuation, or eliminating inconsistencies."

Hoffman, C. G. "Fact and Fantasy in Orlando: Virginia Woolf's Manuscript Revisions," Texas Studies in Literature and Language, 10 (Fall 1968): 435-444.

"The manuscript version of Orlando ... is quite close to the published version. However, there are significant differences between the two which are worth examining because they help clarify Virginia Woolf's intentions, particularly in relation to the various aspects of Orlando's character and the history of the Sackville family. The most obvious difference is that structurally the manuscript version is divided into four chapters, not six as in the novel, one for each major shift in historical and literary period." "Certain key passages in the manuscript which vary from the published novel reveal more explicitly important themes and character conflicts that are later modified to make them more subtle and complex."

Lavin, J. A. "The First Editions of Virginia Woolf's To the Lighthouse," Proof, 21 (1972): 185-211.

"... When To the Lighthouse was published simultaneously in London and New York on 5 May, 1927, the American edition actually was a revised text superior to the one published in England by Woolf's own company." "... They differ in hundreds of ways in both substantives and accidentals." "The American text ... is supremely important ... because it records a significant stage in the revision of the novel." Minor "changes are all significant because individually and collectively they have a cumulative effect which must make the reader respond differently to the American and English texts. More important still, however, are the additions and deletions which affect tone, meaning, and characterization." Two appendixes provide nine pages of columned comparisons that show differences between the first English and first American editions and the London Everyman edition of 1938.

Graham, T. W. Virginia Woolf's "The Waves": The Two Holograph Drafts. Toronto: University of Toronto Press, 1976.

Unseen.

Hoffman, C. G. "Virginia Woolf's Manuscript Revisions of The Years," Publications of the Modern Language Association, 84 (1969): 79-89.

The manuscript notebooks of The Years reveal Virginia Woolf's practice in writing the first section by alternating chapters of factual exposition with chapters of fiction in an attempt to develop an essay-novel form. Later revisions integrated the essay chapters into the fictional ones. "Although she extricated herself from the literalness of the essay-novel theory, she depends at times in The Years on authorial commentary in order to state the external facts. As a result, there is a lack of necessary balance between fact and vision to achieve a more meaningful interaction between the two narrative methods."

WILLIAM WORDSWORTH

Hunt, Bishop C., Jr. "Wordsworth, Haydon, and the 'Wellington'

Sonnet," Princeton University Library Chronicle, 36 (Winter 1975): 111-132.

The first draft of William Wordsworth's sonnet "On A Portrait of the Duke of Wellington upon the Field of Waterloo," written in 1840, is presented in the context of eight letters from Wordsworth to the artist of the painting upon which the poem is based, Benjamin Robert Haydon. The poem was sent along in the second of the letters, and the following letters included the poet's decisions for changes. The final version of the sonnet, published in Poems, Chiefly of Early and Late Years (April 1842), is also presented. "An important difference between this and later versions is the speed or 'pace' of the sonnet. Here all seems leisurely, meditative, even anguished in its slow, understated solemnity, an effect heightened by Wordsworth's original punctuation dividing the poem into six separate and complete sentences. The 1842 version, by contrast, has only three full stops and reads measurably quicker (perhaps Wordsworth's first thoughts, as often in his work, may have been better than his second, third, or fourth thoughts)."

Wordsworth, William. The Prelude: A Parallel Text. Edited by J. C. Maxwell. Middlesex: Penguin Books, 1971.

"The purpose of this edition is to offer, in a form which will make comparisons as easy as possible, the two main texts of The Prelude: that which Wordsworth completed in May 1805, and that which, after a final revision in 1839, he laid aside for publication after his death (1850)."

Jaye, Michael C. "Wordsworth at Work: MS. RV Book II of The Prelude," Papers of the Bibliographical Society of America, 68 (1974): 251-265.

William Wordsworth wrote MS. RV, an intermediate state of Book II of The Prelude, between midsummer of 1799 and early 1800. Jaye establishes this time span for the writing, presents examples of revisions made upon the manuscript so that earlier and later versions of passages can be compared, and describes the process of composition in factual, non-critical terms. "In deciding to expand The Prelude beyond one book Wordsworth drew upon previously written material, drafted new material, and organized it in the copying of RV, continuing roughly the chronological sequence established in Book I and using the address to Coleridge as a unifying force. Even while the material was being copied, Wordsworth was at work making substantial revisions and additions to the book and drafting the last part of the poem in the manuscript itself before once again revising the book for transcription in MSS. U and V."

Schell, Richard. "Wordsworth's Revisions of the Ascent of Snowden," Philological Quarterly, 54 (Summer 1975): 592-603.

Schell examines the changes made in the Snowden episode of The Prelude between the 1805-06 version and the 1850 version. "The circumstances of Wordsworth's re-evaluation of his original conception of the Snowden ascent, and the exact process of revision by which he arrived at the version in A will perhaps never be known, since no manuscripts between W and A are extant. But whatever the intermediary stages may have been, it is clear Wordsworth took what had been a long and somewhat discursive celebration of the powers of Nature, and made from it a 'meditation' dealing almost exclusively with the powers of the mind."

Schell, Richard. "Three Versions of the Self: The Prelude 1789-1806," Dissertation Abstracts International, 37 (October 1976): 2205A.

"Between 1798 and 1806 Wordsworth's Prelude developed through three distinct conceptual and compositional stages. The first was a two-part poem completed in late 1799, which dealt with the poet's first thirteen years; the second, a much more tentative five-book version in 1804, which attempted to include another three or four years of his life; and the thirteen-book Prelude of 1805-06, which extended the narrative through his experiences in France, his subsequent crisis, and the final affirmation of his poetic identity. These successive attempts to incorporate more and more of his past into The Prelude presented Wordsworth with some complex problems of structure and thematic unity, for in expanding his poem he seldom discarded what he had previously written (even as his perspective on the past and his conception of the poem changed), and he almost never simply added on to it. Instead, as he composed important new materials, he reorganized whole sections of the poem, relocating key passages, changing interpretations and emphases (often radically), inserting summaries and correctives--all in order to accommodate the old design to the new."

Wordsworth, William. "She Dwelt Among the Untrodden Ways," The Norton Anthology of English Literature, Vol. II, M. H. Abrams, et al., eds. New York: Norton, 1979, pp. 2516-17.

"Our transcriptions from the poet's drafts attempt to reproduce, as accurately as the change from script to print will allow, the appearance of the original manuscript page."

SIR THOMAS WYATT

O'Neel, Michael C. "Wyatt's MS Revisions," Dissertation Abstracts International, 32 (May 1972): 6387A-6388A.

"This study of Wyatt's own revisions in the Egerton MS, because it substantiates things observable in a reading of his poetry, can aid in defining his poetical style. Setting aside several limitations of this study, MS difficulties, Wyatt's frequently indeterminate decasyllabic lines, supra-segmental transcriptions of some features of Wyatt's rhythm, and the difficulty of knowing Wyatt's feelings from reading his poems, this study can also make several statements about Wyatt's life as artist and man. Most changes demonstrate his deliberately careful craftmanship and they improve his poems, but always in relation to the particular and local rhetorical strategy."

W. B. YEATS

Yeats, W. B. "After Long Silence," "Leda and the Swan," "The

Sorrow of Love," The Norton Anthology of English Literature, Vol. II, M. H. Abrams, et al., eds. New York: Norton, 1979, pp. 2528-33.

"Our transcriptions from the poets' drafts attempt to reproduce, as accurately as the change from script to print will allow, the appearance of the original manuscript page."

Marcus, Philip. "'I make the truth': Vision and Revision in Yeats's The Death of Cuchulain," Colby Library Quarterly, 12 (June 1976): 57-64.

"The extant manuscript materials for the play give no indication that Yeats had any major difficulties in articulating his stance concerning that most crucial of questions [death]: composition seems to have proceeded rather smoothly (by Yeatsian standards)...." Marcus bases his discussion on the revisions of one key passage that describes the relationship between Cuchulain and Eithne.

Ackerman, Cara. "Yeats's Revisions of the Hanrahan Stories, 1897-1904," Texas Studies in Literature and Language, 17 (Summer 1975): 505-524.

"As Yeats moved away from 'the artificial, elaborate language' he had employed in the nineties, he came 'to hate' The Stories of Red Hanrahan, and thus it was that in 1904, with the aid of Lady Gregory, they came to be rewritten. The changes in large part are the result of the pruning of verbal deadwood."

Stallworthy, Jon. "W. B. Yeats's 'Under Ben Bulben'," Review of English Studies, 17 (1966): 30-53.

This complete account of the composition of "Under Ben Bulben" makes available and analyzes eight versions of the poem, divided into four stages of composition: (1) three prose drafts; (2) a first attempt to utilize rhyme in a draft; (3) the first complete verse draft; and (4) three typescript drafts. The first complete verse draft "shows the evolution of the poem's title from 'Creed' to 'His Convictions' and, finally, the impersonal 'Under Ben Bulben.' A similar movement from the subjective to the objective is visible...."

Croft, Barbara Lea. "'Stylistic Arrangements': A Comparative Study of the Two Versions of W. B. Yeats's A Vision," Dissertation Abstracts International, 39 (September 1978): 1545A-1546A.

"When the two versions are compared it becomes clear that, whereas the 1925 version takes the system quite seriously, the 1937 version is riddled with self-mockery and self-dramatization and the system itself is placed in an absurd context."

Witt, Marion. "A Competition for Eternity: Yeats's Revision of His Later Poems," Publications of the Modern Language Association, 64 (1949): 40-58.

W. B. Yeats's later poems usually appeared first in a periodical edition, then in book form from his sister's press, in book form from commercial publishing houses, and in collected editions. Witt discusses Yeats's revisions made to effect changes in diction, syntax, meter, and rhyme. Some of the poems examined are:

(1) Easter, 1916; (2) The Song of the Happy Shepherd; (3) The Folly of Being Comforted; (4) The Fisherman; (5) Ego Dominus Tuus; (6) Under Saturn; (7) Among School Children; (8) The Seven Sages; (9) Crazy Jane on the Day of Judgment; (10) The Tower; (11) Solomon and the Witch; (12) Nineteen Hundred and Nineteen; (13) On Being Asked For a War Poem; (14) Meditations in Time of Civil War; (15) Sailing to Byzantium; (16) To a Shade; (17) The Resurrection; (18) The Sad Shepherd; (19) At Algeciras--A Meditation Upon Death; (20) Crazy Jane and the Bishop; (21) A Dialogue of Self and Soul; (22) Fallen Majesty; (23) Leda and the Swan; (24) Those Images; (25) Three Marching Songs. "The poet at work to enhance the half-hypnotic suggestions of sound is everywhere evident, and alterations of diction for greater exactness or intensity dot almost every page." Sections of poems are compared in following order and in parallel columns.

Alspach, Russell K. "Some Textual Problems in Yeats," Studies in Bibliography, (1957): 51-67.

This essay was written after Alspach had been working on the variorum edition of Yeats's poetry for ten years. A quatrain by Yeats is quoted:

The friends that have it I do wrong
Whenever I remake a song,
Must know what issue is at stake:
It is myself that I remake.

Alspach makes several major points: (1) Scholars and critics should be careful in drawing conclusions from Yeats's revisions; statements have been made based upon an incomplete knowledge of the poet's final changes. (2) Yeats's "early" poems include those written up to 1892; the "later" poems include everything from The Wind Among the Reeds (1899) to Last Poems and Plays (London, New York, 1940). (3) Many of Yeats's revisions are reversions to earlier texts. Alspach makes at least some comparisons among revised versions of a large sample of Yeats's poems, e. g.: (1) "The Ballad of the Foxhunter"; (2) "The Song of the Happy Shepherd"; (3) "Ephemera"; (4) "The Wanderings of Oisin"; (5) "The Rose of Battle"; (6) "The Lake Isle of Innisfree"; (7) "When You Are Old"; (8) "The Two Trees"; (9) "The Man Who Dreamed of Faeryland"; (10) "Cuchulain's Fight with the Sea"; (11) "The Second Coming"; (12) "The Folly of Being Comforted"; (13) "The Three Beggars"; (14) "The Scholars"; (15) "Lullaby"; (16) "Adam's Curse."

Yeats, W. B. The Variorum Edition of the Poems of W. B. Yeats. Edited by Peter Allt and Russell K. Alspach. New York: Macmillan, 1957.

Using the two-volume definitive edition of 1949 as the text of the poems, variants are given from 100 other publications. Footnotes display the variants and indicate the publication source of each. Appendix I is divided into "Notes on Particular Poems" and "General Notes," all of which were written by Yeats. Appendix II is composed of his prefaces and dedications. The editors of this volume have drawn no special conclusions about the nature of Yeats's revisions; they have rather let this massive accumulation of his changes speak for itself. "The record begins with the March 1885 number of The Dublin University Review that contained his first two published poems; it ends with the two-volume definitive edition of his poetry in 1949, the proofs of which he had corrected shortly before his death in 1939."

Stallworthy, Jon. Between the Lines: Yeats's Poetry in the Making. Oxford: Clarendon Press, 1963.

Stallworthy has selected the poems for this work largely because of the manuscript material available: "The Second Coming," "A Prayer for My Daughter," "The Sorrow of Love," "The Gift of Harun Al-Rashid," "Sailing to Byzantium," "Byzantium," "Chosen: Parting," "In Memory of Eva Gore-Booth and Con Markiewicz," "Coole Park, 1929," "The Black Tower," and seven shorter poems. Yeats's pattern of composition is represented by the kinds of versions he produced for most of his career: prose draft, rough verse drafts, fair copy, magazine publication, revisions for the first book form, and revisions for further book editions. Three characteristics of the process by which Yeats made poems are (1) to start with a rhyme scheme and rhyming words predetermined, but to discard any of this blueprint if it obstructs the development of substance, (2) to work from the metrically formal to the informal, freeing his rhythms as he moved from draft to draft, and (3) to cut and prune his original material, seldom adding to it.

Bradford, Curtis B. Yeats at Work. Carbondale: Southern Illinois University Press, 1965.

Bradford analyzes successive manuscript versions of selected poems, plays, and prose:

I. Poems
   A. Poems from The Wind Among the Reeds
   B. "Nineteen Hundred and Nineteen"
   C. "The Tower," Section III, and "Lullaby"
   D. "Words" and "The Wild Swans at Coole"
   E. Poems Written in the 1930's
II. Plays
   A. At the Hawk's Well
   B. The Words Upon the Window-pane
   C. The Resurrection
   D. A Full Moon in March
   E. Purgatory
III. Prose
   A. The Celtic Twilight, The Secret Rose, and Discoveries
   B. Autobiographies and On the Boiler

Three purposes are suggested for the study of manuscripts: correcting or improving the text, avoiding wrong readings, and gaining new critical insights into the work. One of the primary insights into Yeats's work gained by studying his manuscripts turns out to be the fact that, when he failed, the failure was a result of his not being able to control his accidence. "Yeats almost always began work on a poem by composing what he called a 'sketch' or 'subject' in prose. These subjects state the content of the poems and note the principal images to be developed in them. They were often brief, though sometimes they were put through successive drafts. Some subjects are as long as the poems that grew out of them, some rough poems already."

Stallworthy, Jon. Vision and Revision in Yeats' "Last Poems." Oxford: Clarendon Press, 1969.

"Four of the six essays in this book explore certain of Yeats's Last Poems through a reconstruction of their growth from manuscript to print." (1) "Lapis Lazuli"; (2) "The Man and the Echo"; (3) "The Three Bushes"; (4) "The Lady's First Song"; (5) "The Lady's Second Song"; (6) "The Lady's Third Song"; (7) "The Lover's Song"; (8) "The Chambermaid's First Song"; (9) "The Chambermaid's Second Song"; (10) "The Spur"; (11) "The Long-legged Fly"; (12) "The Statues"; (13) "Under Ben Bulben." Chapters open with the Variorum texts of the poems to be studied, followed by the versions with cancelled sections marked through and additions indicated. Kinds of changes pointed out include rhythm changes, compression, and movement from the subjective to the objective. These essays may be seen as an extension of Stallworthy's Between the Lines: Yeats's Poetry in the Making.

Bushrui, S. B. Yeats's Verse-plays: The Revisions 1900-1910. Oxford: Clarendon Press, 1965.

Bushrui studies the revisions of five Yeats plays by comparing different published versions: (1) The Shadowy Waters (1900, 1906, 1907); (2) On Baile's Strand (1903, 1906); (3) The King's Threshold (1904, 1906, 1922); (4) Deirdre (1908, 1911, 1922, 1934); (5) The Green Helmet (The Golden Helmet 1908, The Green Helmet 1910). A significant portion of the comparisons is presented by displaying different versions in parallel columns. The revisions fall into two major categories: (1) the craft of the dramatist, (a) dialogue; (b) developing minor characters; (c) technical matters (entrances, exits, costumes, lighting, settings) and (2) "... a sustained effort to find a new style, or poetic language." Bushrui concludes that Yeats's full-time devotion to dramatic writing for more than five years enabled him to find a new expression of his lyricism.

Alspach, Russell K., Editor. The Variorum Edition of the Plays of W. B. Yeats. Assisted by Catherine C. Alspach. New York: Macmillan, 1966.

The Collected Plays of W. B. Yeats (London: Macmillan 1952) stands as the basic text in this volume, and variants are given from 97 other publications. Footnotes present the variants and refer to their publication sources. In the case of some of the plays that were very heavily reworked (e. g. The Countess Cathleen) the first version is displayed on verso pages and the basic text on facing recto pages with variants in other versions specified in recto page footnotes. The Green Helmet, on the other hand, is set up with each page divided into a top section for the basic text, a middle section for the two prose texts with variations between them marked within the lines, and a bottom section for the variant notes on the basic verse text. Notes by Yeats on each play directly follow the texts of the play, with general notes, prefaces, and dedications assigned to Appendix I and Appendix II. "... The chief impressions one gets from a chronological study of Yeats's plays are the same impressions one gets from a similar study of the poetry; he was never content, he revised constantly, and he almost always improved."

PART II:

WRITERS TALK ABOUT THE CREATIVE PROCESS

Allen, Walter, ed. *Writers on Writing.* Boston: The Writer, Inc., 1958.

"I have tried to make the sort of book that would have stimulated me and, I think, have helped me too when I first began to write fifteen years ago," says the editor, Walter Allen, who is both a critic and a novelist. He has divided the book into brief comments by practicing poets of the past and present, under various headings, and comments by fiction writers, about 70 writers in all. See especially sections on style and "The Novelist at Work." Tolstoy: "In a writer there must always be two people--the writer and the critic." Tolstoy seldom re-read his published writing, but "if by chance I come across a page, it always strikes me: All this must be rewritten; this is how I should have written it...."

Allott, Miriam, ed. *Novelists on the Novel.* New York: Columbia University Press, 1966.

Fifty English, French, and Russian novelists talk about the purposes and techniques of fiction under many headings. An index to authors and subjects is included. Brief comments are quoted in chronological order under three general headings: "The Nature of Prose Fiction," "The Genesis of a Novel," and "The Craft of Fiction." Those headings are broken down further, as in the "Craft of Fiction" section: structural problems, unity and coherence, plot and story, the time-factor, narrative technique, characterization, dialogue, background, style. This is an excellent source of comment by writers themselves. SEE ALSO Walter Allen, *Writers on Writing,* a similar format. Dostoevsky: "Yes, that was and ever is my greatest torment--I never can control my material." Robert Louis Stevenson: the writer "must ... suppress much and omit more." George Eliot: "Beginnings are always troublesome." Chekhov: "at the end of a novel ... I must artfully concentrate for the reader an impression of the entire work." Andre Gide: "the difficult thing is inventing when you are encumbered by memory...."

Barry, Elaine. *Robert Frost on Writing.* New Brunswick, N.J.: Rutgers University Press, 1973.

The scope of Frost's criticism is demonstrated. In Part I, Ms. Barry examines Frost as critical theorist and practical critic; Part II consists of letters, prefaces, reviews, lectures, interviews, parodies, and marginalia which demonstrate the scope of Frost's literary criticism. Speaking of the poet, Frost says, "His style is the way he carries himself toward his ideas and deeds." In one place, he says, "I have never been good at revising. I always thought I made things worse by recasting or retouching. I never knew what was meant by choice of words." But in another place, he says of a line in one poem that it "is manifestly redundant as well as retruse and I must invent one to supplant it."

Baumbach, Jonathan, ed. Writers as Teachers: Teachers as Writers. New York: Holt, Rinehart and Winston, 1970.

"This book is about how eleven diverse writers who teach make sense to themselves of their roles as teachers of writing.... A writing class ... is an action course in the humanities--one of the rare school occasions where the individual is valued for being uniquely himself...." Contributors are Jonathan Baumbach, Wendell Berry, Robert Creeley, George P. Elliott, George Garrett, Ivan Gold, John Hawkes, Denise Levertov, Wright Morris, Grace Paley, L. S. Simckes. Talking about teaching others, these writers reveal insights into their own writing, including the revision process.

Bellamy, Joe David, ed. The New Fiction: Interviews with Innovative American Writers. Urbana: University of Illinois Press, 1974.

"... suddenly writers have emerged who face us with compelling new 'versions of reality'--more aesthetically advanced though no less stylized than 'realism,' highly contemporaneous, and written in decidedly idiosyncratic, imaginative, and personal idioms.... American writers of the present moment--all either well known or with rising reputations, those who seem to be most involved in effecting significant change, whose artistic innovations, impressive or exotic sensitivities, and/or critical formulations or aesthetic theories seem most compelling, provocative, or influential..." John Barth, Joyce Carol Oates, William H. Gass, Donald Barthelme, Ronald Sukenick, Tom Wolfe, John Hawkes, Susan Sontag, Ishmael Reed, Jerzy Kosinski, John Gardner, Kurt Vonnegut, Jr. Oates: "I am interested in formal experimentation, yes, but generally this grows out of a certain plot. The form and the style seem naturally suited to the story that has to be told." Gass: "There are no events but words in fiction."

Berg, A. Scott. Max Perkins, Editor of Genius. New York: E. P. Dutton, 1978.

This major biography of Perkins includes accounts of his editorial relationship with Thomas Wolfe, Ernest Hemingway, F. Scott Fitzgerald, James Jones, Ring Lardner, Sherwood Anderson, and many other American writers, involving revision problems as part of the larger publishing process. See especially passages recounting Perkins' classic editorial relationship with Thomas Wolfe. SEE Perkins, Editor to Author, Part II.

Berg, Stephen, and Robert Mezey. Naked Poetry: Recent American Poetry in Open Forms. Indianapolis: Bobbs-Merrill, 1969. (Revised as The New Naked Poetry, 1976.)

"... we invited each poet ... to write an essay or statement or letter to accompany his poems ... talking about their notion of poetry, about open forms, what they were doing, how they felt, why they considered themselves to be etc." The poets are Kenneth Rexroth, Theodore Roethke, Kenneth Patchen, William Stafford, Weldon Kees, John Berryman, Robert Lowell, Denise Levertov, Robert Bly,

Robert Creeley, Allen Ginsberg, Galway Kinnell, W. S. Merwin, James Wright, Philip Levine, Sylvia Plath, Gary Snyder, Stephen Berg, Robert Mezey. Gary Snyder: "... each poem grows from an energy-mind-field-dance...." James Wright: "If any principle of structure can be disentangled from the poems that I have written in free verse, it is, I suppose, the principle of parallelism...." Denise Levertov: "For me, back of the idea of organic form is the concept that there is a form in all things (and in our experience) which the poet can discover and reveal."

Birmingham, Frederic A., ed. The Writer's Craft. New York: Hawthorn Books, 1958.

An informal, quirky, sometimes useful commentary on "the professional techniques of the art of writing as demonstrated by" Birmingham, formerly editor of Esquire, "with the help of some of the world's greatest authors and editors," in poetry, fiction, and nonfiction. Generous quotes from Sinclair Lewis, Sean O'Casey, Theodore Dreiser, Thomas Wolfe, Maxwell Perkins, and others provide a collage of workshop bits and pieces.

Block, Haskell M., and Herman Salinger, eds. The Creative Vision: Modern European Writers on Their Art. New York: Grove Press, Inc., 1960.

"The Creative Vision is a collection of essays by major European literary figures of the twentieth century. In these essays, the writer discusses and interprets either his own writings or those of kindred spirits or the problems of the literary artist generally." Many of the pieces are very difficult to find elsewhere. "The universal characteristic of twentieth-century European literature is its extreme self-consciousness.... The essays collected in this book are decisive evidence of the dominance of critical intelligence in recent European literature. Any sharp distinction between critical and creative activity has all but fallen away." These poets, playwrights, and novelists talk about language, structure, the nature of art and of the artist, and the artist's relation to the audience. Paul Valéry, Rainer Maria Rilke, André Gide, Marcel Proust, Thomas Mann, Luigi Pirandello, Federico García Lorca, Jean Giraudoux, Jean Anouilh, Bertolt Brecht, André Malraux, Jean-Paul Sartre, Friedrich Duerrenmatt.

Borges on Writing. Norman Thomas di Giovanni, Daniel Halpern, and Frank MacShane, eds. New York: Dutton, 1973.

"The text of this book is based on tape-recorded transcripts" of the three informal meetings Borges had in the spring of 1971 with "the students enrolled in the graduate writing program at Columbia University ... devoted primarily to a single topic: to the writing of fiction, poetry, and of translation." Borges is blind. Di Giovanni read a story, "The End of the Duel," aloud; and Borges interrupted to comment on it, passage by passage. The same procedure was used with a poem, "June 1968." Borges discusses his methods and his conceptions about writing.

Braine, John. Writing a Novel. New York: Coward, McCann and Geoghegan, 1974.

"This is a practical manual, a conducted tour of my workshop.... I am sure that, if you have the necessary ability, observing my rules will enable you to write a novel which will be accepted for publication." The first ten chapters are discussions of basic techniques of fiction, with illustrations and quotations from British and American novelists. The eleventh chapter is "the history of my own first novel," Room at the Top. "What follows, in roughly chronological order, are the actual extracts from my notes and first drafts." An excellent demonstration, by a writer, of the revision process, this is one of the better books by a writer on writing.

Breit, Harvey. The Writer Observed. Cleveland: World, 1956.

These short articles are based on interviews with 60 well-known British and American authors, from 1948 to 1955, usually on the occasion of the publication of a new book, by Harvey Breit of the New York Times Book Review. Poets, fiction writers, both popular and serious, and critics and nonfiction writers are represented.

Brooks, Cleanth, and Robert Penn Warren. "How Poems Come About: Intention and Meaning," Understanding Poetry. New York: Holt, Rinehart and Winston, 1938 (1950, 1960), pp. 514-550.

"What we can learn about the origin of a poem may, if we do not confuse origin and poem, enlarge our understanding and deepen our appreciation." Footnote: "This gain in understanding and appreciation is not merely, in fact not primarily, of the poem whose development we can trace.... It is, rather, a gain in our understanding and appreciation of poetry in general; when we learn about the materials of poetry and about the poetic process, we also learn something about the nature of poetry." As they discuss "the materials of the poem" and "the process whereby the poem is made," Brooks and Warren look very closely at Housman's "I Hoed and Trenched and Weeded" and "The Immortal Part," and at Keats's "Ode to Autumn." They offer Randall Jarrell's long, detailed analysis of his own poem, "The Woman at the Washington Zoo." They provide versions of "The Immortal Part" and "To an Athlete Dying Young" for comparison. Some comment on Wordsworth's "I Wandered Lonely as a Cloud," Yeats's "Upon a Dying Lady," Coleridge's "Kubla Kahn," Poe's "The Raven," by the author's themselves, is offered; Frost and Eliot are quoted, speaking of the creative process in general terms.

Brooks, Cleanth, and Robert Penn Warren. "Fiction and Human Experience: How Four Stories Came to Be Written," Understanding Fiction. New York: Appleton-Century-Crofts, 1943 (1959), pp. 526-643.

"... in our attempt to read fiction more fully and enjoy it more deeply, it may be of use to see what four writers have to say of the origins of their four stories.... The creative process is concerned with bringing things together; but we may add that, in general, what it brings together is not even the same kind of elements that critical analysis distinguishes.... Katherine Anne Porter and John Cheever ... do not speak of technical questions at all--yet both are accomplished technicians." Welty does discuss atmosphere and point of view; Warren discusses structure and feeling. The four writers and their selections are Eudora Welty, "No Place for You, My Love"; John Cheever, "Goodbye, My Brother"; Katherine Anne Porter, "Noon Wine"; Robert Penn Warren, "Blackberry Winter."

Brooks, Van Wyck (introduced by). Writers at Work: The Paris Review Interviews, Second Series. New York: Viking Press, 1963.

Robert Frost, Ezra Pound, Marianne Moore, T. S. Eliot, Boris Pasternak, Katherine Anne Porter, Henry Miller, Aldous Huxley, Ernest Hemingway, S. J. Perelman, Lawrence Durrell, Mary McCarthy, Ralph Ellison, Robert Lowell. Bio-bibliographical notes, with sample manuscript pages, are included. Robert Frost: "No tears in the writer, no tears in the reader. No surprise for the writer, no surprise for the reader.... What do I want to communicate but what a hell of a good time I had writing it? The whole thing is performance and prowess and feats of association. Why don't critics talk about those things--?" Ernest Hemingway: "I rewrote the ending to A Farewell to Arms, the last pages of it, thirty-nine times before I was satisfied.... Getting the words right."

Buckler, William E., ed. Novels in the Making. Boston: Houghton Mifflin, 1961.

"In Novels in the Making the editor's object has been to provide representative primary documents--distributed by time, type, and nationality--which suggest the problems and perceptions that have gone into the making of the modern novel," and of specific novels, classic and modern. The documents are authors' prefaces, letters, notebook entries, sketches, outlines. The authors are Defoe, Fielding, Smollett, Cooper, Dickens, Flaubert, Turgenev, Tolstoy, Eliot, Zola, de Maupassant, Conrad, James, Bennett, Lawrence, Gide, Bowen. Of unusual interest are Dickens' numbered plans for David Copperfield; Eliot's notes, outlines, lists for Middlemarch; James's notebook entries for and preface to The Wings of the Dove; and Zola's sketches for L'Assommoir. Zola: "Plan in Brief: Chapters of 20 pages, average uneven in size, the shortest ten pages, the longest 30 pages. The style in full flight."

Burnett, Whit, ed. This Is My Best. New York: The Dial Press, 1942.

"America's 93 greatest living authors present ... over 150 self-chosen and complete masterpieces, together with their reasons for their selections." Authors' comments are generally very brief; several are long enough to be significant. Forms represented are poetry, short fiction, novels, plays (by excerpts), and nonfiction (essays, biography, reportage, autobiography, editorials).

Burnett, Whit, ed. The World's Best. New York: The Dial Press, 1950.

"105 Greatest Living Authors," represented by stories, humor, drama, biography, history, essays, and poetry, select their personal favorites and briefly give their reasons for the selections.

Burnett, Whit, ed. This Is My Best, in the Third Quarter of the Century. Garden City, N. Y.: Doubleday & Company, 1970.

From a ballot of over 500 authors, six thousand selected authors, librarians, critics, editors, and other readers chose eighty-five of the "greatest living American authors" to be represented in this anthology. Each author presents his "best" selection with an explanation of his choice. "Specifically, of the eighty-five authors, thirty write novels or short stories, nineteen are poets, fifteen are historians, biographers or journalists, five are dramatists, and sixteen are essayists covering everything from natural history and human behavior to theories of space."

Burnett, Whit, and Hallie Burnett, eds. The Modern Short Story in the Making. New York: Hawthorn Books, 1964.

Twenty-two short stories by 22 authors are included, with comments by each author: Norman Mailer, Jesse Stuart, James T. Farrell, Lord Dunsany, Mary O'Hara, Whit Burnett, Gladys Schmitt, Dorothy McCleary, Erskine Caldwell, Kay Boyle, Truman Capote, William Saroyan, Hallie Burnett, George Hitchcock, George Sumner Albee, Kressman Taylor, Howard Nemerov and W. R. Johnson, John Knowles, Guido D'Agistino, Luigi Pirandello, Katherine Anne Porter. The editors, who are also fiction writers, and are represented in this collection, provide commentary by fictional categories and techniques. The book "is designed ... to tell the reader something about the circumstances of the publication of the story; to tell something about the author's life; and to engage the author in such editorial inquiry as to elicit from him personally, as a reflective assessment, afterthoughts or words of wisdom as a professional--how he felt as he sat at his typewriter, what went before and where the idea came from, what took place in the construction and the writing, at what particular period in his life and career he wrote his particular tale, and how it fits into his own development as a writer."

Caldwell, Erskine. Call It Experience: The Years of Learning How to Write. New York: Duell, Sloan and Pearce, 1951.

Caldwell's personal account of his writing life extends from his boyhood in Georgia to the height of his financial and professional success in 1950. His determination, in spite of many obstacles, to succeed in becoming a professional writer is the theme that is repeated over and over. "Perhaps the reason I am unable to give explicit directions that would assure anyone of becoming a successful writer is because I consider creative writing to be motivated by a certain state of mind; and believe that only those who are born with the gift or who acquire the indefinable urge to express themselves in print can accomplish it."

Camus, Albert. Notebooks: 1935-1942. Translated from the French with a Preface and Notes by Philip Thody. New York: Alfred A. Knopf, 1963.

Lists of newspaper articles published by Camus between 1938 and 1940 and plays performed between 1935 and 1939 are included. Thody says it is "for the light which the Notebooks throw on the way he worked that they are most valuable." The entries fall into three general categories: "philosophical ideas, the fragments of description, the scraps of conversation overheard.... Camus often wrote passages that needed very little revision before being incorporated into the final version of his works." He speaks often of the books he read. We may follow his notes on his early version of The Stranger which was published as A Happy Death, then his notes on The Stranger itself while he was still working on A Happy Death. "Notes, scraps of paper, reverie, which all might go on for years. Then, one day, I have the idea or conception that makes all these isolated fragments coagulate together. There then begins a long and painful putting them into order." It is "through a desire to shine too early that some authors did not agree to rewrite."

Camus, Albert. Notebooks: 1942-1951. Edited and translated, with annotations, by Justin O'Brien. New York: Alfred A. Knopf, 1965.

These notebooks cover the years of the writing of most of the plays, The Misunderstanding, Caligula, The Just Assassins, and State of Siege, and end as Camus has just finished The Rebel.

Cane, Melville. Making A Poem: An Inquiry Into the Creative Process. New York: Harcourt, Brace and World, 1953 (1960, 1962).

This book is a response to the questions writers often hear: "But how do you go about writing your poems?" Cane answers that question for "Linda," "Humbly, Wildly," "Hokinson," "Bed-time Story," "The Dismal Month," "The Fly," "Bullet-Hunting" (in the 1962 Harvest paperback edition), among others. He conducts an "interior exploration of the creative process as I have experienced it." He reports "the step-by-step, trial-and-error operations from the first tappings on the door of the unconscious to the emergence of the final form, the completed expression." The book became an act of self-discovery.

Carr, John, ed. Kite-Flying and Other Irrational Acts: Conversations with Twelve Southern Writers. Baton Rouge: Louisiana State University Press, 1972.

These interviews were done by John Carr and other young Southern poets and fiction and nonfiction writers. Poets and writers of fiction and non-fiction are represented. When they were interviewed, each had just published a book and talked about the experience of writing it: Shelby Foote, Walker Percy, Marion Montgomery, Reynolds Price, Willie Morris, Larry L. King, Doris Betts, George Garrett, Jesse Hill Ford, Fred Chappell, Guy Owen, James Whitehead.

Cary, Joyce. Art and Reality: Ways of the Creative Process. New York: Anchor Books, 1961.

Thirty-five short chapters are presented on intuition, originality, style, conception, idea and form, creativity and the subconscious, symbolism, and allegory by the novelist Joyce Cary. "... Every student must have a form of expression, and he must learn it by a purely technical and conceptual education." Cary writes out of his training in aesthetics and his practical experience as the author of 11 novels.

Cassill, R. V. Writing Fiction. 2nd edition. Englewood Cliffs, N. J.: Prentice-Hall, 1975.

This is the best book on the writing of fiction. A fine novelist, short story writer, and teacher, Cassill "emphasizes analytical reading as an integral part of learning to write fiction," as do most teachers of writing, because too many young writers are severely deficient in reading background. The book is in three parts: One: "The Mechanics of Fiction"; Two: "An anthology of stories used for purposes of illustration"; Three: "The Concepts of Fiction." The first edition, published by Permabooks (1963), contains three excellent pages on revision, including Cassill's account of his own typical revision process. "Almost always I had to rewrite the beginning extensively for the sake of economy and to make it conform to developments I hadn't foreseen when I began. The endings I had first written were usually too abrupt and had to be modulated and paced better."

Cheever, John, "Goodbye, My Brother" and "What Happened."
SEE Brooks and Warren, Understanding Fiction.

Ciardi, John. Mid-Century American Poets. New York: Twayne, 1950.

Poet-critic Ciardi asked fifteen poets to respond to these questions about "the technical problems of your own writing": 1) the oral quality of the poem, 2) the audience, 3) the language, 4) the function of overtone, 5) levels of meaning, 6) subject matter, 7) imagery, 8) symbolism, 9) rhyme, 10) line length and function of line-endings, 11) total structure, 12) rhythm and meter. About ten poems by each of the following poets are also included: Richard Wilbur, Peter Viereck, Muriel Rukeyser, Theodore Roethke, Karl Shapiro, Winfield Townley Scott, John Frederick Nims, E. L. Mayo, Robert Lowell, Randall Jarrell, John Holmes, Richard Eberhart, John Ciardi, Elizabeth Bishop, Delmore Schwartz. Several drafts of "The Minute" by Karl Shapiro are reproduced without comment. "The writing principles of the poem must be implicit in that process, and by observing the process itself, the reader will be able to trace the principles with a minimum of distortion." Among Ciardi's own answers to his own questions is this one: "A line of poetry is a conceived unit, not a typographical fragment."

Cocteau, Jean. Beauty and the Beast: Diary of a Film. Introduction by George Amberg. New York: Dover, 1972 (1950).

"The incredible difficulties under which the production ... suffered from beginning to end," says Amberg, are "thoroughly documented...." "As everywhere in his writings, there is ample evidence of Cocteau's pervading fear of falling into the trap of poetic conventions.... the Diary reveals everything the film disguises.... there is, most of all, the compelling urge to justify ... every thought and action.... It is enormously instructive to follow scene by scene ... the problems the director encountered and the ingenuity with which he resolved them.... one is simply amazed at the superhuman control Cocteau exerted over the whole production.... Cocteau had no reservations whatever about revealing usually closely guarded professional secrets, the technical tricks with which he achieved his magic effects, the way he worked his visual wonders. These passages are endlessly fascinating, even for the layman who is privileged to witness the birth of an illusion and the creation of art."

Cole, Toby, ed. Playwrights on Playwriting: The Meaning and Making of Modern Drama from Ibsen to Ionesco. Introduction by John Gassner. New York: Hill and Wang, 1961.

"Part I, Credos and Concepts, with its fervent expressions of artistic conviction, its battle cries and proclamations, reflects the modern dramatist's restless search for form toward and away from realism. The marvelous ways in which these abstractions have been substantiated in many of the finest plays of the period comprise Part 2, Creations," in which the playwrights comment on individual plays. Henrik Ibsen, Emile Zola, August Strindberg, Anton Chekhov, Maurice Maeterlinck, William B. Yeats, John Galsworthy, Bernard Shaw, Federico García Lorca, Jean Giraudoux, Eugene O'Neill, Bertolt Brecht, Thornton Wilder, Jean-Paul Sartre, Christopher Fry, Friedrich Duerrenmatt, John Osborne, Eugene Ionesco, John Millington Synge, Luigi Pirandello, Ernst Toller, Jean Cocteau, Sean O'Casey, T. S. Eliot, Arthur Miller, Tennessee Williams, Friedrich Hebbel.

Conrad, Joseph. Joseph Conrad on Fiction. Edited by Walter F. Wright. Lincoln: University of Nebraska Press, 1964.

The sections are entitled: "Essays on Divers Books and Authors," "Literary Reflections and Reminiscences," "Author's Notes and Prefaces." The editor states: "His tone ranges from the bitterness of revulsion, when he sometimes mocks a story that has been exhausting his nervous energy for weeks, to a nearly ecstatic reminiscence of the adventures of composition." Conrad said, "Give me the right word and the right accent and I will move the world--"

Corliss, Richard. Talking Pictures. Woodstock, N. Y.: The Overlook Press, 1974.

A critical survey of thirty-eight screenwriters and over a hundred of their movies. Ben Hecht, Preston Sturges, Norman Krasna, Frank Tashlin, George Axelrod, Peter Stone, Howard Koch, Borden Chase, Abraham Polonsky, Billy Wilder, Samson Raphaelson, Nunnally Johnson, Ernest Lehman, Betty Comden and Adolph Green, Garson Kanin (and Ruth Gordon), Robert Riskin, Dudley Nichols, Joseph L. Mankiewicz, Herman J. Mankiewicz, Dalton Trumbo, Jules Furthman, Sidney Buchman, Casey Robinson, Morrie Ryskind, Edwin Justus Mayer, Delmer Daves, Charles Lederer, Charles Brackett, Frank S. Nugent, Ring Lardner, Jr., Terry Southern, Erich Segal, Buck Henry, Jules Feiffer, David Newman, and Robert Benton. There is some discussion of revision--by the screenwriters themselves, but also by the directors, actors, producers, etc., and by other writers who are brought in to "revamp" a script.

Cowley, Malcolm, ed. Writers at Work: The Paris Review Interviews. New York: The Viking Press, 1959.

The sixteen authors represented are E. M. Forster, Francois Mauriac, Joyce Cary, Dorothy Parker, James Thurber, Thornton Wilder, William Faulkner, Georges Simenon, Frank O'Connor, Robert Penn Warren, Alberto Moravia, Nelson Algren, Angus Wilson, William Styron, Truman Capote, Françoise Sagan. Bio-bibliographical notes and sample manuscript pages are presented. Robert Penn Warren: "People deeply interested in an art are interested in the 'how'." "I try to think a lot about the craft of other people.... When it comes to your own work you have made some objective decisions, such as which character is going to tell the story. That's a prime question, a question of control." William Styron: "I seem to have some neurotic need to perfect each paragraph--each sentence, even--as I go along," an average of three pages a day.

Dembo, L. S., and Cyrena N. Pondrom, eds. The Contemporary Writer. Madison: University of Wisconsin Press, 1972.

Isaac Singer, Jorge Luis Borges, Vladimir Nabokov, John Barth, John Hawkes, Kenneth Rexroth, Louis Zukovsky, James Merrill, George Barker.

Dostoevsky, Fyodor. The Notebooks for "The Brothers Karamazov." Edited and with an introduction by Edward Wasiolek. Chicago: Chicago University Press, 1971.

"The character of the notes that follow is different from that of the other major novels, in that the distance between notes and novels is shortest." "The notebooks for other novels show Dostoevsky searching for theme, narrative structure, technique, and the identity of his characters.... The notes for The Brothers Karamazov are not those of germination, quest, and discovery. Dostoevsky knows what he is writing about; the subject is firm, the identities of the chief characters are fixed, and the basic dramatic situation is clear.... The differences between notes and novel are differences between schematic representation and dramatic embodiment, summary and amplification, between ideas and the dramatization of the ideas." Wasiolek provides photocopies of several manuscript pages.

Dostoevsky, Fyodor. The Notebooks for "Crime and Punishment." Edited and with an introduction by Edward Wasiolek. Princeton: Princeton University Press, 1967.

"What do the wrong turns, mistakes, blind alleys, and unmined possibilities tell us? How do we go from possibilities to the fact itself? They remind us, first of all, that the marvelous coherence of Crime and Punishment, the creative logic that takes us from what seems to be inevitable movement from beginning to end, was once uncertain, halting, and far from clear. They tell us something about the way Dostoevsky's creative imagination works: its habits, mannerisms, logic; something about his concern for technique; and something about what was recurrent in his thinking about the novel. The notebooks tell us much about the content of the novel itself: what was left out, what was different, what was undeveloped, and what was at some point more fully developed. At times they may help us clear up what is obscured in the novel, and resolve what has been critically disputable." "The right point of view evidently gave him a great deal of trouble, for he returns to reflection on it again and again, and he considers a variety of modes of narration." Photocopies of several pages of manuscript are provided.

Dostoevsky, Fyodor. The Notebooks for "The Idiot." Edited and with an introduction by Edward Wasiolek. Chicago: Chicago University Press, 1967.

The format is very similar to that for the other Dostoevsky notebooks edited by Wasiolek. SEE other entries, Crime and Punishment, The Possessed, A Raw Youth, The Brothers Karamazov.

Dostoevsky, Fyodor. The Notebooks for "The Possessed." Edited and with an introduction by Edward Wasiolek. Chicago: University of Chicago Press, 1968.

"The notes for The Possessed consist of some autobiographical materials; the accounts of several dreams and a record of fits for more than a year; notes for several related but unpublished works, notably those for 'The Life of a Great Sinner'; and, in great bulk, variants, outlines of plots, sketches of scenes, and analyses of characters for The Possessed itself. This is the longest of the notebooks, and the distance between the first notes and the final version is also the greatest." Photocopies of several pages of manuscript are provided.

Dostoevsky, Fyodor. The Notebooks for "A Raw Youth." Edited and with an introduction by Edward Wasiolek. Chicago: Chicago University Press, 1969.

"Throughout a significant portion of the notes Dostoevsky carries on a dialogue with himself about the relative advantages of the first or third person point of view.... 'Think over the possibility of a first-person narrative. Many advantages; much freshness, the figure of the Youth would emerge more typical, nicer. I'll be able to cope better with the character, with the personality, with the essence of that personality.' On the other hand he realizes that in giving the point of view to the Youth he will not be able to express certain important thoughts and feelings of others." Judging by the standards set by his best novels, Dostoevsky's A Raw Youth is not successful. But the notebooks "are as much a preparation for The Brothers Karamazov as they are for A Raw Youth." Wasiolek provides photocopies of several pages of manuscript.

Du Maurier, Daphne. Myself When Young: The Shaping of a Writer. Garden City, N.Y.: Doubleday & Company, 1977.

Based on du Maurier's diaries for the years 1920-1932 (age 12 to age 24), this partial autobiography furnishes the background for much of her later writing; and the last section, "Apprenticeship," recounts the writing and publishing of her first novel, The Loving Spirit. A quotation from her diary describes her cutting this first book down to size. "No sentimentality about this job. I was ruthless, and crossed out passages that had given me exquisite pleasure to write. But it teaches me a hell of a lot, and does me no end of good for the future."

Duras, Marguerite. Hiroshima, Mon Amour. New York: Grove Press, 1961.

Included with the film script are Duras' interpretative synopsis of the film, her notes on sequences set in Nevers, called "Nocturnal Notations, " not included in the film, further notes on Nevers and the Frenchwoman, often speaking in her own voice, and on the Japanese lover. These notes suggest something of Duras' creative method, the conception and evolution of the work.

Ellison, Ralph. Shadow and Act. New York: Random House, 1953.

Ralph Ellison, author of the novel Invisible Man, is a conscious and articulate artist. "... these essays are a witness of that which I have known and that which I have tried and am still trying to confront ... they are an embodiment of a conscious attempt to confront, to peer into, the shadow of my past and to remind myself of the complex resources for imaginative creation which are my heritage. " In "That Same Pain, That Same Pleasure: An Interview, " Ellison quotes Richard Wright, who told him, "You have to go about learning to write consciously. People have talked about such and such a problem and have written about it. You must learn how Conrad, Joyce, Dostoevsky get their effects.... " SEE ALSO "The Art of Fiction: An Interview. "

Engle, Paul, ed. On Creative Writing. New York: E. P. Dutton, 1966.

Paul Engle: Criticism is "a constant part of the writer's job, beginning with his rejection of one concept in favor of another, one image, one phrase, rather than others. " Paul Engle opens with an essay on "The Writer on Writing. " R. V. Cassill writes about the short story, Jean Todd Freeman about the commercial short story, Brock Brower about the article, Donald Justice about poetry, George P. Elliott about the novel, Lionel Abel about the play. Each chapter is followed by several excerpts from works in each form, with commentary.

Engle, Paul, and Langland Joseph, eds. Poet's Choice. New York: Dell, 1962.

"When we invited one hundred living poets, " British and American, "to select a favorite or crucial poem from their own work and comment on it, we were not surprised... to find that they did so with fervor, insight and eloquence. Nor were we startled at the intensity of devotion to the craft of poetry expressed by many poets.... An almost endless working and reworking of words and lines is at least the partial lot of good poets, and many of them speak with an almost painful affection of the number of times they revised a favorite poem.... The one obsession that seems to persist with many is, indeed, hard work.... It is apparent that poets today are sharply and self-consciously aware of sources, purposes, and manners of their own work. They not only feel, they know. "

Gwynn, Frederick L., and Joseph L. Blotner, eds. Faulkner in the University: Class Conferences at the University of Virginia 1957-1958. Charlottesville: University of Virginia Press, 1959.

During thirty-seven group sessions, Faulkner "encouraged groups to ask questions about his writing... which resulted in his answering publicly over two thousand queries.... We have selected what seemed to us the most typical and significant questions and answers...." Session twenty-seven offers "A Word to the Young Writer." The index directs the reader to numerous comments on writing and on Faulkner's own works and the creative process that produced them.

Fitzgerald, F. Scott. The Crack-Up. Edited by Edmund Wilson. New York: New Directions-James Laughlin, 1945.

The volume consists of autobiographical essays, of which "The Crack-up" is major, and notebooks and letters that reveal Fitzgerald's struggles, psychological and technical, as a writer. The notebook entries, says Edmund Wilson, "make ... extremely good reading ... they really ought to be read with Tender Is the Night, The Last Tycoon, and the pieces in the first part of this volume for their record of the final phases of the milieux in which Fitzgerald lived and of his sensations, emotions and ideas in the last years before his death."

Ford, Ford Madox. Joseph Conrad: A Personal Remembrance. London: Duckworth, 1924.

Sinclair Lewis called this "the one great book on the technique of writing a novel that I have ever read."

Frenz, Horst, ed. American Playwrights on Drama. New York: Hill and Wang, 1965.

"... this is the only collection of essays by twentieth-century American playwrights." They are Eugene O'Neill, Maxwell Anderson, John Howard Lawson, Thornton Wilder, Tennessee Williams, Paul Green, Arthur Miller, William Inge, Robinson Jeffers, S. N. Behrman, Archibald MacLeish, Elmer Rice, Lorraine Hansberry, Edward Albee. "Producers, directors, actors, and even the audiences help to create the final versions" of American plays. "The changes that make a play usable for the stage are incorporated in the text" that is published. "The American drama could almost be called a by-product of the stage. Hence the curious--at times perhaps even healthy--fusion of practical with literary matters.... The essays in this collection attempt to cope with almost every complex question that could be raised in connection with the drama and theater of the United States. If nothing else, all of them tell us a great deal about the author as a playwright and a human being."

Froug, William, ed. The Screenwriter Looks at the Screenwriter. New York: Macmillan, 1972.

Twelve screenwriters talk about their craft, their techniques, and their role in shaping a film. Lewis John Carlin, William Bowers, Walter Brown Newman, Jonathan Axelrod, Ring Lardner, Jr., I. A. L. Diamond, Buck Henry, David Giler, Nunnally Johnson, Edward Anhalt, Stirling Silliphant, Fay Kanin. Screen credits are given for each writer, and pages of revised manuscripts for The Fox, M. A. S. H., Catch 22, and others are given. The editor is himself a writer-producer of twenty years' experience.

Gardner, Dorothy, and Kathrine Sorley Walker, eds. Raymond Chandler Speaking. Cambridge, Mass.: Houghton Mifflin, 1962.

In letters and articles, Raymond Chandler, the best-selling tough-guy mystery writer, talks about himself, the mystery novel, the craft of writing, films and television, publishing, and famous crimes; and of specific interest are comments on his own novels and short stories and his famous character, Marlowe. Several pieces of fiction found among his papers are published here for the first time.

Ghiselin, Brewster, ed. The Creative Process. Berkeley: University of California Press, 1952.

Thirty-eight artists, writers, composers, scientists, dancers, philosophers, and psychiatrists comment in letters, essays, etc., on the creative process, with a very good introduction by the editor. The poets and fiction writers are: D. H. Lawrence, John Dryden, William Wordsworth, Jean Cocteau, Samuel Taylor Coleridge, A. E. Housman, Paul Valéry, William Butler Yeats, Amy Lowell, Stephen Spender, Brewster Ghiselin, Allen Tate, Henry James, Rudyard Kipling, Gertrude Stein, Dorothy Canfield, Llewellyn Powys, Henry Miller, Thomas Wolfe, Katherine Anne Porter.

Gibson, Walker, ed. Poems in the Making. Boston: Houghton Mifflin, 1963.

Walker Gibson offers several approaches to a study of "the making of poems": 1. Examination of various drafts and work sheets used by the poet: Keats' "the Eve of St. Agnes"; 2. The same approach, plus the poet's own later comments: Stephen Spender on "Seascape"; 3. An explanation by literary origins: John Livingston Lowes on Coleridge's "Kubla Khan"; 4. Unreliable testimony by a poet on his poem: Poe on "The Raven"; 5. "Disorder in the Making and Order in the Poem": three critics on Pope's "An Essay on Man"; 6. A critic-poet's warning about the study of the creative process: I. A. Richards. Each section is augmented by the comments of critics, in some cases poet-critics: Kenneth Burke, T. S. Eliot, Karl Shapiro. The book offers pro and con arguments on the usefulness of studying early versions of a work to aid in understanding the finished work. There is a further, more pertinent question: How does a study of the creative process facilitate an understanding of literature generally?

Gibson, William. The Seesaw Log, A Chronicle of the Stage Production, with the text of "Two for the Seesaw." New York: Alfred Knopf, Inc., 1959.

The Seesaw Log is a 112-page account of the trials and tribulations of a playwright (The Miracle Worker) and novelist (The Cobweb) as he sees his play go from conception to dubious success (1953-1958). Gibson tells little about the writing and pre-production revisions of the play; rather, he stresses changes forced upon him by the collaborative nature and economic entanglements of Broadway theater.

Gibson, William. Two for the Seesaw.

SEE The Seesaw Log, above.

Gide, André. The Journals of André Gide: 1889-1949. Edited and translated by Justin O'Brien. New York: Vintage Books, 1956. Volume I: 1889-1924. Volume II: 1924-1949.

"... love of truth is apparent from one end to the other of André Gide's monumental Journals. From the age of twenty in 1889 until the last entry of 1949 written in his eightieth year he carefully set down his reflections about men, ideas, events, and himself.... Originally begun as a literary exercise, the Journals little by little assumed more importance in his own eyes until ... they became almost an obsession.... To a growing number of readers the Journals appear as Gide's greatest and most enduring work ... whose very informality allows them to reproduce the Protean multivalence of their creator.... In the journals, we see Gide as naturalist, musician, teacher, individualist, moral philosopher, critic, and artist.... Frequently in these pages the author also discusses his stylistic problems. He tells why he purified his language of metaphors in his first book and then longed for an even poorer, nuder style, for which he sought inspiration in Stendhal. Later, he confesses his desire to achieve inimitability by dint of the secret perfection of his sentences. On the other hand, he often sees the Journals themselves as an exercise in spontaneous and rapid composition...."

Graham, John, interviewer, and George Garrett, ed. Craft So Hard to Learn. New York: William Morrow, 1972.

This condensed version of The Writer's Voice focuses on "the teaching of writing." James Whitehead: "A writer is a performer. He is performing in the language and he is trying to predict his effects, to a great extent, on his audience. I don't mean he calculates this during a first draft, or necessarily becomes highly conscious of this in a second draft. But at some point or another he becomes aware of his audience, and begins to calculate effects to one extent or another."

Graham, John, interviewer, and George Garrett, ed. The Writer's Voice: Conversations with Contemporary Writers. New York: William Morrow, 1973.

In June of 1970, nineteen poets and fiction and nonfiction writers met with 268 students from 48 states to talk about writing, their own and the students'. John Graham of the University of Virginia taped interviews with them for his radio show, The Scholar's Bookshelf. Novelist-poet George Garrett edited those interviews, supplied biographical sketches and impressionistic "snapshots" of each of the writers; he also wrote the preface. The writers are: R. V. Cassill, William Peden, Margaret Sayers Peden, Brian Moore, Richard Wilbur, Shelby Foote, Henry Taylor, Michael Mewshaw, William Manchester, James Seay, James Whitehead, Sylvia Wilkinson, Jonathan Baumbach, Ralph Ellison, James Dickey, David Slavitt, William Harrison, R. H. W. Dillard.

Graham, Sheilah. College of One. New York: Viking, 1967.

Graham offers a photo copy of her 25-page "fictional account" of her "meeting and falling in love with F. Scott Fitzgerald." "I had titled it Beloved Infidel after his poem to me." The piece is interesting because of Fitzgerald's "severe editing."

Gundell, Glenn, ed. Writing--From Idea to Printed Page: Case Histories of Stories and Articles Published in The Saturday Evening Post. New York: Doubleday & Company, Inc., 1949.

Gundell, advertising and promotion manager of the Post, describes the book as "merely a record of how individual writers and an artist went about creating an acceptable product. It is a reporting job with no attempt to pass judgment on whether 'this is good' or 'that is bad'." In the preface, Frank Luther Mott, an expert on the history and workings of magazines, says, "In the fall of 1944 the School of Journalism at the University of Missouri experimented with the use of The Saturday Evening Post in connection with certain of its courses." Gundell offered to open up Post techniques and lay them "before students of journalism in understandable form." A portfolio method was designed, offering "exhibits designed to show the building and processing of an article from idea to publication...." Eventually, 800 colleges and universities used the Post's Case Histories in their classrooms. This book is an attempt to make them more available. "It is an educational aid of the highest value," says Mott. "It is living, breathing stuff. It shows the student how good, effective writing gets that way. It will not suit the 'art for art's sake' writers...." It is "the most practical commentary on the method and technique of magazine writing ever published.... Perhaps the author and editor are collaborators to a larger degree than most of us realize. For the young writer, the book is the next best thing to internship." The case histories, "in their clear, comprehensive and intimate use of the case method ... introduce a new and exciting technique in education for writing." The book offers three fact-writing case histories, two fiction writing case histories and a fiction-illustration case history.

Hall, Donald, ed. The Modern Stylists: Writers on the Art of Writing. New York: The Free Press, 1968.

Poet Donald Hall has gathered short essays, augmented by paragraph-length selections, in which contemporary fiction writers and poets talk about style: James Thurber, Robert Graves, George Orwell, Ernest Hemingway, William Carlos Williams, Virginia Woolf, Robert Frost, Edmund Wilson, E. B. White, Katherine Anne Porter, Marianne Moore, Georges Simenon, Mary McCarthy, Truman Capote, Gertrude Stein, Herbert Read, and several non-fiction writers. Hemingway: "Prose is architecture, not interior decoration, and the Baroque is over."

Helterman, Jeffrey, and Richard Layman. Dictionary of Literary Biography, Volume Two: American Novelists Since World War II. Detroit: Gale Research, 1978.

Most entries include one page of manuscript, photocopy.

Hemingway, Ernest. A Moveable Feast, Sketches of the Author's Life in Paris in the Twenties. New York: Scribner's, 1964.

This account concerns the years 1921 to 1926 when Hemingway wrote the short stories that gave a new dimension to the form and one of his best novels, The Sun Also Rises. He tells of the circumstances in which he wrote and of his writing and rewriting habits. "It was in that room too that I learned not to think about anything that I was writing from the time I stopped writing until I started again the next day. That way my subconscious would be working on it and at the same time I would be listening to other people and noticing everything, I hoped; learning, I hoped; and I would read so that I would not think about my work and make myself impotent doing it.... I was learning something from the painting of Cézanne that made writing simple true sentences far from enough to make the stories have the dimensions that I was trying to put in them." SEE The Nick Adams Stories.

Hersey, John, ed. The Writer's Craft. New York: Alfred A. Knopf, 1974.

Poets and fiction writers write about writing under Hersey's seven general headings: "The Aim of Art," "The Whole Intricate Question of Method," "Words Have to Do Everything," "Writing and Survival," "The Writing Process," "The Writer's Life," "The Writing Itself." A selected bibliography is included. The writers are: Conrad, James, Tolstoy, Faulkner, Flannery O'Connor, Percy Lubbock, E. M. Forster, Elizabeth Bowen, Robbe-Grillet, Gertrude Stein, Orwell, Grass, Solzhenitsyn, Coleridge, Poe, Housman, Kipling, Gorky, Sartre, Cummings, Pasternak, Trollope, Auden, Ellison, Bellow, Burroughs, Flaubert, Mailer, Mann, Woolf, Thomas Wolfe, John Fowles. Elizabeth Bowen: "Much irrelevance is introduced into novels by the writer's vague hope that at least some of this may turn out to be relevant, after all. A good deal of what might be called provisional writing goes to the first drafts of first chapters of most novels. At a point in the novel's progress, relevance becomes clearer. The provisional chapters are then recast .... To direct ... an author's attention to the imperative of relevance is certainly the most useful--and possibly the only--help that can be given."

Heyen, William. American Poets in 1976. Indianapolis: Bobbs-Merrill, 1976.

"American Poets in 1976 represents twenty-nine contemporaries writing on their own lives and work, on their art and on the people and landscapes that have entered their poems." The poets are: Robert Bly, John Malcolm Brinnin, Robert Creeley, John Haines, John Haislip, William Heyen, Richard Hugo, David Ignatow, John Logan, William Matthews, Jerome Mazarro, William Meredith, Joyce Carol Oates, Linda Pastan, Raymond R. Patterson, John Peck, Stanley Plumly, Ishmael Reed, Adrienne Rich, M. L. Rosenthal, Anne Sexton, Louis Simpson, Dave Smith, William Stafford, Primus St. John, Lucien Stryk, Lewis Turco, James Wright, Paul Zimmer.

Hicks, Granville, ed. The Living Novel: A Symposium. New York: Collier, 1962.

At Hicks' request, Saul Bellow, Paul Darcy Boles, John Brooks, Ralph Ellison, Herbert Gold, Mark Harris, Wright Morris, Flannery O'Connor, Harvey Swados, and Jessamyn West offer "their reflections on some of the problems of the novelist and of the novel.... All of them are passionately concerned with the craft of fiction.... They are likely to talk ... about how a writer feels when he is writing rather than about what he does." Saul Bellow: "There are critics who assume that you must begin with order if you are to end with it. Not so. A novelist begins with disorder and disharmony, and he goes toward order by an unknown process of the imagination."

Hildick, Wallace. Thirteen Types of Narrative. New York: Clarkson N. Potter, 1970.

Novelist Hildick discusses and gives numerous excellent examples of thirteen point-of-view techniques. His study is short, simple, clever, witty, and very useful for students, teachers, and writers.

Hills, Rust, ed. Writer's Choice. New York: David McKay, 1974.

Twenty American writers choose and introduce briefly what each considers to be his/her best story: John Barth, Donald Barthelme, Hortense Calisher, Truman Capote, R. V. Cassill, Evan S. Connell, Jr., Stanley Elkin, George P. Elliott, Bruce Jay Friedman, Herbert Gold, James Jones, Norman Mailer, Reynolds Price, James Purdy, Philip Roth, Terry Southern, John Updike, Thomas Williams, Richard Yates. "What I am interested in," says Barthelme, "is the ugly sentence that is also somehow beautiful." And Elkin says about his story that "in writing it, I discovered my style.... I recall tinkering with the first paragraph of that story for more than a week, remember a dozen variants...." SEE ALSO Burnett, This Is My Best.

Horgan, Paul. Approaches to Writing. New York: Farrar, Straus and Giroux, 1974.

Novelist Horgan's "reflections and notes on the art of writing," are derived from a career of half a century. Part One: Talking Shop; Part Two: Notebook Pages: I Process, II Of the Mode, III Glimpses of the Actual, IV Behind the Word; Part Three: Memories of an Apprentice. A kind of practical guide to writing emerges from the book. He believes in a "sustained study in every approach" to the art of writing. "... revision word by word and sentence does follow, for me, not once, but many times, each for a different value."

Housman, A. E., "The Immortal Part."

SEE Brooks and Warren, Understanding Poetry.

Housman, A. E. The Name and Nature of Poetry. New York: The Macmillan Company, 1933.

The Leslie Stephen lecture was delivered at Cambridge, England, 9 May 1933. "I cannot satisfy myself that there are any such things as poetical ideas.... Poetry is not the thing said but a way of saying it.... Meaning is of the intellect, poetry is not... Poetry indeed seems to me more physical than intellectual." Poetry belongs to the class of "natural secretions," often morbid, "like the pearl in the oyster." Housman then gives a brief account of the writing of one of his own poems.

Housman, A. E., "To an Athlete Dying Young."
SEE Brooks and Warren, Understanding Poetry.

Hull, Helen, ed. The Writer's Book. New York: Harper, 1950 (1956).

Hull offers "practical advice by experts in every field of writing." Pearl Buck, Thomas Mann, John Hersey, Arthur Koestler, James A. Michener, Paul Gallico, Frederick Lewis Allen, Babette Deutsch, Ira Wolfert, Ann Petry, Rex Stout, Faith Baldwin, W. H. Auden, Niven Busch, and many non-fiction writers. Forty pieces are included, 28 written expressly for this volume.

Ibsen, Henrik. "Notes For A Doll's House and Ghosts," The Collected Works of Henrik Ibsen. Vol. 12 (From Ibsen's Workshop). Translated by A. G. Chater. New York: Charles Scribner's Sons, 1913, pp. 91-95; 185-190.

"The play [Ghosts] is to be like a picture of life. Belief undermined. But it does not do to say so." However, Ibsen's focus in these notes is plot and the meaning or implications of the plot.

James, Henry. Partial Portraits. New introduction by Leon Edel. Ann Arbor: The University of Michigan Press, 1970 (first published 1888).

The famous essay, "The Art of Fiction," is included, as are essays on George Eliot, Anthony Trollope, Robert Louis Stevenson, Alphonse Daudet, Guy de Maupassant, and Ivan Turgenieff. Edel says of "The Art of Fiction" that it "remains the most significant statement ever made by a working novelist about his art ... he was little aware at the time that he was writing a veritable manifesto on behalf of his art." "... impressions are experience.... 'Try to be one of the people on whom nothing is lost!'" "Of course it is of execution that we are talking--that being the only point of a novel that is open to contention.... We must grant the artist his subject, his idea, his donnée: our criticism is applied only to what he makes of it." "We are discussing the Art of Fiction; questions of art are questions ... of execution; questions of morality are quite another affair...." "Remember that your first duty is to be as complete as possible--to make as perfect a work."

James, Henry. The Art of the Novel, Critical Prefaces. With an introduction by Richard P. Blackmur. New York: Charles Scribner's Sons, 1934 (1962).

"These notes," said James, "represent, over a considerable course, the continuity of an artist's endeavor...." Blackmur summarizes the character of the book: "In short, James felt that his Prefaces represented or demonstrated an artist's consciousness and the character of his work in some detail, made an essay in general criticism which had an interest and a being aside from any connection with his own work, and that finally, they added up to a fairly exhaustive reference book on the technical aspects of the art of fiction." In these prefaces, James tried to "remount" "the stream of composition," "to make an ex post facto dissection, not that we may embalm the itemized mortal remains, but that we may intellectually understand the movement of parts and the relation between them in the living body we appreciate." Blackmur sees five connected subject areas: "The Relation of Art and the Artist. The Relation of Art and Life. Art, Life, and the Ideal. Art and Morals. Art as Salvation for its Characters." He breaks these down further in his long introduction into numerous other categories and directs the reader to those prefaces in which James makes comments in those categories about his own work. James notes "the author's instinct everywhere for the indirect presentation of his main image. I note how, again and again, I go but a little way with the direct," but rather he approaches his main character, Milly, for instance, in The Wings of the Dove, "through the successive windows of other people's interest in her."

Janeway, Elizabeth, ed. The Writer's World. New York: McGraw-Hill, 1969.

"A series of panel discussions sponsored by The Authors Guild, Inc. and given at The New School in New York City in 1965 and 1966 by writers on writing," in many genres. Fiction: Louis Auchincloss, Joseph Heller, Wallace Markfield, John Cheever, Shirley Hazzard, Harry Mark Petrakis, Elizabeth Janeway, Peter S. Feibleman, Isaac Bashevis Singer, Sol Yurick, Glenway Wescott, William Styron, Robert Penn Warren. Poetry: Robert Graves, Marianne Moore, Howard Nemerov, Stanley Kunitz, Susan Sontag, Uwe Johnson. "This is a book of conversations--of writers, talking to writers about their work.... A great deal that is taught in sensible creative writing courses is implicit in these conversations, and sometimes explicit: Heller, for instance, on beginning a novel." Other genres are represented.

Jarrell, Randall, "The Woman at the Washington Zoo."

SEE Brooks and Warren, Understanding Poetry, Part II.

Kilmer, Joyce, ed. Literature in the Making, By Some of Its Masters. New York: Harper and Brothers, 1917.

"This book," says poet Joyce Kilmer, in his brief introduction, "is an effort to bridge the gulf between literary theory and literary practice." These essays grew out of Kilmer's interviews with William Dean Howells, Kathleen Norris, Booth Tarkington, Rex Beach, Robert Herrick, Arthur Guiterman, John Erskine, Amy Lowell, Fannie Hurst, Ellen Glasgow, Edwin Arlington Robinson, Percy MacKaye (poets, fiction writers, playwrights), plus 11 other writers who were his contemporaries but whose reputations have not survived. These writers explain "their literary creeds and practices." Arthur Guiterman offers "Sixteen Don'ts for Poets," a few of which are: "Don't write poems about unborn babies," "Don't--don't write hymns to the great god Pan. He is dead; let him rest in peace!"

Kuehl, John, ed. Creative Writing and Rewriting: Contemporary American Novelists at Work. New York: Appleton-Century-Crofts, 1967.

Comparisons are made of drafts on facing pages of ten works

of fiction--short stories and novels. The book is designed for creative writing classes but the author argues well for its use in literature classes as well because "A comparison of drafts ... derives meaning by uncovering some of the author's intentions." There are other good reasons, argued by this bibliography, as well. The pieces are Eudora Welty's "Where Is the Voice Coming From?"; Kay Boyle's "The Ballet of Central Park"; James Jones's novella The Pistol; Bernard Malamud's "Idiot's First"; Wright Morris' One Day; F. Scott Fitzgerald's The Great Gatsby; Philip Roth's Letting Go; Robert Penn Warren's All the King's Men (the poetic play version, Proud Flesh, is compared with the novel); John Hawkes's "The Nearest Cemetery," worked into his novel Second Skin; William Styron's The Long March, a facsimile of a draft. Problems demonstrated are in the areas of language, characterization, structure, setting, symbolism, narrative focus. The editor provides biographical-bibliographical information and commentary on each piece, often quoting the author's own comments. The finest book of its kind.

Lewis, Sinclair. The Man from Main Street: Selected Essays and Other Writings 1904-1950. Edited by Harry E. Moule and Melville H. Cane. New York: Random House, 1953.

See Part V, pp. 187-232, "Problems of the Craft." Included are "No Flight to Olympus," "A Letter on Style," "My Maiden Effort," "Rambling Thoughts on Literature as a Business," "How I Wrote a Novel on Trains and Beside the Kitchen Sink," "Obscenity and Obscurity," "Introduction to Main Street," "Introduction to Selected Short Stories," "The Art of Dramatic Action," "Novelist Bites Art." Other parts are called, "Declarations," "S. L. Remembers," "Early Writings," "Literary Views," "People and Events," "Places on the Journey," "Social Questions." Two pages from a notebook never before published and the outline for Babbitt are included. The editors were Lewis's friends.

McCormack, Thomas, ed. Afterwords: Novelists on Their Novels. New York: Harper & Row, 1969.

Fourteen novelists offer "after-the-fact prefaces." The editor invited each to "take one of your novels ... and write about it; give a sort of craftsman's journal, a report describing the campaign of the book--how it began, what it looked like to you at various stages, what problems came up and what solutions you devised, how explicit were the considerations of craft we think we see--in other words, what was going on when you worked." The value the editor sees for the book is for general readers, creative writers, and students who wish to gain greater insight into the works discussed. These pieces offer "news from the inside," "technical tips," better understanding of "what the writers were after and what they actually did," and "some good stories about stories." Louis Auchincloss writes about The Rector of Justin; Wright Morris about One Day; Anthony Burgess, Nothing Like the Sun; Robert Crichton, The Secret of Santa Vittoria; Mark Harris, Trumpet to the World; Mary Renault, The King Must Die; William Gass, Omensetter's Luck; Reynolds Price, A Generous Man; George P. Elliott, Among the Dangs; Truman Capote, Other Voices, Other Rooms; Ross Macdonald, The Galton Case;

John Fowles, The French Lieutenant's Woman; Vance Bourjaily, Confessions of a Spent Youth; Norman Mailer, The Deer Park. John Fowles: "During the revision period I try to keep some sort of discipline. I make myself revise whether I like it or not; in some ways, the more disciplined and dyspeptic one feels, the better--one is harsher with oneself. All the best cutting is done when one is sick of the writing."

McCullers, Carson. The Mortgaged Heart. Edited by Margarita G. Smith. Boston: Houghton Mifflin Company, 1971.

A large selection of McCullers' unpublished work, from age seventeen to posthumously published work, short stories, essays and poetry, including eight stories never before published. The selections were chosen, says the editor, McCullers' sister, "to illuminate in part the creative process and development of Carson McCullers ... to give some idea of the early work of a writer and to illustrate, within the range of material chosen from her least-known work, the development of that talent." Of special interest is the author's outline of "The Mute" (The Heart Is a Lonely Hunter). "This book is planned according to a definite and balanced design. The form is contrapuntal throughout.... There are five distinct styles of writing --one for each of the main characters who is treated subjectively and an objective, legendary style for the mute.... This book will be complete in all its phases. No loose ends will be left dangling and at the close there will be a feeling of balanced completion." See also "How I Began to Write" and "The Flowering Dream: Notes on Writing." "The dimensions of a work of art are seldom realized by the author until the work is accomplished. It is like a flowering dream. Ideas grow, budding silently, and there are a thousand illuminations coming day by day as the work progresses."

Madden, Charles, ed. Talks with Authors. Carbondale: Southern Illinois University Press, 1968.

These are transcripts of conversations with writers by telephone; students and teachers in classes at three different colleges asked questions of each writer about the techniques of writing, the search for identity, religious themes, the theme of initiation, and the comic element in their works. The writers interviewed are John Dos Passos, James T. Farrell, Karl Shapiro, Muriel Rukeyser, Anne Sexton, Richard Wilbur, Vance Bourjaily, Kay Boyle. Horace Gregory talks about Sherwood Anderson, Arthur Mizener about F. Scott Fitzgerald, Carvel Collins about William Faulkner, Warren Beck about John Steinbeck, Carlos Baker about Ernest Hemingway. Ms. Sexton: "I'll tell you exactly why I did it this way...."

Madden, David. "Cassandra Singing--On and Off Key," in The Poetic Image in Six Genres. Carbondale: Southern Illinois University Press, 1969, pp. 174-196.

An account of the origin and revisions of Cassandra Singing as a one-act play and a three-act play, as a short story, and as a novel, from 1954-1967, is related to other work written during that period, and to autobiographical elements. "Since I have dealt with the same raw material in two radically different forms and over such a long stretch of time, I think my experience, though possibly unique, may offer exaggerated illustrations of certain creative problems which every writer encounters."

Madden, David. "Cassandra Singing, Novel, Play, Movie," Contemporary Literary Scene. Englewood Cliffs, N. J.: Salem Press, 1979, pp. 181-193.

This article is an expansion into a discussion of revisions of the movie version of an earlier article, "Cassandra Singing--On and Off Key." "Novelistic preoccupations and freedoms allowed by the novel medium spawned problems in the play, and the play versions spawned problems for the novel. Problems in the play and the novel versions obstructed progress with the screenplay, too, but with the play and the novel finally finished, I devoted my attention completely to characteristics of the nature of the film medium. Using the same characters, theme, and story in two different media--play and novel--working on them simultaneously, I learned about the one while working in the other; and while working in the film medium, I learned about drama and fiction as media."

Madden, David, ed. Creative Choices. Glenview, Ill.: Scott, Foresman, 1975.

Madden's "The Day the Flowers Came" is included with the author's notes discussing revisions printed in the margin. Also included in the margins are revised passages, with the early version crossed out in the text of the story. In a prologue and an epilogue Madden discusses the origin and publishing history of the story and more general technical problems in the writing and revising of the story. "My choice of point of view determined the special quality of the experience I tried to subject you to. The effective use of point of view makes a greater demand on a writer's skills than any other technique."

Madden, David. "Introduction," in The Poetic Image in Six Genres. Carbondale: Southern Illinois University Press, 1969, pp. xi-xxx.

A partial account of Madden's writing career (from 1956 to 1969) discusses the influence of the mountain oral tradition of story telling, the movies, radio, popular literature, serious literature, people and places, and the origin and revision of several works, especially the short story, "The Singer" (reprinted in the book), relating those elements to his essays on the short story, the novel, poetry, film, theater, and autobiography collected in the volume. "Looking back, I see that my own compulsion to tell a story, on one or another level of sophistication, has always, consciously and unconsciously, reached out to explore every possible medium in which to express what has always been a rich and abundant raw material. Each medium and genre had its own special attraction, offered its peculiar way into the relationship between teller and listener. My reactions since childhood to movies, radio, magazines, books, and theater, purely as media, explain my experiences as a writer."

Madden, David. "Performing 'The Singer'," Dramatics, 50 (September-October 1978): 22-32.

Madden discusses the influence upon his work, especially "The Singer," of the oral tradition of story telling in the Southern Appalachians and the genesis, composition, and revision of the story (which is reprinted in the same issue of Dramatics). He also discusses his technique in giving dramatic readings of this story. "I want to stress that the technical inspiration was just as crucial as the real-life inspirations: the singer and the landscape. Most of the story's effects can be traced to the technical solution: the use of film images and of the two voices (with no authorial intrusion to describe the church setting or the characters). The movies show images and the living voices of the story-tellers evoke images.

Madden, David. "No Trace," Studies in the Short Story. Virgil Scott and David Madden, eds. 5th edition. New York: Holt, Rinehart, and Winston, 1980, pp. 282-310.

David Madden gives details of his revisions of this story in an accompanying essay. Also included are two sets of notes for the first two drafts. "One way to study the nature of fiction is to analyze the creative process itself. If in one story students can see instances in which the author made a series of choices--effective or inept, ranging over every element of fiction--in various drafts, if they can see relationships between the way it was done and the finished work, they may understand better how those elements function in other fiction.... Drawing on criticisms of the four editors who had rejected the story, I wrote draft four ... and ... draft five.... Most of the revisions of my fiction deal with style."

Mailer, Norman. Advertisements for Myself. New York: G. P. Putnam's Sons, 1959.

There is nothing in the history of American literature that can quite compare with this book, a miscellany with two tables of contents: "Beginnings," "Middles," "Births," "Hipsters," "Games and Ends" is the first. The second is "Fiction," "Essays and Articles," "Journalism," "Interviews," "Poetry," "Plays," "Biography of a Style." The pieces on the conception, writing, rewriting, and publishing perils of The Deer Park are especially interesting. The book is a multi-faceted self-portrait of a famous, public writer in mid-career. "If I wanted to improve my novel, yet keep the style, I would have to make my narrator fit the prose, change his past, make him an onlooker.... If, however, I wanted to keep that first narrator-- ... well to keep him I would need to change the style from the inside of each sentence.... I never enjoyed work so much."

Mann, Thomas. "The Making of The Magic Mountain," in The Magic Mountain. New York: Alfred A. Knopf, 1961.

Published first in the Atlantic in 1953, this is a 10-page essay. Conceived as a short story, the novel became monumental. Just as the writer rewrites, Mann suggests his reader re-read the novel, as one listens again to music. "To me the novel was always like a symphony, a work in counterpoint, a thematic fabric; the idea of the musical motif plays a great role in it."

Mansfield, Katherine. Journal of Katherine Mansfield. Edited, with an introduction and notes by John Middleton Murry. New York: Alfred A. Knopf, 1927.

The time-span of the Journal is February 1914 to October 1922 (three months before her death). "The ... material of which the Journal is composed is of various kinds--brief (and sometimes difficult) notes for stories, fragments of diaries, unposted letters, comments and confessions scattered throughout her manuscripts." "Wrote The Dove's Nest this afternoon. I was in no mood to write; it seemed impossible. Yet when I had finished three pages, they were all right. This is proof (never to be too often proved) that once one has thought out a story nothing remains but the labour."

Mansfield, Katherine. The Scrapbook of Katherine Mansfield. Edited by J. Middleton Murry. New York: Alfred A. Knopf, 1940.

These previously unpublished fragments are arranged in chronological order. "When the full tide of inspiration came, she wrote till she dropped with fatigue--sometimes all through the night, in defiance of her illness." A valuable companion to her letters, her Journal, and her collected stories.

Martz, William J. The Distinctive Voice. Glenview, Ill.: Scott, Foresman, 1966.

Some of these 40 modern poets give very brief comments on their own poetry or the creative process in general, with focus on "voice." Richard Wilbur: "The 'poet's voice' is the natural voice of the man who is writing the poem, but it is that voice moved to attempt its maximum range. It is that natural voice trying to invent a version of itself in which all of the man's selves, worlds, and tongues may speak at once, and clearly, and without apparent strain."

Maugham, W. Somerset. The Summing Up. New York: Doubleday, 1938.

"In this book I am going to try to sort out my thoughts on the subjects that have chiefly interested me during the course of my life." One of those subjects is the creative process, and Maugham's comments are practical and lucid. "It seemed to me that I must aim at lucidity, simplicity, and euphony." Maugham has variously been called "competent" or a "masterly writer." SEE A Writer's Notebook.

Maugham, W. Somerset. A Writer's Notebook. New York: Doubleday and Company, Inc., 1949.

The time-span is from 1892, when Maugham was 18, to 1949, when he was 75. In 1944, he added a postscript, and in 1949 another. "I never made a note of anything that I did not think would be useful to me at one time or another in my work, and though, especially in the early notebooks, I jotted down all kinds of thoughts and emotions of a personal nature, it was only with the intention of ascribing them sooner or later to the creatures of my invention. I meant my notebooks to be a storehouse of materials for future use and nothing else.... I publish it because I am interested in the technique of literary production and in the process of creation, and if such a volume as this by some other author came into my hands I would turn to it with avidity. By some happy chance what interests me seems to interest a great many other people." SEE The Summing Up.

Moynihan, William T., Donald W. Lee, and Herbert Weil, Jr., eds. Reading, Writing and Rewriting. Philadelphia, New York: J. B. Lippincott Company, 1964.

A freshman English college textbook, unusual in its emphasis on re-writing. Consult table of contents and index. Four checklists for rewriting are included. Two versions of essays by Francis Bacon and three contemporary non-fiction writers, "Design," a poem by Robert Frost, and four student themes are provided. "Three closely related and practical assumptions underline this book. Effective writing most frequently stems from intelligent reading. Effective writing also presumes informed self-criticism. And informed self-criticism is best put into practice by learning how to rewrite."

Meredith, Robert C., and John D. Fitzgerald. Structuring Your Novel: From Basic Idea to Finished Manuscript. New York: Harper & Row, 1972.

This is a typical how-to-do-it manual, a guide for beginning novelists. Examples drawn from classic and contemporary novels. Consult index for advice on revision. Some problems that prompt rewriting are faulty exposition, scene drags, motivation weak, prose awkward, chapter rambles, dialogue stiff, poor transition, narrative where action is required.

Miller, Henry. Henry Miller on Writing. Selected by Thomas H. Moore, from the Published and Unpublished Works. Norfolk, Conn.: New Directions Books, 1964.

I. "The 'Literary' Writer"--"Miller's struggles to perfect his style by imitating various writers he admired" (1917-1927). II. "Finding His Own Voice"--"a record of his successful search within himself for his own way of writing" (1930 to the present). III. "The Author at Work"--"methods Henry Miller used in preparing his books." IV. "Writing and Obscenity"--"on obscenity and its relation to his own idea of the artist as writer." Miller helped in making the final selection of the passages. "Concentrate. Narrow down. Exclude." "Work according to Program and not according to mood. Stop at the appointed time!"

Mirrielees, Edith Ronald. Story Writing. Preface by John Steinbeck. New York: The Viking Press, 1939; 1962, revised.

A sensible, balanced, witty, long-respected introduction to the art of the short story. See especially IX "Verbal Revision," p. 191. "More often than not, sentences made by an inexpert hand are overloaded with clauses as well as modifiers." "Three fourths of verbal revision is elimination...." John Steinbeck, one of her early students, praises her.

Morris, Wright. About Fiction: Reverent Reflections on the Nature of Fiction, with Irreverent Observations on Writers, Readers, and other Abuses. New York: Harper & Row, 1975.

"The writer learns to write, the reader learns to read." "It seems the writer's intent is to involve the reader not merely in the reading, but in the writing...." "What we choose to call 'style' is the presence in the fiction of the power to choose and mold its reader." This book does not deal directly with Morris's own work, but when he speaks of writing in general and of other writers, Morris, more than most other writers, provides the reader with perspectives on his own work and on the creative process that produces it. The first two chapters of Morris's The Territory Ahead are also helpful.

Morris, Wright. Earthly Delights, Unearthly Adornments: American Writers as Image Makers. New York: Harper & Row, 1978.

Morris opens with "Of Memory, Emotion and Imagination," and continues with brief essays on Melville, Whitman, Twain, James, Crane, Cather, Stein, Sherwood Anderson, Lardner, Eliot, Katherine Anne Porter, Fitzgerald, Dos Passos, Faulkner, Hemingway, Richard Wright, James Agee, Carson McCullers, focussing on a few quoted passages to reveal the image-making power of each author's style. Morris looks at his own work in "Origins: The Self-Imaged Image Maker," and at the paintings of Hieronymous Bosch in the final essay. Morris speaks often in the first person and recounts personal experiences that relate to the authors and passages he discusses. About Stein's "The Good Anna," Morris writes, "The life is simple, the words are simple but the mind of the writer is complex." "First we make these images to see clearly: then we see clearly only what we have made. In my own case, over forty years of writing what I have observed and imagined has replaced and overlapped what I once remembered. The fictions have become the facts of my life." "The reader exclaims, 'What a memory you have!' But it is what escaped memory that stirred the writer to write." "To make an image that is adequate to his sensations, he will have to imagine more than he remembers, intuit more than he saw." The writer has at his "instant disposal the inexhaustible powers of light and darkness, the ceaseless, commonplace, bewildering interlacing of memory, emotion and imagination."

Nemerov, Howard. Journal of the Fictive Life. New Brunswick, N. J.: Rutgers University Press, 1965.

This is a strange, but witty, and somewhat unusual self-scrutiny by a writer suspended in fearful hesitation and dissatisfaction between the two genres in which he has already proven himself successful: fiction and poetry. The "fictive life" is one that deals with the creative process, and this journal is an account of complex and subtle psychological strivings. "That may be a reason, too, for its taking me so long between one fiction and the next; not 'having an idea,' but having ten or twenty ideas, and having to wait as patiently as possible for the relations among them to reveal themselves.... Much the same thing appears to happen in the course of these notes, when the mind, unable to bear the richness of consequence entailed upon one idea, forthwith produces another instead."

Nemerov, Howard. Poets on Poets. New York: Basic Books, 1965.
While Consultant in Poetry at the Library of Congress, Nemerov, a distinguished poet and writer of fiction, asked nineteen poets: 1) Do you see your work as having essentially changed in character or style since you began? 2) Is there, has there been, was there ever, a "revolution" in poetry... ? 3) Does the question whether the world has changed during this century preoccupy you in poetry? 4) What is the proper function of criticism? Poets generally ignore, evade, elude Nemerov's questions; some talk about the techniques of poetry. The poets are: Conrad Aiken, Marianne Moore, Richard Eberhart, J. V. Cunningham, Ben Belitt, Barbara Howes, John Brinnin, John Berryman, Jack Gilbert, Vassar Miller, Robert Duncan, May Swenson, Richard Wilbur, Gregory Corso, William Jay Smith, Reed Whittemore, Theodore Weiss, James Dickey, and Nemerov himself. "I discovered," says James Dickey, "that the simple declarative sentence, under certain circumstances and in certain contexts, had exactly the qualities I wanted my lines of poetry to have.... I liked poems which had a basis of narrative, that described an action.... I also discovered that I worked most fruitfully in cases in which there was no clear-cut distinction between what was actually happening and what was happening in the mind of a character in the poem."

Nin, Anaïs. The Novel of the Future. New York: Macmillan, 1968.
"The purpose of this book is to study the development and techniques of the poetic novel.... To analyze and observe the process of creation I have had to use my own work simply because here I know the steps, and the gradual evolution, and by putting it under the microscope, can more clearly indicate the way to achieve such an integration." Chapter titles: "Proceed from the Dream Outward," "Abstraction," "Writing Fiction," "Genesis," "Genesis of the Diary," "Diary versus Fiction," "The Novel of the Future." "Spontaneity belongs in the first jet of writing, but some disciplined selectivity and cutting should follow in editing."

O'Connor, Frank. The Lonely Voice. New York: The World Publishing Company, 1963. A special anthology edition: New York: Bantam Books, 1968.
See the "Epilogue," which precedes his own story "Guests of the Nation," which he revised, after it had been published and anthologized, before including it in his later collections. "... the rest is rereading and rewriting. The writer should never forget that he is also a reader, though a prejudiced one, and if he cannot read his own work a dozen times he can scarcely expect a reader to look at it twice. Likewise what bores him after the sixth reading is quite liable to bore a reader at the first, and what pleases him after the twelfth may please a reader at the second. Most of my stories have been rewritten a dozen times, a few of them fifty times."

O'Neill, Eugene. "Working Notes and Extracts from a Fragmentary Work Diary," in Theatre and Drama in the Making. Edited by John Gassner and Ralph G. Allen. Boston: Houghton Mifflin, 1964.
Notes on Mourning Becomes Electra. "Technique--for the

first draft use comparatively straight realism--this draft only for purpose of plot material into definite form--then lay aside for period and later decide how to go to final version--what departures necessary--whether to use masks, soliloquies, asides, etc.--"

Orwell, George. "Why I Write," in Decline of the English Murder. Harmondsworth, Middlesex, England: Penguin Books, 1965.

"Putting aside the need to earn a living, I think there are four motives for writing ... Sheer egoism ... Aesthetic enthusiasm ... Historical impulse ... Political purpose.... What I have most wanted to do throughout the past ten years is to make political writing into an art.... And looking back through my work, I see that it is invariably where I lacked a political purpose that I wrote lifeless books and was betrayed into purple passages, sentences without meaning, decorative adjectives and humbug generally."

Ostroff, Anthony. The Contemporary Poet as Artist and Critic. Boston: Little, Brown, 1964.

"The plan of this book may be simply explained: In each of our eight symposia, three distinguished poets write independent critiques of a recent poem by an important contemporary--who then write a commentary in response; the poem, the three critiques, and the author's comment together constitute the finished symposium ... the scheme introduces something new in literary criticism, first, in calling upon poets to perform the essential critical task; second, in calling upon the authors of the poems under consideration to comment directly on their own work and on criticism of it...." In "the dramatic interplay of ideas among the contributors ... we are granted considerable insight into the nature of poetry and the creative process itself...." "The participants all served at the editor's invitation." The poems discussed are "Love Calls Us to the Things of This World" by Richard Wilbur; "In a Dark Time" by Theodore Roethke; "Father and Son" by Stanley Kunitz; "Skunk Hour" by Robert Lowell; "Master's in the Garden Again" by John Crowe Ransom; "Am I My Neighbor's Keeper?" by Richard Eberhart; "A Change of Air" by W. H. Auden; selections from The Bourgeois Poet by Karl Shapiro.

Perkins, Maxwell. Editor to Author: The Letters of Maxwell Perkins. Selected and edited, with commentary and an introduction, by John Hall Wheelock. New York: Charles Scribner's Sons, 1950.

In these letters, arranged chronologically, to Thomas Wolfe (of special note), F. Scott Fitzgerald, Ernest Hemingway, Ring Lardner, Sherwood Anderson, James Jones, and many other American writers, Maxwell Perkins reveals the interaction between author and editor in all phases of publishing, including the revision process. He "comments upon specific elements or episodes in a manuscript or outlining detailed plans for its organization. They reveal an extraordinary insight, a wealth of creative criticism far beyond the range of the usual editorial routine. It is not surprising that many well-known authors welcomed suggestions so perceptive and, later, came to feel that these had played an important part in the final achievement. There were some who even went so far as to claim that whatever they knew about writing they had learned from Max." SEE Berg, Max Perkins.

Plimpton, George, ed. Writers at Work: The Paris Review Interviews, Third Series. Introduction by Alfred Kazin. New York: The Viking Press, 1968.

Poets, novelists, playwrights: William Carlos Williams, Blaise Cendrars, Jean Cocteau, Louis-Ferdinand Céline, Evelyn Waugh, Lillian Hellman, William Burroughs, Saul Bellow, Arthur Miller, James Jones, Norman Mailer, Allen Ginsberg, Edward Albee, Harold Pinter. Bio-bibliographical notes, with sample manuscript pages. Evelyn Waugh: "But look, I think that your questions are dealing too much with the creation of character and not enough with the technique of writing. I regard writing not as investigation of character, but as an exercise in the use of language, and with this I am obsessed."

Plimpton, George, ed. Writers at Work: The Paris Review Interviews, Fourth Series. Introduction by Wilfred Sheed. New York: The Viking Press, 1976.

Isak Dinesen, Conrad Aiken, Robert Graves, John Dos Passos, Vladimir Nabokov, Jorge Luis Borges, George Seferis, John Steinbeck, Christopher Isherwood, W. H. Auden, Eudora Welty, John Bergman, Anthony Burgess, Jack Kerouac, Anne Sexton, John Updike. Bio-bibliographical notes, with sample manuscript pages. Christopher Isherwood revises "a great deal. What I tend to do is not so much pick at a thing but sit down and rewrite it completely. Both for A Single Man and A Meeting by the River I wrote three entire drafts. After making notes on one draft I'd sit down and rewrite it again from the beginning. I've found that's much better than patching and amputating things. One has to rethink the thing completely." Isherwood's method is unusual.

Poe, Edgar Allan. "The Philosophy of Composition," in The Portable Poe. Edited by Philip Van Doren Stern. New York: Viking Press, Inc., 1945.

"I have often thought how interesting a magazine paper might be written by any author who would--that is to say who could--detail, step by step, the processes by which any one of his compositions attained its ultimate point of completion.... Most writers--poets in especial--prefer having it understood that they compose by a species of fine frenzy--an ecstatic intuition--and would positively shudder at letting the public take a peep behind the scenes, at the elaborate and vacillating crudities of thought--at the true purposes seized only at the last moment--at the innumerable glimpses of idea that arrived not at the maturity of full view--at the fully matured fancies discarded in despair as unmanageable--at the cautious selections and rejections--at the painful erasures and interpolations--in a word, at the wheels and pinions--the tackle for scene-shifting--the step-ladders and demon-traps--the cock's features, the red paint and the black patches, which in ninety-nine cases out of the hundred, constitute the properties of the literary histrio.... For my own part, I have neither sympathy with the repugnance alluded to, nor, at any time the least difficulty in recalling to mind the progressive steps of any of my compositions.... I select 'The Raven,' as most generally known. It is my design to render it manifest that no one point in its composition is referrable either to accident or intuition--that the work proceeded, step by step, to its completion with the precision and rigid consequence of a mathematical problem."

Porter, Katherine Anne. "'Noon Wine': the Sources."
SEE West, Reading the Short Story and Brooks and Warren, Understanding Fiction, Part II.

Porter, Katherine Anne. "Notes on Writing," New Directions 1940. New York: New Directions, 1940.
(1936) "Perhaps in time I shall learn to live more deeply and consistently in that undistracted center of being where the will does not intrude, and the sense of time passing is lost, or has no power over the imagination.... Now and again thousands of memories converge, harmonize, arrange themselves around a central idea in a coherent form, and I write a story.... I must know a story 'by heart' and I must write from memory."

Romains, Jules. The Death of A Nobody. New York: Alfred A. Knopf, 1911 (1944).
Romains discusses the conception (l'unanimisme), style (simple), technique (cinematic omniscience, ensembles, and simultaneities), and influence (upon other writers and upon his own 16-volume Men of Good Will) of his first novel.

Roth, Philip. Reading Myself and Others. New York: Farrar, Straus and Giroux, 1975.
"These twenty-three pieces were written sporadically over the last fifteen years, between the time my first book of fiction was published in 1959 and my eighth in 1974 ... they are largely the by-products of getting started as a novelist, and then of taking stock.... Together these pieces reveal to me a continuing preoccupation with the relationship between the written and the unwritten world." The book is divided into two parts, each chronological. Part I "consists mainly of interviews in which I describe what I think has generated my work, the means employed from book to book, and the models with which I associate my efforts...." Part II "is made up of selected articles and essays," on books, writers, fiction in general, world events, and on adaptations of his stories to the stage, and on Portnoy's Complaint.

Spender, Stephen. The Making of a Poem. New York: The Norton Library, W. W. Norton & Company, Inc., 1962.
Essays on poetry and fiction under the headings, "Contemporaries," "Romantics," and "Situation" (including "The Situation of the American Writer"). In "The Making of a Poem," Spender describes the genesis and rewriting of his own poem "Seascape," with subheadings: "Apology," "Concentration," "Inspiration," "Memory," "Faith," "Song." He gives seven versions of the same two lines.

Stein, Gertrude. Lectures in America. Boston: Beacon Press, 1957.

Essay titles: "What Is English Literature," "Pictures," "Plays," "The Gradual Making of the Making of Americans," "Portraits and Repetition," "Poetry and Grammar." "In The Making of Americans I tried it in a variety of ways. And my sentences grew longer and longer, my imaginary dependent clauses were constantly being dropped out, I struggled with relations between they and them and then, I began with a relation between tenses that sometimes almost seemed to do it. And I went on and then one day after I had written a thousand pages, this was in 1908, I just did not go on any more." "So now to come to the real question of punctuation, periods, commas, colons, semi-colons and capitals and small letters. I have had a long and complicated life with all these."

Steinbeck, John. Journal of a Novel. New York: The Viking Press, 1972.

A journal in the form of letters. "The writing covered the period from January 29 through November 1, 1951," a note from the publisher tells us. "There was a letter for every working day until the first draft of 'East of Eden' was finished ... the letters were ... full of serious thinking about this novel, his longest and most ambitious; about novel-writing in general; and about some of Steinbeck's deepest convictions. Not a formal act of literary creation for its own sake, this document casts a flood of light on the author's mind and on the nature of the creative process.... The letters, of course, refer to the first draft of East of Eden. After it was copied by a typist, Steinbeck made extensive revisions, omitted whole passages, and rearranged some of the chapters."

Tooker, Dan, and Roger Hofheins, eds. Fiction: Interviews with Northern California Novelists. New York: Harcourt Brace Jovanovich, 1976.

Peter S. Beagle, Kay Boyle, Don Carpenter, Evan S. Connell, Jr., Alfred Coppel, Ernest J. Gaines, Leonard Gardner, Herbert Gold, James Leigh, Janet Lewis, Wallace Stegner, Jessamyn West. Evan S. Connell, Jr.: "I've never had a sentence turn up in the final form as it was in the beginning."

Trask, Georgianne, and Charles Burkhart, eds. Storytellers and Their Art: An Anthology. Garden City, N.Y.: Doubleday, 1963.

"The purpose of this book is to bring together what writers of the short story have said about it." Brief comments under 33 headings by over 60 writers, classic and contemporary. Section Titles: "The Story," "The Storyteller," "The Creative Process," "Technical Aspects," "Storyteller as Critic." Katherine Mansfield: "In 'Miss Brill' I choose not only the length of every sentence, but even the sound of every sentence. I choose the rise and fall of every paragraph to fit her, and to fit her on that day at that very moment."

Turner, Alberta T. Fifty Contemporary Poets: The Creative Process. New York: McKay, 1977.

Fifty out of a hundred poets responded to Ms. Turner's questionnaire: "Select one of your recent poems which you feel is representative of your best current work and answer the following questions about it. 1. How did the poem start? 2. What changes did it go through from start to finish? 3. What principles of technique did you consciously use? 4. Whom do you visualize as your reader? 5. Can the poem be paraphrased? How? 6. How does this poem differ from earlier poems of yours in (a) quality (b) theme (c) technique? Please add any other remarks about the poem which you consider pertinent." These poets responded: Ray Amorosi, Jon Anderson, Marvin Bell, Michael Benedikt, Philip Booth, Hayden Carruth, Laura Chester, Norman Dubie, Richard Eberhart, Russell Edson, Peter Everwine, Robert Francis, Stuart Friebert, Gary Gildner, Louise Glück, John Haines, Donald Hall, James Baker Hall, Michael S. Harper, Phil Hey, Donald Justice, Shirley Kaufman, X. J. Kennedy, Peter Klappert, Maxine Kumin, Denise Levertov, Lou Lipsitz, Cynthia Macdonald, Sandra McPherson, William Matthews, Jerome Mazarro, Vassar Miller, Judith Minty, Linda Pastan, David Ray, James Reiss, Dennis Schmitz, Richard Shelton, Charles Simic, Louis Simpson, William Stafford, Frank Stanford, Joan Swift, James Tate, Robert Wallace, Richard Wilbur, Nancy Willard, John Woods, Charles Wright, David Young. Some of the poets include early drafts, marked for deletions and showing insertions.

Valéry, Paul. <u>The Art of Poetry.</u> New York: Vintage Books, Random House, 1961.

Introduction by T. S. Eliot. "This volume," says Valéry "contains various essays which have appeared here and there, and which deal with the poet's state and the art of verse." Valéry also comments on his own development as a poet, especially in the long essay "Memoirs of a Poem." In "On Literary Technique," he observes, "Literature is the art of playing on the minds of others.... Given an impression, a dream, a thought, one <u>must</u> express it in such a way as to produce the maximum effect <u>in the</u> mind of a listener--an effect entirely calculated by the Artist." The poet "will take care not to hurl on to paper everything whispered to him in fortunate moments by the Muse of Free Association. On the contrary, everything he has imagined, felt, dreamed, and planned will be passed through a sieve, weighed, filtered, subjected to <u>form</u>, and condensed as much as possible so as to gain in power what it loses in length...."

Van Gelder, Robert. <u>Writers and Writing.</u> New York: Scribner's, 1946.

Brief essays based on interviews with 89 writers, mostly novelists; usually on the occasion of the publication of a new book or some other literary event. SEE Breit, <u>The Writer Observed</u>, which is similar.

Vidal, Gore. <u>The City and the Pillar.</u> New York: E. P. Dutton & Co., Inc., 1948, revised edition, 1965.

Compare the original edition with the revised edition. "Recently I reread <u>The City and the Pillar</u> for the first time since it was published," Vidal says in "An Afterword," "and I was startled to find that the book I had written was not at all the one I remembered. Midway through what I meant to be a commonsense redefinition of the homosexualist in American life, the narrative turned melodramatic. Nor was the actual theme of the book entirely clear .... And of course the coda was unsatisfactory.... I have now altered the last chapter considerably. In fact, I have rewritten the entire book (my desire to imitate the style of Farrell was perhaps too successful), though I have not changed the point of view nor the essential relationships."

Warren, Robert Penn, "'Blackberry Winter': A Recollection."
SEE Brooks and Warren, Understanding Fiction, Part II.

Watkins, Floyd C., and Karl F. Knight, eds. Writer to Writer: Readings on the Craft of Writing. Boston: Houghton Mifflin, 1966.

"The common theme of the selections in this volume is down-to-earth advice about writing. The principles which are stated simply, however, are those which must be studied by the beginner and remembered by the wise old novelist writing his tenth volume.... The most useful guide to the book may be the index," which groups "topics and kinds of errors," and includes an entry on revision. "In summary, the writers of these essays tend to agree on two major points: writing well is a stupendously difficult task; but to the reader good writing looks simple, almost easy." John Steinbeck, Thomas Wolfe, William Saroyan, John Ciardi, William Faulkner, W. Somerset Maugham, Arnold Bennett, Sean O'Faolain, Ernest Hemingway, Robert Frost, Aldous Huxley, George Orwell, Herbert Read, Jesse Stuart, and several nonfiction writers. Sean O'Faolain: "the art of writing is rewriting."

Welty, Eudora. The Eye of the Story, Selected Essays and Reviews. New York: Random House, 1977.

Ms. Welty reveals few insights into her own work directly, but in talking about writing (and reading) generally, she suggests many insights into her own writing. Pieces "On Writing" reprinted are "Looking at Short Stories," "Writing and Analyzing a Story," "Place in Fiction," "Words into Fiction," "Must the Novelist Crusade?" "'Is Phoenix Jackson's Grandson Really Dead?'," "Some Notes on Time in Fiction." "... I rode out of the old story on the back of the girl and then threw away the girl; but I saved my story, for, entirely different as the second version was, it was what I wanted to tell." "Indeed, learning to write may be a part of learning to read. For all I know, writing comes out of a superior devotion to reading."

Welty, Eudora. "No Place for You, My Love," and "How I Write," Understanding Fiction, pp. 530-545.
SEE Brooks and Warren, Understanding Fiction, Part II.

West, Ray B. Reading the Short Story. New York: Thomas Y. Crowell Co., 1968.

This standard approach to the short story includes "Two Short

Stories and How They Were Written," "Noon Wine" by Katherine Anne Porter and "Dovisch in the Wilderness" by Herbert Wilner. They attempt to "reconstruct how their stories came to be written. In so doing, they suggest the importance to the author of knowing as much as possible about what he is doing; in short, reading his own work of fiction."

Williams, William Carlos. I Wanted to Write a Poem: The Autobiography of the Works of a Poet. Reported and edited by Edith Heal. New York: New Directions, 1958.

"For five months I met with the poet and his wife, the Bill and Floss you will hear talking in these pages." Williams takes each of his books, including the fiction, from his shelves chronologically and comments in an engaging, rambling sort of way. "To me, at that time, a poem was an image, the picture was the important thing." The book is a kind of living, breathing bibliography.

Wilner, Herbert, "Dovisch: Things, Facts, and Rainbows."
SEE West, Reading the Short Story.

Woolf, Virginia. The Letters of Virginia Woolf, Volume One: 1888-1912. Edited by Nigel Nicolson and Joanne Trautman. New York: Harcourt Brace Jovanovich, 1976.

"The letters of Virginia Woolf are of supreme interest because she became a writer of genius. The origins of her style and the newness of her vision are all to be found here. 'The way to get life into letters,' she wrote to Vanessa, 'is to be interested in other people.' The same is true of her novels.... The letters are a record of her daily observations, the novels a distillation of it. In both she sought 'clarity,' avoiding triteness of thought and expression, disdaining convention and humbug." Woolf writes to Clive Bell about her first novel, The Voyage Out: "When I read the thing over (one very grey evening) I thought it so flat and monotonous that I did not even feel 'the atmosphere': certainly there was no character in it. Next morning I proceeded to slash and rewrite, in the hope of animating it; and (as I suspect for I have not re-read it) destroyed the one virtue it had--a kind of continuity; for I wrote it originally in a dream-like state, which was at any rate, unbroken.... I have kept all the pages I cut out; so the thing can be reconstructed precisely as it was."

Woolf, Virginia. A Writer's Diary: Being Extracts from the Diary of Virginia Woolf. Edited by Leonard Woolf. With an afterword by Louise Bogan and Josephine Schaefer. New York: New American Library, 1968.

Covers the period 1918-1941. Woolf's husband has extracted from the 26 volumes of her diary "practically everything which referred to her own writing." Three other kinds of extracts: those "in which she is obviously using the diary as a method of practising or trying out the art of writing"; those which describe "scenes and persons" who contributed to the raw material of her art and those that comment upon the books she was reading. "The book throws light upon Virginia Woolf's intentions, objects, and methods as a writer.

It gives an unusual psychological picture of artistic production from within.... The diaries at least show the extraordinary energy, persistence, and concentration with which she devoted herself to the art of writing and the undeviating conscientiousness with which she wrote and rewrote and again rewrote her books." Woolf: "And I have just finished ... the last sentence of The Waves.... But I have never written a book so full of holes and patches; that will need rebuilding, yes, not only re-modelling. I suspect the structure is wrong ... unlike all my other books in every way, it is unlike them in this, that I begin to re-write it, or conceive it again with ardour, directly I have done." "I finished my re-typing of The Waves. Not that it is finished--oh dear no. For then I must correct the re-retyping ... no one can say I have been hasty or careless this time; though I doubt not the lapses and slovenliness are innumerable."

Wordsworth, William. "I Wandered Lonely as a Cloud."
SEE Brooks and Warren, Understanding Fiction.

Wordsworth, William, and Samuel T. Coleridge. "Preface," Lyrical Ballads. 2nd ed. (1800). The text of the 1798 edition with the additional 1800 poems and the Prefaces edited with introduction, notes and appendices by R. L. Brett and A. R. Jones. London: Methuen, 1963 (revised 1965).

In the preface, Wordsworth says "that poetry is the spontaneous overflow of powerful feelings; it takes its origin from emotion recollected in tranquility." "... the feeling therein developed gives importance to the action and situation, and not the action and situation to the feeling." "My purpose was to imitate, and, as far as possible, to adopt the very language of men.... There will also be found in these volumes little of what is usually called poetic diction; as much pains has been taken to avoid it as is ordinarily taken to produce it." Wordsworth maintains that nothing in the poet differs "in kind from other men, but only in degree."

INDEX 1: GENRES

INDEX 2: REVISION PROBLEMS

INDEX 3: SCHOLARS AND TITLES OF THEIR ARTICLES AND BOOKS

INDEX 4: NAMES OF WRITERS AND THE WORKS IN WHICH THEY COMMENT ON THE CREATIVE PROCESS

INDEX 5: NAMES OF WRITERS AND THE WORKS REVISED